Basic V

GRAMMAR AT A GLANCE

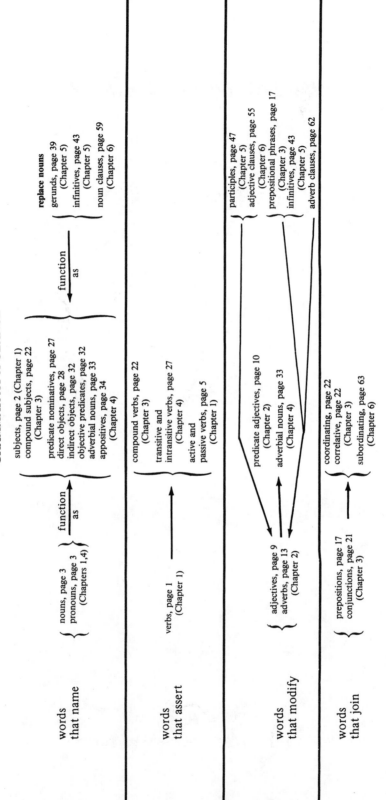

words that name

nouns, page 3
pronouns, page 3
(Chapters 1,4)

function as →

subjects, page 2 (Chapter 1)
compound subjects, page 22
(Chapter 3)
predicate nominatives, page 27
direct objects, page 28
indirect objects, page 32
objective predicates, page 32
adverbial nouns, page 33
appositives, page 34
(Chapter 4)

replace nouns

gerunds, page 39
(Chapter 5)
infinitives, page 43
(Chapter 5)
noun clauses, page 59
(Chapter 6)

words that assert

verbs, page 1
(Chapter 1)

compound verbs, page 22
(Chapter 3)
transitive and
intransitive verbs, page 27
(Chapter 4)
active and
passive verbs, page 5
(Chapter 1)

words that modify

adjectives, page 9
adverbs, page 13
(Chapter 2)

predicate adjectives, page 10
(Chapter 2)
adverbial nouns, page 33
(Chapter 4)

participles, page 47
(Chapter 5)
adjective clauses, page 55
(Chapter 6)
prepositional phrases, page 17
(Chapter 3)
infinitives, page 43
(Chapter 5)
adverb clauses, page 62

words that join

prepositions, page 17
conjunctions, page 21
(Chapter 3)

coordinating, page 22
correlative, page 22
(Chapter 3)
subordinating, page 63
(Chapter 6)

Basic Verbal Skills

FOURTH EDITION

RICHARD LEDERER
&
PHILIP BURNHAM

St. Paul's School
Concord, New Hampshire

WAYSIDE PUBLISHING
CONCORD, MASSACHUSETTS

PRINTED IN THE UNITED STATES
ISBN 1-877653-31-4

Contents

Preface

"The more things change," says a well-known remark by Alphonse Karr in 1849, "the more they are the same." So in this third edition of *Basic Verbal Skills*, though there have been a considerable number of changes, of improvements, the book is essentially and firmly the same text that was in the first two editions. Comments on the earlier two editions have indicated that the approach to writing through immediate application of grammatical principles is effective and should be retained. And so it has been.

The directness and light tone of each chapter have been retained and further strengthened. Again, prayerful adjurations to students have been eliminated and invocations to virtues ("You must remember," "Be sure that you . . . ," etc.) have been studiously avoided. As a result the text is less patronizing, more appealing to intelligence and understanding.

Words in sentences, we all recognize, do one of four things: they assert, they name, they modify, they join. So *Basic Verbal Skills* deals, at appropriate length, with each of the four, moving on thereafter through the relative complexities as each relates to the others and are interrelated in writing.

Punctuation is given proper attention, especially as it may be seen as more than a high class game of put-and-take, of sprinkling salt and pepper (possibly sugar?) throughout the substance of the feast. Rather, recognition of the sense of signal, and of added and heightened communication are the foundation for appropriate punctuation.

Similarly, the basic rules of spelling are explained and illustrated in individual chapters. Attention is also centered on those spellings that defy rules or logic — the so-called spelling "demons." When experience tells us that words of similar spelling or of close yet different meanings cause troubles, such words are separately (that's one of the demons!) discussed and illustrated in use.

Basic verbal skills, once learned and understood, are of minimal use or significance until they are turned into background or source from which direct applications are made to the neverending problems of improving sentences, of acceptable form in written language, and of effective expression. Then these basic verbal skills are of extraordinary value. To a committee member who asked a complex question in a cumbersome and circumlocuted way, ending with the plea of "What shall I do?" the chairman responded with humor and sympathy, "Straighten out your sentence is the first thing."

So *Basic Verbal Skills* practices what it preaches. The seventeen sections called "Improving Sentences" will help students to take pleasure in revising the sentences of others, and thereby come to see how to revise their own. Students can also take considerable satisfaction in recognizing effective sentences in the writings of others and similarly be aware of their own stylistic strengths. *Basic Verbal Skills* will bring to students understanding of the bedevilments in English spelling and ways to avoid spelling errors, just as it will do the same for troublesome words and for usage and rhetoric.

For possibly the first time students may come to recognize that sentence patterns and sentence variations are neither whimsical nor routine, but are related to emphasis and clarity and meaning.

Since for many students objective tests of matters in sentence construction, in rhetoric, in usage are very much a part of experience, Chapter 14 reproduces, through the courtesy of the College Entrance Examination Board and the Educational Testing Service, items similar to those used on their exams. Each of these items is clued to the pages of *Basic Verbal Skills* that discuss the principle behind the proper choice or correction to be made.

Richard Lederer
Philip Burnham

These Comments are for Students (and even Teachers)

"Why care for grammar as long as we are good?" wrote Artemus Ward, an American humorist of the nineteenth century. He was joking, of course, as the nonsense logic of that question shows. So also — and in spite of the difference in fourteenth century spelling and today's — the complaint made by a character in Chaucer's *Canterbury Tales* is clear enough: "I lerne song, I kan but smal grammeere." And that brings to mind Artemus Ward again, for he made this comment about Chaucer: "It is a pity that Chaucer, who had geneyus, was so unedicated. He's the wuss speller I know of." As is readily evident — here and in all of his writing — Ward made deliberate misspelling one part of his style.

But grammar and spelling don't always get kidded or joked about. Another fourteenth century poet, William Langland, called grammar "The ground of all." The great literary figure of the eighteenth century (sometimes given to rather heavy, sententious statements — yet all full of great wisdom and sincerity) once remarked, "I have laboured to refine our language to grammatical purity, and to clear it from colloquial barbarisms, licentious idioms, and all irregular combinations." A tall order! But one that all of us, as writers — usually expressing it less ponderously — strive to follow in all kinds of composition.

Few skills are more important than being able to speak and write well. It will become increasingly important after school; for almost every adult occupation requires the ability to speak well, and many require also the ability to write well. Fortunately, the ability to use language effectively can be acquired — if you are sufficiently interested to master the skills.

Skills come from practice. And this book will help you acquire language skills, by providing the necessary material and by showing you how to make the best use of it.

You will, for example, study grammar, not to acquire an extensive vocabulary of grammatical terms, but to learn how you can improve your sentences. You will study punctuation, not for the sake of memorizing a list of rules, but to help you punctuate written sentences so that your intended meaning will be clear to your readers. The spelling lessons — concerned with common, everyday words rather than strange, tricky words of an old-fashioned spelling bee — will help you avoid mistakes in your writing. The usage lessons will familiarize you with the forms appropriate in standard English.

Finally, and of considerable importance, the lessons on improving sentences will show you how you can apply the fundamental verbal skills you have learned to the editing and revising of faulty English sentences, and to the creation of your own sentences.

Does all this sound like work? It is work, of course, and takes patience and time and effort. So do practicing scales, performing chemistry experiments, rehearsing lines or dance steps, running through new football plays, doing typewriter exercises. (Only very few people believe the advertisements that promise to make them experts in six easy lessons.) But the effort you put into acquiring any skill is always well repaid, especially when the skill is one as useful as the ability to talk and write well. Your everyday life is filled with occasions in which you want to express your thoughts clearly — in conversations with family and friends, in giving directions to strangers, in asking for information, in class recitations, in speaking before a club, in writing reports and examinations, in friendly and business letters. What is more valuable than knowing how to use our language effectively?

Would you like to speak well? Then this book can help you. Would you like to write well? Then this book can help you. "Help you" is the key phrase: if you bring to each of the lessons of this book a desire to achieve these goals, a willingness to give the effort that will master each one to the best of your ability, you cannot fail to improve your speaking and writing.

P.B.
R.L.

Basic Verbal Skills

Verbs and Subjects of Verbs

Verbs: foundations of sentences

To know whether a group of words is or is not a sentence is to have "sentence sense." Since every sentence has a verb, expressed or clearly implied, the first step in acquiring sentence sense is learning to recognize verbs. In the six sentences that follow, the words used as verbs are italicized:

The teacher *was* not sure about the answer given in the book.
Laura *could*n't *sew* well enough to make her own clothes.
The question *has* often *been* vigorously *argued* in public forums.
Sneaking through back alleys, Luke *may have been seen* by one of the neighbors.
Don't you *care* for chocolate topping on your frozen custard?
Push on the latch gently before trying to open the door.

The word *not* is never a part of the verb, even when its contraction *n't* is attached directly to the verb. Nor are such words as *sure, well, often, by, for,* and *on* parts of verbs, however closely connected in meaning they may be. Only the words in italics are verbs.

A verb is a word or group of words that makes a statement or asks a question or gives a command. It may consist of one, two, three, or four words, and these words may be separated from each other.

Verbs of more than one word are made in five ways:

1) With *do, does,* and *did,* usually in questions or with *not:* Do you admire them? It does not fit me. They didn't believe me.

2) With *have, has,* and *had:* have told, has lost, had received

3) With *am, is, are, was,* and *were:* am asking, am asked; is fighting, is fought; are doing, are done; was telegraphing, was telegraphed; were trying, were tried

4) With *have been, has been,* and *had been:* have been watching, have been watched; has been seeing, has been seen; had been writing, had been written

5) With *may, can, must, might, could, shall, should, will, would:* may have found, can be doing, must have been seen, might go, might have gone, might have been going, could swim, could have written, shall know, shall be elected, should have seen, will arrive, will have arrived, will be forgotten, would have driven, would have been driven

These examples are given as reminders of how verbs look.

EXERCISE 1. Find the verb in each of the sentences. Find the whole verb — and nothing but the verb. Then on a sheet of paper write each verb, numbering it with the number of the sentence. For the first sentence write: *1. could be grown*

1. Nothing could possibly be grown in the wasteland beyond the hills.
2. The star of the play became more conceited every day.
3. Driving will be difficult because of the blinding snowstorm.
4. Look up the meanings of all French words and phrases in the article.
5. Grandfather's bark, like old Rover's, was far worse than his bite.
6. Fast thawing is one of the treatments for frostbite.
7. Regardless of his skimpy education, he should be adequate for the job.
8. Violin music almost drives our spaniel out of his mind.
9. Ted's attempts to impress his friends with his new wealth and importance ended in failure.
10. Janie was going around and around in the revolving door at the hotel.

Subjects of verbs

The second step in acquiring sentence sense is learning to recognize the subjects of verbs. After recognizing the verb in a sentence, find the subject simply by asking "Who or what?" of the verb. In the following sentences the verbs are italicized:

The photograph on the piano *was taken* by Jim White. The beautiful collie near the center of the picture *is* Lassie, Jim's favorite model. She *appears* in several of his prize-winning photos.

To find the subject in the first sentence, ask "Who or what was taken?" The answer is *photograph,* since the sentence is not about taking a piano. The word *photograph* is the subject of the verb. Now what word is the subject of the verb in the second sentence? The question "Who or what is?" shows that the subject of the verb is *collie.* And "Who or what appears?" shows that the word *She* is the subject of the verb in the third sentence.

Two kinds of words may be subjects of verbs — **nouns** and **pronouns.** The subjects of the first two example sentences, *photograph* and *collie,* are nouns. Nouns may be divided into three groups:

1) The *common nouns,* or ordinary names: river, house, library, cat, purse, bus
2) The *proper nouns,* or special names: Janet, Mr. Simpson, Kansas City, Brooklyn Bridge, National Geographic Society
3) The *abstract nouns,* or names of qualities and conditions: truth, heroism, contentment, politeness, grief

2

One simple explanation will cover all nouns:

A word used as a name is called a noun.

A word is a noun if it is used as a name in a sentence. For instance, in "My watch has stopped" and "Paint dries slowly," the words *watch* and *Paint* are used as names and so are nouns. But in "Our neighbors watch us all the time" and "Paint more carefully," the words *watch* and *Paint* are used as verbs. See how a word is used in a sentence in order to determine whether it is a noun or a verb.

The needless repetition of nouns is avoided by using other words in their place. Look again at the examples. Notice that instead of repeating the proper noun *Lassie* as the subject of the third sentence, the writer used the pronoun *She,* which means the same as *Lassie.*

A word used in place of a noun is called a pronoun.

The pronouns generally used as subjects of sentences are:

1) The *personal* (directly naming) pronouns: I, we, you, he she, it, they

2) The *demonstrative* (pointing) pronouns: This, that, these, those

3) The *indefinite* (indirectly naming) pronouns: all, another, both, each, either, neither, few, many, none, one, other, several, some, etc.

4) The *interrogative* (question-raising) pronouns: who, which, what

In statements the subject usually comes before the verb, but not always. For example, find the words used as subjects of the italicized verbs in the following sentences:

Down the hot, dusty road *waddled* an old cow.
On some Sundays there *have been* over thirty singers in the choir.
Never before *has* our club *asked* the student body for contributions.

"Who or what waddled?" The subject in the first sentence is *cow.* In the second sentence the subject *singers* follows the verb, as it does also in sentences beginning with "There is," "Here are," and so on. Now look at the third sentence. Who or what has asked? The subject is *club.* Notice that it comes between two parts of the verb.

In questions the subject frequently comes after the verb or between parts of the verb. Here are a few examples:

Are the new neighbors nice people?
Where was she yesterday?
Who is Sylvia?
Where have you been all morning?

When will the next game be played?
Could this problem have been more easily decided at the meeting?

One easy way of finding the subject in questions is to put them into the form of statements and ask "Who or what?" of each verb:

The new neighbors *are* nice people.
Yesterday she *was* where.
Sylvia *is* who.
You *have been* where all morning.
The next game *will be played* when.
This problem *could have been decided* more easily at the meeting.

You will see that the subjects are *neighbors, she, Sylvia, you, game,* and *problem.* Except for questions that already are in the form of statements — such as "Who goes there?" "Which is cheaper?" "What caused that noise?" — it is simpler to put each question into the form of a statement before asking "Who or what?" of the verb.

In commands the problem is different. If you ask "Who or what?" of the verbs in commands such as "Close the door" and "Turn to page 100," you will see that the command is addressed to a listener or a reader. For this reason the subject is understood by everyone to be *you.* When the pronoun *you* is omitted — and it almost always is — we say that the subject of the verb is *you* "understood."

Now look at the next two sentences:

James, will you collect the papers for me?
Mary, come here at once.

The first sentence is a question, not a command. What word is subject of the verb *will collect?* The subject is the pronoun *you,* since the proper noun *James* merely shows for whom the question is meant. In the second sentence — a command — the name *Mary* tells which person is being spoken to, but it is not the subject. The subject of the verb *come* is *you* "understood," just as it would be if the word *Mary* were omitted or put last.

Studying subjects and verbs strengthens your knowledge of what a sentence is. A sentence is made by combining a verb and its subject. Any student who realizes that a verb and its subject may make a sentence will understand why the following groups of words are independent units:

Don't shove!
My foot is caught.
Can't you see?

4

If groups like these come together in a composition, they must be treated as separate sentences:

Don't shove! My foot is caught. Can't you see?

Keep in mind, however, that not every group of words having a subject and a verb is a grammatically complete sentence. For example, a verb and its subject do not form a sentence if they are preceded by what is called a subordinating conjunction (*"after* the curtain rose"*) or a relative pronoun (*"which* we had noticed"*). Later chapters will explain such groups more fully. The concern now is only with the first steps — learning to recognize verbs and their subjects in simple sentences.

EXERCISE 2. First find the verb in each sentence. Then find each subject by asking "Who or what?" of the verb. On a sheet of paper, write each verb and its subject. Begin each subject with a capital letter. Put a period after each verb. If the sentence is a command, write the understood subject *you* in parentheses. For the first group you should write: *1. (you) run. You do see.*

1. Run! Don't you see that huge dog?
2. The new clerk didn't want any cracked cups and plates on the neat cabinet shelves. So he threw away several prized antiques.
3. You should have been warned about those rapids near Elbow Bend. Can your canoe be repaired?
4. Who is that odd-looking woman? She has been waiting here in the station for hours.
5. The number of copies of orders could be reduced from six to four. Why should we waste valuable filing space?
6. Kate, don't whip the pony. That isn't the way to handle him.
7. Around the mountain steamed the aged little locomotive. Daily it puffed its way along that same route.
8. Grief did not soften the king's heart. It made him even more cruel and bitter.
9. Long ago the penguin lost the art of flight. Now it moves swiftly in an unbirdlike way.
10. Amy could hardly wait until the next day to spring her idea on the principal. Promptly at eight o'clock she was knocking on the office door.

Active and passive verbs

Notice the following sentences:

Sheriff Ellis *questioned* the two men.
The smoke *ruined* all her clothes.

The verbs in both these sentences are **transitive.** Each expresses an action that passes to a person or thing named in the sentence. The object *men* receives the action expressed by *questioned;* the object *clothes* receives the action expressed by *ruined.* Who questioned the men? Sheriff Ellis did. The subject *Sheriff Ellis* tells who is the doer of the action that passes to the object *men.* What ruined the clothes? The smoke did. The subject *smoke* tells what is the doer of the action that passes to the object *clothes.* In sentences like these, in which the subject tells who or what is the doer of the action expressed by a transitive verb, the verb is called **active.**

Now look at these two sentences:

The two men *were questioned* by Sheriff Ellis.
All her clothes *were ruined* by the smoke.

The verbs in both these sentences also are transitive. Each expresses an action that passes to a person or thing named in the sentence, but there is no object in either of the sentences. In each it is the subject that tells who or what receives the action of the verb. In sentences like these, in which the subject tells who or what is affected by the action expressed by the verb, the verb is called **passive.**

A passive verb can be changed to an active verb by making the doer of the action the subject of the sentence:

Our team was badly beaten by Central High last night.
Central High beat our team badly last night.

The word *team,* the subject of the passive verb *was beaten,* becomes the object of the active verb *beat.*

Passive verbs are useful wherever the doer of the action is obvious, unknown, or unimportant, or wherever special emphasis is wanted for the receiver of the action:

Hank was elected class treasurer.
Two banks were robbed last night.
The hedges in front of the courthouse should be pruned.
Most of the hand work was done by Aunt Helen.

In the first sentence it is obvious that the class elected Hank. In the second it is not known who robbed the banks. In the third it makes no difference who prunes the hedges. And in the fourth the writer calls attention to the receiver of the action by using the passive voice. Except in sentences like these, however, active verbs are generally preferred; for they give sentences added force and vigor. An abundance of passive verbs is often a mark of a heavy, sluggish style. The active voice is generally crisper and more direct.

6

Improving sentences

1. Use an active verb

In conversation, students rarely overuse passive verbs. For example, a student will usually say "I will call you tonight" — not "You will be called by me tonight." Or "Tom bought a new set of golf clubs" — not "A new set of golf clubs was bought by Tom." But in writing, students often use too many passive verbs. They weaken their compositions by writing sentences like these:

Many beautiful dresses were seen by them in the gaily decorated shop windows along Michigan Boulevard.
The June prom was dreamed about by Alice for months in advance.
The class was read several humorous poems by Mr. Mitchell.

Passive verbs are useful when the doer of the action is obvious, unknown, or unimportant. But in each of the example sentences the doer of the action is important and has been expressed in a phrase beginning with *by.* The sentences all sound awkward, and the last one is confusing as well. No one can tell whether Mr. Mitchell wrote the poems or read them. Such sentences are improved by using active verbs:

They *saw* many beautiful dresses in the gaily decorated shops along Michigan Boulevard.
Alice *dreamed* about the June prom for months in advance.
Mr. Mitchell *read* the class several humorous poems.

In revising written work, watch for awkward sentences in which the doer of the action expressed by a passive verb is in a phrase beginning with *by.* If the doer is obvious or unimportant, cross out the phrase. If the doer is important, use an active verb and make the doer the subject of the verb.

EXERCISE 3. Each of the sentences contains a passive verb. Revise any sentence that might be improved by changing a passive verb to an active verb. Be ready to read the revised sentences aloud. For the first sentence you might say: *Bob cooked thick, juicy steaks in the fireplace in the back yard.*

1. Thick, juicy steaks were cooked by Bob in the fireplace in the back yard.
2. Dick was arrested for speeding by Officer Cooney.
3. Dorothy was asked to play a violin solo by the program committee.
4. Before the end of the semester Helen was offered an opportunity to study painting in Paris by Mrs. Barnes.

5. The ugly old building next to the library will be torn down soon.
6. No attempt was made to change the tire by the boys.
7. Miss Johnson's papers had been neatly stacked by the custodian on one corner of her desk.
8. The ice cream was made by my grandmother in a huge, old-fashioned freezer.
9. My gym shoes might have been taken from the locker room by someone in the sixth-hour gym class.
10. Some of the people in the audience were asked to give their opinions on government spending by the newspaper reporter.

6. The boys made no attempt to change the tires

7. The custodian neatly stacked Mrs Johnson's

8. My grandmother made the ice-cream in an old-.

9. Someone in our 6th gym hour gym class prob...

10. #?.

Chapter 2

Modifiers

Adjectives

Notice how the italicized words affect the meanings of the nouns and pronouns in the following sentences:

An old woman in *a black linen* dress peered over *the candy* counter.
No one likes *that leather* chair as much as *this small metal* one.
Which team won *first* place in *the city* tournament *last* week?

The italicized words make the meanings of the nouns and pronouns more definite by telling which persons or things are meant. Words that affect the meaning of — or "modify" — other words are called **modifiers.** Modifiers of nouns and pronouns are called **adjectives.**

An adjective is a word used to modify a noun or a pronoun.

Adjectives modify nouns and pronouns in different ways. They "turn" the meaning of the nouns or pronouns in a specific direction, thereby limiting or restricting the generalized nouns or pronouns to particular meaning. They tell what kind by giving details of color, material, size, use, or type: a *black* linen dress, *leather* chair, *small* metal one, the *candy* counter, the *city* tournament. Here the words *linen, leather, metal, candy,* and *city,* which are often used as nouns, are used as adjectives.

Adjectives tell which one or how much or how many by giving details of number, amount, order, or place: *no* one, *several* men, *thirteen* dollars, a *few* mistakes, *more* sugar, *first* place, the *third* time, the *east* wall, the *front* windows. They may be **demonstratives,** used to point out: *this* one, *that* chair, *these* cards, *those* shrubs. Or they may be **interrogatives,** used in asking which person or thing is meant: *Which* team won? *Whose* pen is this? *What* time is it?

Because the adjectives *a* and *an* point out any one of a group, they are called **indefinite articles.** Because the adjective *the* points out a certain one of a group, it is called the **definite article.**

Nouns and pronouns that show possession are often used as modifiers: *Elaine's* sister, *his* turn, the little *boy's* favorites. But since these possessives may themselves be modified by adjectives (as in "The little *boy's* coat was torn"), they are usually called possessive nouns and pronouns "used like adjectives."

Adjectives do not always precede the words they modify. They may follow the words, as in these sentences:

Try to write about something *different*.
Haven't you any cloth *wider* than this?
The only sound *audible* was the pounding of my heart.

Adjectives modifying the subject of a sentence sometimes follow the verb:

Joan will be *angry*, of course.
The theater was *empty*.

Because the verb and the words used with it to tell about the subject are called the **predicate** of the sentence, adjectives that follow the verb and modify the subject are called **predicate adjectives.** Predicate adjectives usually follow some form of the verb *be* or of such verbs as *look, taste, feel, smell, grow, sound, become* or verbs of more than one word like *were painted, has been considered,* and *should have been made:*

Jim has been *sick* all week.
Sue feels *bad* about the mistake.
Sour milk doesn't taste *good*.
The window frames were painted *green*.
Darrel has always been considered *lazy*.
The assignments should have been made *shorter*.

In questions predicate adjectives usually come right after the subject or after a part of the verb:

Were the boys *late* again this morning?
Hasn't Jane grown *tall* in the last two years?

By changing the questions to statements — "The boys were late again this morning" and "Jane hasn't grown tall in the last two years" — it is clear that *late* and *tall* are predicate adjectives.

EXERCISE 1. Each of the sentences has one or more adjectives or possessives modifying the subject. Divide a sheet of paper into three columns. In the first column, write the subjects. In the second, write the adjective modifiers that come before or directly after the subject. In the third, write any predicate adjectives. Do not list the articles *a, an, the* or adjectives that modify words other than the subject. Number your answers with the numbers of the sentences. For the first sentence you should write:

1. shrieks | cousin's | louder

1. My little cousin's shrieks became louder.

2. Both kitchen chairs should have been painted white.
3. Miss Reed's first-period English class always looks attentive.
4. Every one of the girls turned pale on seeing the mouse.
5. The proud, stately president of their corporation is not considered trustworthy by even his closest friends.
6. Our next-door neighbors grew more and more friendly.
7. The three wide-awake children would not keep quiet for a minute.
8. In our own state there are no navigable rivers.
9. Often during the long, depressing years their goal seemed unattainable.
10. What is the real proof of this man's greatness?

Another use of adjectives is to explain or add to the meanings of other words by setting the adjectives alongside nouns or pronouns:

The baby, *hungry* and *restless,* began to wail loudly.
Tall, wiry, and *fast* on his feet, Ned Hopkins made a good forward.
The little girl strolled through the crowd, quite *unconscious* of her strange appearance.

Such adjectives are called **appositive adjectives.** As you can see, they may be placed after or before or at some distance from the words they explain, and they are set off on both sides.

Improving sentences

2. Choose exact modifiers

Adjectives make the meanings of nouns and pronouns more definite. But sometimes adjectives are carelessly used merely to show approval or disapproval.

Notice the italicized words in the following sentences:

The speaker had a *nice* manner, a *swell* voice, and a *cute* smile. Everyone thought he would be *grand.* But he made one *horrible* mistake after another, and his talk turned out to be *awful.*

Such words are "lazy" adjectives. They express approval or disapproval, but they do not tell what caused it. Do the italicized words help a listener or reader know what kind of manner the speaker had? What kind of voice? What sort of mistakes he made? What was wrong with his talk? Notice that the sentences have more meaning when exact adjectives are used:

The speaker had a *confident* manner, a *rich baritone* voice, and a *friendly* smile. Everyone thought he would be *excellent.* But he made one *ridiculous* mistake after another, and his talk turned out to be *tiresome.*

One way of improving sentences is to replace lazy adjectives with exact modifiers.

Some adjectives give facts: *wavy black* hair, a *wooden* bridge, a *gray stucco* house, a *freckle-faced fourteen-year-old* girl, a *square blue* purse with a *green leather* lining, an *old Model-T* sedan. Other adjectives give impressions: *beautiful* hair, an *ugly* bridge, an *attractive* house, a *surly* girl, a *smart* purse with a *gaudy* lining, a *paint-hungry* sedan.

Both kinds of adjectives are useful. The facts help the reader "see" what the writer saw with his or her eyes. The impressions help the reader know the writer's thoughts about what was observed. Sometimes a combination of the two kinds is effective: *beautiful black* hair, an *ugly wooden* bridge, an *attractive gray stucco* house, a *surly freckle-faced fourteen-year-old* girl, a *smart blue* purse with a *gaudy green* lining, an *old paint-hungry Model-T* sedan. But when reporting a news event or the results of an investigation — where facts and not impressions are wanted — it is important to choose adjectives that tell only what was seen and heard.

There is no simple rule to tell how many adjectives to use. Sometimes none is needed. Sometimes five are not too many. But using several adjectives to express the same idea is almost always wearying to the reader:

> On a *pleasant, warm, sunny autumn* afternoon a *tiny, gay, little brown* bird perched on a *gnarled, twisted* limb of the *huge, ancient oak* tree near my *grandmother's lovely old white frame* farmhouse.

A *warm, sunny* autumn afternoon is usually *pleasant.* A *tiny* bird is *little.* The adjectives *gnarled* and *twisted* express the same idea; both could be omitted, since the limb is part of an old oak tree. And an oak tree that is *huge* is probably also *ancient.* The sentence reads more easily without the unnecessary adjectives:

> On a *pleasant autumn* afternoon a *gay little brown* bird perched on a limb of the *huge oak* tree near my *grandmother's lovely old white frame* farmhouse.

Notice that the five adjectives modifying *farmhouse* have been kept, since each one expresses a different idea.

Adverbs

Adjectives are words used to modify nouns and pronouns. Now see what the italicized words in the following sentences modify:

Mother *promptly* shook her head.
The gray suit was *too* expensive.
Dad *very quickly* agreed.

In the first sentence *promptly* modifies the verb *shook*. In the second *too* modifies the adjective *expensive*. In the third *very* modifies the word *quickly,* which modifies the verb *agreed*. Words like *promptly, too, very,* and *quickly* are called **adverbs.**

An adverb is a word used to modify a verb, an adjective, or another adverb.

Adverbs that modify verbs usually tell how, when, where, or to what extent:

She speaks French *fluently.* Send the money *there.*
I shall write *soon.* You have worked *enough.*

Adverbs that modify adjectives or other adverbs usually tell to what extent:

Neil is *unusually* tall. She arrived *quite* late.
The tomatoes are *rather* good. He *almost* never complains.

Some adverbs indicate to what extent a statement is true:

She will *certainly* call on me. She will *perhaps* call on me.
She will *probably* call on me. She will *not* call on me.

Though adverbs of this kind affect the meaning of the sentence as a whole, they are — grammatically — modifiers of the verb.

Other adverbs show that two sentences are related in meaning:

Kay knew Dad was right. *Therefore* she took his scolding in silence.
The cottage was too small. It was, *furthermore,* too expensive.

The adverb *Therefore* shows a relationship in meaning between the two sentences in the first pair. It also modifies the verb *took*. The adverb *furthermore* shows that the two sentences in the second pair are related in meaning. It also modifies the verb *was*. Other adverbs that may show meaning relationships between sentences are *then, now, still, nevertheless, consequently, however, moreover,* and *otherwise.* Such adverbs always modify the verbs in their own sentences.

Now look at the italicized words in these sentences:

The *night* was clear and cold.
The *night* air was cool and refreshing.
Dave and Uncle Bill arrived last *night*.

In the first sentence *night* is a noun used as subject of the verb *was*. In the second *night* is an adjective modifying the noun *air*. In the third *night* modifies the verb *arrived* by telling when. Because nouns that modify adverbially are often themselves modified by adjectives, as *night* is in the third example, we say that they are nouns "used like adverbs," or **adverbial nouns.** Adverbial nouns usually tell how much, how far, where, when, or how:

It weighs ten *pounds.*   Has Ellen gone *home?*
The fence is six *feet* high.   I'll finish the job next *week.*
He swam three *miles.*   Don't hold your fork that *way.*

EXERCISE 2. Find the adverbial modifiers. Then find the verbs, adjectives, and adverbs they modify. Write the numbers of the sentences and, after them, the adverbs and the words they modify. Use a separate line for each adverb, and put parentheses around the word modified. For the first sentence you should write: *1. too (much)*
much (does cost)
However (will last)
lifetime (will last)

1. The carpet does cost too much. However, it will last a lifetime.
2. Last Wednesday we foolishly hiked ten miles through marshy fields.
3. The previous day we had been practically sure of his assistance.
4. Hank now speaks much more effectively.
5. Jane immediately saw through Ann's obviously false statements.
6. Aunt Martha almost always complains about the meals.
7. Slowly we crawled up the side of the dangerously steep mountain.
8. Perhaps Helen is too smart to advertise her real opinions.
9. Last winter some rather noisy tenants lived upstairs.
10. Seldom does Bob obey Mr. Thompson's orders willingly or graciously.

Improving sentences

3. Begin with an adverb

Adverbs that modify verbs are usually placed directly before the verb or after the verb or between the parts of the verb:

The ragged army *slowly* advanced toward the fort.
The warning bell will ring *soon.*
We have *already* collected five hundred dollars.

See what happens when the adverbs are put first in the sentences:

Slowly the ragged army advanced toward the fort.
Soon the warning bell will ring.
Already we have collected five hundred dollars.

The meanings of the sentences are not changed. But by putting the adverbs first, the writer calls attention to their importance and achieves an emphasis he or she wants the idea of the adverb — *Slowly* or *Soon* or *Already* — to have.

There is another reason for occasionally beginning a sentence with an adverb. When sentence after sentence begins with the subject, a paragraph is likely to seem monotonous. Putting an important adverb first in one or two of the sentences adds variety and can make the paragraph more interesting to read. Compare these two examples:

The champ entered the ring with a great flourish. His colorful robe gleamed brilliantly under the powerful lights. He waved condescendingly to his many fans. His attendants waited on him respectfully. This impressive scene ended abruptly with the sound of the opening gong. The champ was immediately transformed from a genial king to a dangerous assailant.	The champ entered the ring with a great flourish. His colorful robe gleamed brilliantly under the powerful lights. *Condescendingly* he waved to his many fans. His attendants waited on him respectfully. This impressive scene ended abruptly with the sound of the opening gong. *Immediately* the champ was transformed from a genial king to a dangerous assailant.

The paragraph at the right is more interesting because two of the sentences begin with adverbs, breaking the monotony of subject-verb, subject-verb, subject-verb. Notice that adverbs in the other sentences have not been moved. Too many adverb-first sentences would be just as monotonous as too many subject-first sentences. Only an occasional sentence beginning with an adverb is needed and only when the emphasis achieved is desirable in the context.

Never put an adverb first if doing so makes the sentence sound awkward or unnatural. For example, it would be ridiculous to write "Abruptly this impressive scene ended with the sound of the opening gong" or "Fast he always drives through town." In these sentences, the adverbs should follow the verbs they modify. After shifting an adverb, always read the sentence aloud to be sure that it sounds natural.

In revising first drafts of compositions, watch for unnecessary adverbs. For example, in the sentence "The miners descended down into the pit" the adverb *down* is not needed, because *descend* means "go down." No one need write "The warehouse on the corner was completely demolished," because the idea of *completely* is expressed by the verb *demolished*.

Some students tend to overwork the adverb *very,* writing sentence after sentence like this:

> I was very sure she would find the book very helpful, since it has very many new and very attractive drawings.

Used occasionally, *very* adds emphasis. Used too often, it loses its force. Don't forget the boy who cried "Wolf!"

The sentence is more effective without the *very's:*

> I was sure she would find the book helpful, since it has many new and attractive drawings.

In everyday speech we often use adverbs like *awfully, mighty, terribly,* and *dreadfully* as substitutes for *very.* But such "lazy" adverbs are out of place in most writing. In revising written work, try to use more exact modifiers, like *unusually, extremely, quite, somewhat,* and *rather.*

EXERCISE 3. In each of the sentences two adverbs are printed in italics. Decide which adverbs could be put first and which are unnecessary or lazy. Then revise the sentences, beginning with an adverb wherever you can do so without making the sentence sound awkward. Drop the unnecessary adverbs. Substitute a word like *quite, unusually,* or *extremely* for the lazy adverbs. Be ready to read your revised sentences aloud. For the first sentence you might say: *Eventually Mr. Sands will be an extremely wealthy banker.*

1. Mr. Sands will *eventually* be a *mighty* wealthy banker.
2. You would *probably* consider such movies *awfully* childish.
3. Mary must *certainly* have sent the magazines *back* to the library.
4. The fireman *quickly* began to ascend *up* the ladder toward the trapped mother and child.
5. John *enthusiastically* presented Mary's *terribly* clever plan to the committee chairman.
6. At last Uncle Don has *finally* consented to give our manuscript an *awfully* careful reading.
7. Janie *usually* tells one *terribly* stupid joke after another.
8. Raise the window shade *up* *quickly*.
9. The three pirates *eagerly* divided *up* the stolen jewels.
10. Jean *gradually* became *terribly* dependent upon her mother's judgment.

16

Joiners

Chapter 3

Prepositions

Notice the italicized words in these sentences:

He crawled *through* the fence.　　He crawled *under* the fence.
He crawled *past* the fence.　　　He crawled *over* the fence.
He crawled *around* the fence.　　He crawled *toward* the fence.

The sentences have different meanings because the italicized words express different relationships between the noun *fence* and the verb *crawled*. Such words, which join nouns to other words in a sentence, are called **prepositions.**

Now notice the italicized words in the following sentences:

The money in the *box* is Amy's.　The money in the *wallet* is Amy's.
The money in the *cup* is Amy's.　The money in the *bank* is Amy's.

The sentences have different meanings because the words that complete the meaning of the preposition *in* are names of different things. Each of the italicized words is called the **object** of the preposition *in*. So, similarly, the noun *fence* is the object of each of the six prepositions *(through, past, around, under, over, toward)* in the first group of sentences above.

A preposition and its object form a **phrase** that modifies some word in the sentence. In the first group of examples the phrases *through the fence, past the fence,* and so on, modify the verb *crawled* by telling where. Since they do the work of adverbs, they are called "adverb phrases." In the second group of examples the phrases *in the box, in the cup,* and so on, modify the noun *money* by telling which money is meant. Since they do the work of adjectives, they are called "adjective phrases."

A preposition is a word that together with a noun or pronoun called its object forms a modifying phrase.

The prepositions in the following sentence are italicized. What do the phrases modify?

A man *with* one arm *in* a sling jumped *on* the bus *at* the same time.

To find out what word a phrase modifies, ask "What?" about the phrase. What *with one arm?* The answer is *man*. The phrase modifies the noun *man*. Notice that a prepositional phrase may modify a noun that is the object of another preposition. If you ask "What *in a sling?*" you will see that the phrase modifies the noun *arm,* which is the object of the preposition *with*. Notice also that the same word may be modified by more than one phrase. If you ask "What *on the bus?*" the answer is *jumped*. And if you ask "What *at the same time?*" the answer is *jumped*. The verb *jumped* is modified by both phrases, one telling where and one telling when.

Two or more words that do the work of a single preposition are called **compound prepositions:**

> The game was called *because of* rain.
> She brought cookies *instead of* cake.
> Mrs. Keith resigned *on account of* poor health.
> We drove *in spite of* his warning.

You can see that compound prepositions have objects just as single prepositions do. The objects are *rain, cake, health,* and *warning.*

Do not confuse adverbs and prepositions. An adverb never has an object; a preposition always has. An adverb is a modifying word. A preposition, by itself, is not; it is merely part of a modifying phrase. Notice the different uses of the word *outside* in these two sentences:

> A crowd had gathered *outside.*
> A crowd had gathered *outside* the courthouse.

In the first sentence *outside* is an adverb. It modifies the verb *had gathered.* In the second sentence *outside* is a preposition. It has an object, *courthouse;* and the whole phrase, *outside the courthouse,* modifies the verb.

EXERCISE 1. Find the prepositions and their objects in the sentences. Then decide what words the prepositional phrases modify. Divide a sheet of paper into three columns. In the first column, write the words modified by the phrases. In the second, write the prepositions. In the third, write the objects. Use a separate line for each preposition. Number your answers with the numbers of the sentences. For the first sentence you should write:

1. Several	*of*	*friends*
have enrolled	*in*	*class*
class	*at*	*school*

1. Several of my friends have enrolled in the aviation class at the vocational school.
2. Meg ran quickly toward the alley alongside the warehouse.
3. A boy with a slingshot was hiding inside the garage.
4. We chose the small apartment back of the store because of the great difference in rent.
5. Near Dundee the car behind ours turned off the highway.
6. After her death the money was divided among her many relatives.

7. The girl between us fidgeted nervously during the first few numbers on the program.
8. The ball sailed over the fence and through the front window of the store across the street.
9. Before winter we must go to the grove beside Crystal Lake for a picnic.
10. They built several cottages along the river road outside the city limits.

Improving sentences

4. Begin with a preposition

Students seldom think of beginning a sentence with a prepositional phrase. Yet a simple way of breaking the monotony of a series of subject-first sentences is to begin an occasional sentence with a prepositional phrase. Compare the first-draft paragraph at the left on the next page with the revision at the right:

Mr. Cowling was the last one on the program. He read his speech from a sheaf of note cards. We listened attentively to his droning voice for a half hour or so. We finally lost interest. None of us could understand the point of his remarks. He shifted constantly from one topic to another. Most of the audience was yawning and squirming impatiently by the end of his speech.

Mr. Cowling was the last one on the program. He read his speech from a sheaf of note cards. *For a half hour or so* we listened attentively to his droning voice. We finally lost interest. None of us could understand the point of his remarks. He shifted constantly from one topic to another. *By the end of his speech* most of the audience was yawning and squirming impatiently.

Notice that two simple changes — shifting the prepositional phrases of two sentences to the beginning — make the revised paragraph more interesting to read. A prepositional phrase modifying the verb usually comes at the end of a sentence. Putting the phrase first calls attention to its importance. See the difference in emphasis in these sentences:

Father makes all important decisions at our house.
At our house Father makes all important decisions.

And see how beginning sentences with prepositional phrases makes the contrast in these pairs of sentences clear:

Doing long division is hard work for me. *For Bill* even quadratic equations are easy.
Before breakfast Uncle Will is sullen and silent. *After breakfast* he talks incessantly.

Changing the position of a prepositional phrase is not always a matter of gaining variety or emphasis. Sometimes a change is needed to make the writer's meaning clear. Notice the following sentences:

He could see the baggage crew busily unloading heavy crates *through the tiny window.*

The woman lowered the awning, splashing dirty water all over the new suit I was wearing *without the slightest warning.*

An old man was standing next to my little brother *with a long, gray beard.*

These sentences are ridiculous because of the phrases at the end. The italicized phrase in the first sentence seems to modify *unloading,* making the meaning absurd. The italicized phrase in the second seems to modify *was wearing.* And the italicized phrase in the third should modify *man,* not *brother.* Sentences like these become easier to understand when the phrases are moved closer to the words they modify. The first two sentences should begin with the phrase:

Through the tiny window he could see the baggage crew busily unloading heavy crates.

Without the slightest warning the woman lowered the awning, splashing dirty water all over the new suit I was wearing.

The phrase in the third sentence should come right after *man:*

An old man *with a long, gray beard* was standing next to my little brother.

In revising first drafts of your written compositions, watch for opportunities to use this trick of beginning a sentence with a prepositional phrase. Use it occasionally to vary the sentences in a paragraph. Use it whenever you want to call attention to an important phrase or a contrast. Use it without fail if it is needed to make your meaning clear. But do not make changes thoughtlessly. It would be no improvement to change "Sam was experimenting with a new electric razor" to "With a new electric razor Sam was experimenting." The goal is always clearer, more forceful, and more interesting sentences.

EXERCISE 2. Each of the following sentences ends with a phrase or group of phrases that is clumsily placed. Revise each sentence, putting the awkwardly placed group of words at the beginning of the sentence or nearer the word it modifies. Be ready to read your revised sentences aloud.

For the first sentence you might say: *After the game the coach went over the blunders made by each of the players.*

1. The coach went over the blunders made by each of the players after the game.
2. People wondered why he had confessed to a crime he had not committed for many years.
3. A man told us about a new poison for getting rid of rats from the county agent's office.
4. We read that the river would continue to rise for several days in last night's paper.
5. Joan pointed to a huge black bear that was coming toward us with a look of horror on her face.
6. The policeman found the jewels that had been stolen from my aunt's hotel room in the trunk of the sedan.
7. Wilson opened the door of his room, which was on a long corridor, with his overcoat still on his arm.
8. A heavy wind had begun to blow after our mishap with the sail from the southwest.
9. I wondered how the men knew when to stop driving the poles into the ground for the first hour or so.
10. We were getting far down the street where the tape-deck stores have their showrooms, by this time.

Conjunctions

While prepositions join nouns to the rest of the sentence in which they appear, **conjunctions** join together words, phrases or clauses. Notice how the conjunctions work in the following sentences:

Her attic room was *small* but *cheerful.*
They should be here *by Monday evening* or *by Tuesday morning.*
The teacher told us *that the test would have four questions* and *that one of these would be a written composition.*

In the first sentence *but* joins two predicate adjectives. In the second sentence *or* joins two adverb phrases. In the third sentence *and* joins two noun clauses used as objects of the verb *told.* When words like *but, or,* and *and* join words, phrases, and clauses that are used in the same way, they are called **coordinating conjunctions.**

The most useful coordinating conjunctions are the following six, which can be remembered by the rhyme:

and, or, nor
but, yet, for

Or you can picture a little boy fanning a large sultan who is sitting in the sun. The little boy would be called a FANBOY:

*F*or
*A*nd
*N*or
*B*ut
*O*r
*Y*et

Notice how the sentence that introduces the FANBOY memory device above itself begins with a coordinating conjunction — *or*. Experienced writers will occasionally begin a sentence with a coordinating conjunction to gain emphasis and enhance sentence rhythm.

Now look at the words *either* and *or* in the sentence below:

Either a streetcar or a North Street bus will take you there.

Words like either . . . *or,* used in pairs as they are above to emphasize the words they join, are called **correlative conjunctions.**

A third kind of conjunction — a **subordinating conjunction** — joins a clause to the word the clause modifies. Subordinating conjunctions will be discussed later.

Compound subjects

What are the subjects of the following sentences?

In the top drawer were many receipted bills and personal letters.
Should Sam or Jerry stop for the hamburgers?
My mother, my aunt, and my grandmother had their first plane ride last Saturday afternoon.

The subject of each sentence consists of more than one noun. "What were in the top drawer?" *Bills* and *letters* were. "Who should stop for the hamburgers?" *Sam* or *Jerry* should. "Who had their first plane ride?" My *mother* and *aunt* and *grandmother* did. Two or more words used as the subject of one verb are called a **compound subject.** Compound subjects are usually joined together by coordinating conjunctions.

Compound verbs

What are the verbs in the following sentences?

Rob skated out too far and fell through the ice.
Holly read the chapter carefully, took several pages of notes, yet

could not answer three of the questions in the test the next day.
The boxes were packed a week ago, but were forgotten in the rush.
John neither sealed the envelope nor put a stamp on it.

In each of these sentences more than one verb is used with the same subject. In the first sentence the verbs *skated* and *fell* tell what Rob did. In the second the verbs *read* and *took* and *could answer* tell about Henry. In the third *were packed* and *were forgotten* tell what happened to the boxes. And in the fourth *sealed* and *put* tell what John did not do. Two or more verbs used with the same subject are called a **compound verb.** Notice that compound verbs are joined by coordinating conjunctions like *and, but, yet,* or by correlative conjunctions like *neither . . . nor.*

A compound verb is often used with a compound subject:

Our *skates,* woolen *mittens,* and heavy knit *socks were* carefully *wrapped* and *were stored* away in the attic.

EXERCISE 3. Each of the sentences contains a compound subject or a compound verb or both. Find the subject and verb of each sentence. Then divide a sheet of paper into two columns. In the first column, write the subjects. In the second, write the verbs. If the subject or verb is compound, write the conjunction that connects the parts, putting parentheses around it. Number your answers with the numbers of the sentences. For the first sentence you should write:

1. Sue (and) Marie | *talked, giggled, rattled, (and) made*

1. During the recital Sue and Marie talked, giggled, rattled candy wrappers, and made themselves generally obnoxious.
2. John wanted a second piece of cake, yet did not dare take it.
3. The new chairman and the committee wasted no time, but plunged into the work enthusiastically.
4. Margaret neither realized the importance of the project nor considered the consequences of failure.
5. Bill slipped on the ice, balanced in mid-air for a split second, and then fell flat on his face.
6. You and Hal either must accept the invitation or must give a good reason for your refusal.
7. Audrey's Southern drawl, her sudden flares of temper, and her fondness for practical jokes attracted others at first, but soon grew tiresome.
8. To talk back to Grandfather Heydrick or to interrupt him during one of his wearisome, endless stories was dangerous.
9. Across the room from Michael, half-hidden by a tall mahogany clock, sat one of the Gordon twins and his friend, Polly Willems.
10. David, still angry about Helen's sarcastic remark, neither spoke nor smiled on passing her in the hall.

Improving sentences

5. Use a compound verb

Experienced writers know how to improve their sentences by using two or more verbs with one subject. Suppose that in revising a composition you find sentences like these:

> The flame flickered wildly for an instant or two. Then it went out with a sputter.
>
> He returned the flasks to the refrigerator. He carefully recorded his observations in his notebook. Then he started for the library to find Dr. Morrison.
>
> The manager had probably forgotten my phone call. Maybe she had decided not to interview any more applicants.
>
> I could hear the alarm clock ringing shrilly. However, I couldn't wake up enough to turn it off.
>
> From that day on Mary Ann would not read the assigned lessons. Also she would not pay attention during the class discussions.
>
> Lucille spends very little money on clothes. Nevertheless, she always manages to look well dressed.

You can see that the verbs in the sentences of each group tell about the same person or thing. Since they do, you can use compound verbs to combine the groups into single sentences that will be more interesting to read:

> The flame *flickered* wildly for an instant or two and then *went* out with a sputter.
>
> He *returned* the flasks to the refrigerator, carefully *recorded* his observations in his notebook, and *started* for the library to find Dr. Morrison.
>
> The manager *had* probably *forgotten* my phone call or *had decided* not to interview any more applicants.
>
> I *could hear* the alarm clock ringing shrilly, but *could*n't *wake* up enough to turn it off.
>
> From that day on Mary Ann *would* neither *read* the assigned lessons nor *pay* attention during the class discussions.
>
> Lucille *spends* very little money on clothes, yet always *manages* to look well dressed.

In using compound verbs to combine related sentences, be sure to choose the conjunction that most accurately expresses the meaning intended. The conjunction *and,* for instance, is appropriate in first and second example sentences. But it would not be suitable in the last sentence, where the meaning is that Lucille manages to look well dressed "in spite of" the fact that she spends little on clothes.

24

EXERCISE 4. Each of the numbered groups consists of two or more sentences that are about the same person or thing. Read each group of sentences, and decide how they can be combined by using a compound verb. Be prepared to read your improved sentences aloud. For the first group you might say: *The mayor's wife looks like an ordinary housewife, yet has a dignity of manner that would distinguish her in any group.*

1. The mayor's wife looks like an ordinary housewife. Still she has a dignity of manner that would distinguish her in any group.
2. I noticed the broken windowpane. ~~However~~, I didn't connect it with the robbery.
3. Hearing the footsteps come closer, Si ducked behind a crate. He pulled a blanket over his head. ~~Then he~~ waited for five endless minutes before daring to peer out.
4. Ken was never given a chance to play in the conference games. Nevertheless he faithfully appeared at every practice.
5. Jennie heard the doorbell ring. She rinsed the soapsuds off her hands. Then she went to the door, none too happy about the interruption.
6. Jerry's cousin would not play with the others. He would not let them use his baseball mitt and bat either.
7. Lorraine finally agreed to take over my baby-sitting job. ~~However~~, she insisted on being paid in advance.
8. Ryan probably stopped to see Sweeney for a while. Maybe he went to the "Y" for a swim.
9. The committee members made elaborate plans for the Halloween party. ~~However~~, they forgot to reserve the auditorium for October 31.
10. Joan Carter gets a large allowance every week. ~~Nevertheless~~, she never has enough money to go to the movies with us on Saturday nights.

Subjects	Verbs
John, he	wanted, take
chairman, committee	wasted, plunged
Margaret	realized, considered
Bill	slipped, balanced, fell
You, Hal	accept, give
Audrey's	drawn, attracted
Grandfather	talk back, interrupt
Gordon twins, Polly	
David, Helen	spoke, smiled

Chapter 4

Other Uses of Nouns and Pronouns

Earlier chapters have shown some of the ways in which nouns and pronouns are used — as subjects of verbs and as objects of prepositions. Here are four more common uses of nouns and pronouns — as predicate nominatives, direct objects, indirect objects, and as appositives — and two occasional uses — as objective predicates and as adverbial nouns.

Predicate nominatives

The subject of a sentence may be modified by an adjective in the predicate, as in "Joan will be *angry,* of course" or "The theatre was *empty*" — sentences used as illustrations in Chapter 2. In some sentences a noun or pronoun in the predicate is used to explain the subject:

Harold is my oldest *brother.*
The first course was onion *soup.*
The one at the desk must have been *he.*

Such nouns and pronouns are called **predicate nominatives.** Predicate nominatives explain a subject by telling who or what it is, or seems to be, or becomes, or is made to be. Like predicate adjectives, most predicate nominatives come after a form of the verb *be.* And they are also used after verbs like *become, seem, remain, are called, were elected,* and *was appointed:*

Before long Allan became *president* of the bank.
Sheila's address has remained a *mystery.*
In the West motherless calves are called *dogies.*
Was Alice appointed *chairman?*

You can see that the predicate nominative and the subject in each of these sentences are different names for the same person or thing. Allan and president are the same person. Sheila's address and a mystery are the same thing to the writer of the second sentence. In one part of the country *dogies* is another name for motherless calves. And changing the fourth example to a statement — "Alice was appointed chairman" — helps you see that *Alice* and *chairman* are different names for the same person.

EXERCISE 1. Some of the sentences have predicate adjectives; some have predicate nominatives; some have neither. Divide a sheet of paper into three columns. In the first column, write the subjects of the sentences. In the second, write the predicate adjectives. In the third, write the predicate nominatives. Number your answers with the numbers of the sentences. For the first sentence you should write:

1. alderman | | politician

1. The alderman in their district must be a clever politician.
2. The interior of the huge mansion on Cooper Road is quite shabby.
3. A universal language has been the dream of many men.
4. Beth's hopes were high before the interview with Mr. Simmons.
5. Mr. Hanson's ancient Maxwell car had been a neighborhood joke for a great many years.
6. In one corner of the back yard there is a comfortable old hammock.
7. Television programs are my little sister's main interest in life.
8. Wasn't Rod's behavior at the game yesterday afternoon inexcusable?
9. Judy was not even considered for the chairmanship of the Assembly Committee this year.
10. The hobby exhibit became the outstanding attraction at the fair.

Direct Objects

Notice the italicized words in the following sentences:

Dave's car struck the *pushcart.*
The principal expelled *them* the very next day.
Amelia believed his *story.*
I have forgotten the *title* and the *author.*

In each sentence the verb expresses a physical or mental action. In each sentence the subject is the doer of that action. The italicized words tell what or who receives the actions expressed by the verbs. What did the car strike? It struck the pushcart. Whom did the principal expel? He expelled them. What did Amelia believe? She believed the story. What have I forgotten? I have forgotten the title and the author.

A noun or pronoun that tells what or who receives the action expressed by the verb is called the object of the verb, or the direct object.

The direct object is almost always a word that means something different from the subject. The only exception is the group of pronouns ending in *self* or *selves.* In the sentence "We burned the toast" the noun *toast* receives the action of the verb *burned* and means something different from the subject *We.* In the sentence "We burned ourselves" the pronoun *ourselves* also receives the action of the verb, though it means the same persons as the subject *We.*

A few cautions: The action expressed by a verb does not always pass to an object:

The traffic *moved* slowly.
Dan *will call* again tomorrow.

The verbs *moved* and *will call* express actions. But there are no objects in these sentences — no nouns or pronouns that tell what or who receives the action.

As has just been said, the action expressed by a verb does not always pass to an object. For example, notice the italicized words in the following sentences:

Bob asked for a *copy* of the letter.
Half of us climbed aboard the rickety old *bus.*

At first glance the nouns *copy* and *bus* may seem to be the objects of the verbs in these sentences. But the meaning shows that this is not so. Bob did not ask a copy. He asked *for* a copy. The noun *copy* is the object of the preposition *for.* And we did not climb a bus. We climbed *aboard* a bus. The noun *bus* is the object of the preposition *aboard.* Nouns or pronouns that do not receive the action expressed by the verb cannot be objects of the verb.

Guard against mistaking predicate nominatives for objects of verbs. Watch particularly for predicate nominatives used after verbs other than *be:*

My brother was considered a skillful *dentist.*
The picnic has become an annual *affair.*

Except for pronouns like *myself* and *themselves,* objects of the verbs always mean something different from the subject. When the answer to a question like "What was my brother considered?" or "What has the picnic become?" is a word meaning the same person or thing as the subject, the word is a predicate nominative, not the object of the verb.

EXERCISE 2. Each sentence contains one subject and one verb. In some of the sentences the verb has an object; in some the verb is followed by a predicate nominative; in others there is no object or predicate nominative. Divide a sheet of paper into four columns. In the first column, write the subjects. In the second, write the verbs. In the third, write the direct objects. In the fourth, write the predicate nominatives.

Number your answers with the numbers of the sentences. For the first sentence you should write:

   1. detective | followed | shoplifter | |

1. A store detective quietly followed the suspected shoplifter ~~from coun-~~
   ~~ter to counter~~.
2. There have been several earthquakes ~~in Ecuador recent~~ly.
3. The city council will give a substantial scholarship to the valedictorian of this year's senior class.
4. Gypsies have always seemed a rather mysterious and fascinating group of people.
5. At the meeting Friday night our principal was made an honorary member of the Pilot Club.
6. Your employer will rate you according to your attitudes ·as well as your work.
7. The old hermit appears in the village once every two or three months.
8. John has been appointed chairman of the newly organized Conservation Club.
9. My sister bought a pair of lovely rhinestone earrings.
10. A car is no longer considered a luxury.

Improving sentences

6. Begin with an object

In most sentences the object of the verb comes after the verb:

Donna left *most* of the work for me to do.
We can buy the *ice cream* later.

Moving the object from its usual place to the beginning of the sentence calls attention to its importance:

Most of the work Donna left for me to do.
The *ice cream* we can buy later.

Sometimes a contrast between two sentences can be made more effective by putting the object first in one or both of the sentences:

Alice washed and ironed the silk blouses. Her wool *skirt* she sent to the cleaners.
The *tables* and *chairs* we sold to the Bennetts. The *cabinet* we donated to the parish house.

Objects of prepositions, like objects of verbs, may also be put first in the sentence when special emphasis is wanted. Compare the sentences in the following pairs:

We have known about this *invention* for several months.
This *invention* we have known about for several months.

I have written to *Wendy* only once.
Wendy I have written to only once.

And notice how vivid the contrast between two sentences is when one or both begin with an object of a preposition:

Some of the adventurers returned to King John with thrilling stories.
Others he never heard from again.

This *painting* we learned about through a radio advertisement. That *one* we came across in a musty little shop on Third Avenue.

Remember this trick of beginning with an object. But be careful. Used thoughtlessly or too often, it may make writing sound artificial and stilted. Used wisely — particularly for emphasis — it can change monotonous sentences to interesting, forceful ones.

EXERCISE 3. Both sentences in each of the numbered groups contain objects. Revise each group, making the meaning more forceful by putting an object first in one or both of the sentences. Make no change if putting an object first causes the sentence to sound awkward or unnatural. Be ready to read your revised sentences aloud. For the first group you might say: *Most of his money Mr. Thomas bequeathed to his favorite charity. The rest he left to his chauffeur.*

1. Mr. Thomas bequeathed most of his money to his favorite charity. He left the rest to his chauffeur.
2. First decide on the time and the place for your party. You can make up the guest list later.
3. Both of the families have moved to California. We shall probably never hear from the Bradleys again.
4. We have only a few items of old business to take up in class meeting. We can dispose of these in ten minutes.
5. I studied the chapter on tariffs very carefully. I merely skimmed the rest of the book.
6. Nancy read and answered one or two of Darrel's letters. She threw Jim's into the waste basket unopened.
7. Mike worked all the easy problems in study hall. He left the hard ones for evening.
8. "Iron only the unstarched pieces," ordered Mrs. Davis. "I will attend to the others myself."
9. We tried calling four more numbers. Each time we drew a blank.
10. I seem to have forgotten his face. However, I remember his name well.

Indirect Objects

Often sentences have two words which seem to be used as objects of the verb. But only one of the words actually receives the action expressed by the verb. Which of the italicized nouns in the following sentences are used as objects of the verbs?

George lent *Clinton* a *dollar* yesterday.
Mr. Evans should buy his *son* a larger *bicycle*.

What did George lend? George lent a dollar. What should Mr. Evans buy? He should buy a bicycle. The nouns *dollar* and *bicycle* receive the action expressed by the verbs. *Clinton* tells to whom George lent a dollar. *Son* tells for whom Mr. Evans should buy a bicycle. In sentences like these the words that receive the action — *dollar* and *bicycle* — are called **direct objects.** The words that tell to whom or for whom the action is done — *Clinton* and *son* — are called **indirect objects.**

The indirect objects are italicized in the following sentences:

He offered *me* a reward.
Mother sends *you* her love.
Has Mrs. Ellis ever refused *Lucy* anything?
I wouldn't give her *remarks* a second thought.

Notice that the indirect object precedes the direct object.

Objective predicates

Occasionally sentences have two words, both meaning the same person or thing, which seem to be used as objects of the verb. But only one of the words actually receives the action expressed by the verb. Which of the italicized nouns in the following sentences are used as objects of the verbs?

The directors appointed my *cousin* assistant *manager*.
The proud parents named the *baby Teresa*.

Whom did the directors appoint? They appointed my cousin. Whom did the parents name? They named the baby. The nouns *cousin* and *baby* receive the action and are direct objects. *Manager* tells what the directors appointed the cousin to be. *Teresa* tells what the parents named the baby. Nouns like *manager* and *Teresa*, which explain the direct object, are called **objective predicates.** An objective predicate is another name for the object. Notice that the objective predicate follows the direct object.

32

Adjectives may also be used as objective predicates:

Alice thought him more *stubborn* than ever.
They had already painted the walls *green.*
She wants dinner *ready* by five-thirty.

The adjective *stubborn* describes the object *him* by telling how Alice thought him to be. *Green* describes the object *walls* by telling how they had painted the walls to be. And *ready* describes the object *dinner* by telling how she wants the dinner to be. Although adjectives are commonly used as objective predicates, they are seldom confusing, since modifying words cannot be objects.

Adverbial nouns

The only other nouns that might be confused with objects of verbs are adverbial nouns, discussed in Chapter 2. Which of the italicized nouns in the following sentences are used as objects of the verbs?

Bill drove his father's *car* to the station.
Rachel drove *home* last *Friday.*

What did Bill drive? He drove his father's car. The noun *car* is the object of the verb in the first sentence. What did Rachel drive? She did not drive a "home"; she did not drive a "Friday." The words *home* and *Friday* in the second sentence are not objects; they are adverbial nouns telling where and when Rachel drove. The second sentence has no object.

Look again at the verbs in the two example sentences. In the first sentence *drove* expresses an action that passes to a person or thing named in the sentence. When verbs are used in this way, they are called **transitive** verbs. In the second sentence *drove* expresses an action that does not pass to a person or thing named in the sentence. When verbs are used in this way, they are called **intransitive** verbs. Remembering that verbs expressing action are not always followed by objects will keep you from mistaking adverbial nouns after intransitive verbs for objects of the verbs. Only a noun or pronoun that receives the action expressed by a verb can be the object of that verb.

EXERCISE 4. Find the verbs in the sentences, and decide which are followed by direct or indirect objects, which are followed by objective predicates, and which are modified by adverbial nouns. Divide a sheet of paper into five columns. In the first column, write the verbs. In the second, write the indirect objects. In the third, write the objects of the verbs. In the fourth, write the objective predicates. And in the fifth, write the adverbial nouns. Number your answers. For the first one you should write:

1. will tell | us | decision | | night

1. The coach will tell us his decision tomorrow night.
2. Until then I had always thought Marjorie a dreadful snob.
3. Why doesn't she dye the curtains blue the next time?
4. Dave drove the car the first hundred miles.
5. How much money did you give Emily last Monday?
6. Uncle Gilbert always calls a spade a spade.
7. The cough syrup didn't do Sandy a bit of good.
8. Miranda lent me a dollar Friday.
9. Which magazines did you send Ellen last week?
10. The following year Pope Pius VII crowned Napoleon emperor.

Appositives

The meaning of nouns and pronouns may often be made clearer by setting other nouns and pronouns alongside them. Notice the italicized words in these sentences:

Their captain, *Joe Simpson,* was hurt in the first play.
One of the parts, the *hairspring,* had to be replaced.
Are there costumes for Joe and Sam, the *pirates* in the first act?
Jean has two tan coats, a cloth *one* for sports wear and *another* with
a brown fur collar.

In the first sentence the proper noun *Joe Simpson* adds to the meaning of the word *captain* by telling the name of the player injured. In the second the common noun *hairspring* explains the word *One* by telling the name of the part replaced. In the third the noun *pirates* with its modifiers adds to the meaning of the two names *Joe* and *Sam.* In the fourth the two pronouns, *one* and *another,* with their modifiers explain the word *coats.* In all four sentences the italicized words are **appositives.** They are said to be "in apposition with" the words that they explain.

A noun or pronoun that is set alongside another word or group of words to explain or add to its meaning is called an appositive.

Appositives are sometimes preceded by *or, like, namely, that is, such as, for example,* and similar introductory expressions:

Next to the brake pedal is the foot throttle, or *accelerator.*
Certain other indoor games, such as *basketball* and *handball,* may
also be played outdoors equally as well.
Any reasonable excuse — for example, *illness, absence* from town,
or a previous *engagement* — will be acceptable.

34

Sometimes an appositive sums up the meaning of a whole group of words:

Ted was always borrowing money — a *practice* that annoyed his friends extremely.
By noon the wind had shifted to the east — a *fact* of considerable importance to the fishermen in their small boats.

In each of the last two sentences the italicized noun is in apposition with the whole group of words preceding it, not with any one word.

Though an appositive usually comes after the word it explains, sometimes it precedes:

An all-American *halfback* in his day, the coach likes to put on a uniform and practice with his team.

And occasionally, for emphasis, an appositive is placed last, even when the word it explains is in the first part of the sentence:

Only one of the students placed in the state meet — *Darrel Keane.*

The noun *halfback* is in apposition with *coach. Darrel Keane* is in apposition with *one.*

EXERCISE 5. Each sentence contains one or more appositives. Find each appositive, and decide what word it is in apposition with. Then divide a sheet of paper into two columns. In the first column, write the words that are explained by the appositives. In the second, write the appositives. Number your answers with the numbers of the sentences. For the first sentence you should write:

1. positions | *quarterback, center, guard*

1. Three positions on the team have not yet been filled — quarterback, center, and left guard.
2. For a souvenir of her trip Elinor brought home a calumet, or peace pipe.
3. Uncle Joe's latest invention, a baby carriage with a small built-in engine, will probably be just another failure.
4. The plane, a Boeing P-26 pursuit ship, was equipped with a 550 horsepower supercharged Wasp engine.
5. After shopping all day, Lisa came home with only two purchases — a hat and a movie magazine.
6. An expert silversmith and engraver, Paul Revere is famous not for his work, but for his midnight ride.
7. One of their musical comedies, *South Pacific,* made a national figure of Ezio Pinza, a Metropolitan Opera star.

8. A few of the rodents — namely, the beaver, the chinchilla, and the muskrat — are valuable for their fur.
9. The only clock in the house, a battered relic left behind by the former tenants, had stopped during the night.
10. House, barn, sheds, machinery, cars — all were destroyed by the flames.

Improving sentences

7. Use an appositive

An untrained writer often fails to make a distinction between what is important and what is not. When he or she wants to express two ideas, he or she regularly puts each idea into a separate sentence. For example:

> John Randall was the speaker at the football banquet. He is an expert on college coaching methods.

Because the sentences look equally important, readers assume the ideas are equally important. This may not be what was intended.

A trained writer might use such sentences, too, but only intentionally. For he or she knows ways to make more important ideas stand out clearly. One way is to use appositives for ideas that are less important:

> John Randall, *the speaker at the football banquet,* is an expert on college coaching methods.
> John Randall, *an expert on college coaching methods,* was the speaker at the football banquet.

The important idea in the first sentence is that John Randall is an expert. The important idea in the second is that John Randall was the speaker. When appositives are used for less important ideas, readers can tell at once what the more important ideas are.

A series of short sentences, each beginning with subject and verb, gives a choppy effect that may become very tiresome to readers. For example, sentences like the following are childish:

> The first prize was an expensive television set. It was donated by Mr. Hartley. He is president of the Video Corporation.

Anybody who knows about appositives can combine the three monotonous sentences:

> The first prize, *an expensive television set,* was donated by Mr. Hartley, *president of the Video Corporation.*

The revised sentence is more interesting to read. And by using appositives for two of the ideas, the writer makes the third idea stand out more clearly.

Watch for sentences that can be combined by using appositives for less important ideas. The goal is not longer sentences, but better ones — sentences that are more interesting to read, sentences that express thoughts more accurately.

EXERCISE 6. Each of the numbered groups consists of two or three sentences. Read the groups, and decide which sentences are merely explanatory. Then change the groups into single sentences, using appositives in place of the explanatory sentences. Be ready to read your revised sentences aloud. For the first group you might say: *Teak, a prized hardwood used in shipbuilding, comes largely from Burma and Siam.*

1. Teak is a prized hardwood used in shipbuilding. It comes largely from Burma and Siam.
2. I found the famed Mexican tortillas most unappetizing. They are pancakes made of corn meal.
3. One of the best subjects for scientific research is the Syrian hamster. This is a strange, furry little animal.
4. Lister was a pioneer in antiseptic surgery. He introduced a number of new surgical instruments and developed many new techniques.
5. Of his own accord Henry went in and apologized to Mrs. Renner. This was a totally unexpected act on the part of this ordinarily thoughtless and selfish boy.
6. Our zoo is one of the best in the Midwest. It houses many relatives of our mild-looking pet cats. These relatives are lions, tigers, leopards, pumas, and jaguars.
7. Walter Haven was the umpire for the city baseball league. He was slow-moving, near-sighted, and as stubborn as a mule.
8. On a dare we bought tickets for a ride on the Loop-o-plane. This is a tinny contraption guaranteed to scare the wits out of the bravest of men.
9. Last month Mabel came late to school only once. It was quite a record for her.
10. Grandfather used to keep his children awake during the hour-long sermons by pinching their arms at the first sign of a nod. This was a method quite common in their little community.

Chapter 5

Verbals and Verbal Phrases

Verbals (gerunds, infinitives, participles) are forms of verbs that are used as nouns, adjectives, or adverbs. When these verbals are joined with certain other words, the resulting word group forms a phrase — a group of closely related words that do the same work as single words.

Gerunds

Notice the italicized words in these sentences:

Effective *studying* usually requires thoughtful *reading*.
Her favorite water sports are *swimming* and *sailing*.
Mary has only two hobbies — French *cooking* and oil *painting*.
The reporters gave his spectacular *hitting* much of the credit for our *winning*.

In the first sentence *studying* is the subject, and *reading* the object, of the verb *requires*. In the second *swimming* and *sailing* are predicate nominatives. In the third *cooking* and *painting* are in apposition with *hobbies*. And in the fourth *hitting* is an indirect object, while *winning* is the object of the preposition *for*. The italicized words are used as nouns. When a verb form ending in *ing* is used as a noun, it is called a **gerund**. Notice that gerunds, like nouns, may be modified by adjectives and possessive pronouns.

A verb form that ends in *ing* and is used as a noun is called a gerund.

Gerunds are not verbs, and they do not make statements. Yet they may have objects and predicate nominatives and predicate adjectives. And they may be modified by adverbs and adverb phrases. Together with a gerund, such words form a **gerund phrase.**

verb + *ing* + $\left\{\begin{array}{l}\text{object} \\ \text{predicate nom.} \\ \text{adverb} \\ \text{predicate adj.}\end{array}\right\}$ $\begin{array}{l}\text{replacing} \\ \text{a noun}\end{array}$ = $\begin{array}{l}\text{gerund} \\ \text{phrase}\end{array}$

Notice the italicized phrases in the following sentences:

Telling everybody your troubles is one way of *being a bore.*
By *having kept quiet,* she can now repeat most of their conversation.
He recalls *having been knocked down.*
Being questioned about low grades annoys almost everyone.

In the first sentence *Telling* has a direct object *troubles* and an indirect object *everybody,* while *being* has a predicate nominative *bore.* In the second *quiet* is a predicate adjective after *having kept.* In the last two *down* is an adverb modifying *having been knocked,* and *about low grades* is an adverb phrase modifying *Being questioned.* The gerund phrases are used as nouns. Gerunds may also be two words or three words, as in the last three example sentences.

Verb forms ending in *ing* are very common. Those used as nouns are gerunds.

EXERCISE 1. Each of the sentences contains one or more gerunds or gerund phrases. Find each gerund or gerund phrase, and decide how it is used in the sentence. Then divide a sheet of paper into two columns. In the first column, write each gerund. In the second, tell how the gerund is used. Use a separate line for each gerund, and number your answers with the numbers of the sentences. For the first sentence you should write:

> *1. painting china plates   in apposition with "accomplishment"*
> *finding a job   object of "in"*

1. Aunt Louisa's only accomplishment, painting china plates, was of little help in finding a job.
2. Merely worrying about your problems will not solve them.
3. The team practiced with just one purpose in mind — trouncing the high school across town.
4. One of Grandmother's chief pleasures is talking about "the good old days" on the farm.
5. Try holding your racquet in your left hand.
6. The Germans are given credit for originating the art of making toys.
7. Mrs. Lee, calling across the street, was loudly congratulating Ed for his latest accomplishment, winning the poster contest.
8. Signing Henry's petition is signing away your freedom.
9. Since winning the popularity contest, Laura doesn't enjoy swimming and picnicking with our gang.
10. Dipping metals in chemicals is replacing much of the mechanical polishing of years gone by.

8. Use a gerund

Gerunds are useful in combining sentences to make important ideas stand out clearly. Writers know which of their ideas are important, but readers cannot always tell. For example:

> Jim's Saturday morning sleep was interrupted by various noises. An eager young soprano screeched. Vacuum cleaners hummed. Children quarreled shrilly in the street.

By using separate sentences, the writer calls attention to the noises. By using gerunds to make appositives of these details, he or she could have called attention to Jim's unsuccessful effort to sleep:

> Jim's Saturday morning sleep was interrupted by various noises — the screeching of an eager young soprano, the humming of vacuum cleaners, the shrill quarreling of children in the street.

Untrained writers often use two sentences to express one important idea, beginning the second sentence with a pronoun:

> Records are packed in excelsior. *This* insures their safe delivery.

The pronoun *this* apparently refers to the meaning of the whole preceding sentence. Notice how the two sentences can be combined:

> *Packing records in excelsior* ensures their safe delivery.

The gerund phrase is used as a subject. The revised sentence is easier to read and understand.

Words like *then* and *but* and *in this way* are helpful in showing how sentences are related. Used too frequently, however, such words can become monotonous:

> Heidi revised her story carefully. *Then* she copied it neatly in ink. *Then* she handed it to the editor of the school paper.
> The chairman called a special meeting. *But* he didn't tell anyone why.
> We mow the grass once a week. *In this way* we keep the weeds down.

By using gerund phrases as objects of prepositions, you can combine such sentences and call attention to the important ideas:

> After *revising it carefully and copying it neatly in ink,* Heidi handed her story to the editor of the school paper.
> Without *telling anyone why,* the chairman called a special meeting.
> By *mowing the grass once a week,* we keep the weeds down.

Such prepositional phrases might also come last. By putting them first, avoid the monotony caused by too many subject-first sentences. But to use too many gerunds in sentences is to replace one kind of monotony with another kind of monotony.

Gerunds almost always name an action. When a phrase containing a gerund comes first in a sentence, readers expect the subject of the sentence to be the same person or thing as the doer of that action. Notice what happens otherwise:

> After riding horseback all afternoon, our supper tasted wonderful.
> Before going to football practice, Bill's grandmother always makes him listen to a long lecture on the dangers of the game.

A supper cannot ride horseback (of course!), and a reader would suspect that Bill's grandmother does not go to football practice! The sentences obviously do not mean what their writers intended them to mean. They need to be revised:

> After riding horseback all afternoon, *we enjoyed a wonderful supper.*
> Before going to football practice, *Bill always has to listen to a long lecture by his grandmother on the dangers of the game.*

When putting phrases containing gerunds first in the sentence, be sure that the subject of the sentence is the same person or thing as the doer of the action named by the gerund.

EXERCISE 2. Each of the numbered groups consists of two or three sentences. Read each group of sentences, and decide how to combine them into one good sentence by using one or more gerunds. Be ready to read your revised sentences aloud. For the first pair of sentences you might say: *Cutting the raw edges of the woolen dresses with a pinking shears keeps them from fraying.*

1. The raw edges of the woolen dresses are cut with a pinking shears. This keeps them from fraying.
2. Dad worked on the radio for over an hour. Then he told me to take it down to the repair shop on the corner.
3. Jane squeezed lemon juice over the sliced apples. In this way she kept them from turning brown.
4. Only one thing annoys Mrs. Gatling. That is to have to stand in a crowded streetcar.
5. Miss Jordan had us choose partners for our lab work. But first she called the roll.
6. Rita played the piano for hours each day. This did not seem to tire her.

42

7. George shot a paper airplane across the room. For this he was sent to the office.

George was sent ~ for shooting

8. My cousin Sara charged three of the sale sweaters. But she didn't phone to ask her mother's permission.

After charging

9. The apples are treated with a calcium chloride solution. This causes them to remain firm and to have superior baking qualities.

Being treated w/ ~

10. Howard argues constantly with the umpires. This is his major fault as a baseball player.

Arguing constantly ~

Infinitives

Gerunds, as has been shown, are verb forms ending in *ing* and used as nouns. Another verb form is used in much the same way. Notice the italicized words in these two sentences:

Apologizing will require real courage.
To apologize will require real courage.

The italicized words are both forms of verbs, but they are not used as verbs. The verb in each sentence is *will require.* "Who or what will require?" shows that the gerund *Apologizing* is the subject in the first sentence, while *To apologize* — called an **infinitive** — is the subject in the second.

Compare the ways in which the italicized words are used in the following pairs of sentences:

Mother hates *cooking* and *ironing.*
Mother hates *to cook* and *to iron.*

Her only answer was *silence.*
Her only answer was *to smile.*

We entered the contest with one thought in mind — *victory.*
We entered the contest with one thought in mind — *to win.*

In the first sentence *cooking* and *ironing* are objects of the verb *hates.* In the next *to cook* and *to iron* are used in the same way. In the second pair *silence* and *to smile* are predicate nominatives. In the third pair *victory* and *to win* are in apposition with the noun *thought.* The italicized words are all used as nouns.

The simple form of a verb, usually preceded by *to* and used as a noun, adjective, or adverb, is called an infinitive.

The *to* is often omitted:

No one dared *refuse* our request.   Who saw it *happen?*
Did you help *cook* the meal?   You should have seen him *go!*
Soon she began to talk, *laugh,* and *act* like the other children.
What are we going to do — *ask* for assistance or *revise* our plans?

Infinitives, like gerunds, may have objects and predicate nominatives and predicate adjectives. And they may be modified by adverbs and adverb phrases. Together with an infinitive, such words form an **infinitive phrase.**

$$\text{to } + \text{ verb} \left\{ \begin{array}{l} \text{object} \\ \text{predicate nom.} \\ \text{adverb} \\ \text{predicate adj.} \end{array} \right\} \begin{array}{l} \text{replacing a} \\ \text{noun,} \\ \text{adjective,} \\ \text{or adverb} \end{array} = \begin{array}{l} \text{infinitive} \\ \text{phrase} \end{array}$$

For example:

The pledge — *to do a good turn daily* — was taken seriously.
Nancy still hopes *to be elected secretary.*
To have become careless would have meant certain disaster.
Not to have been recognized by his closest friends hurt him deeply.

In the first sentence the infinitive *to do* has the object *turn* and is modified by the adverb *daily.* In the second *to be elected* has the predicate nominative *secretary.* In the third *To have become* has the predicate adjective *careless.* And in the fourth *to have been recognized* is modified by the adverb *Not* and the adverb phrase *by his closest friends.* Each of the infinitive phrases is used as a noun. Infinitives may be three or four words, as in the last three examples.

An infinitive used as a subject sometimes follows the verb:

It seemed useless *to complain further about the food.*

"Who or what seemed?" indicates that the real subject is the infinitive phrase *to complain further about the food.* The word *It* does not refer to anything. It is a dummy subject, like the word *There* in "There are ten boys in the class." An *it* or a *there* used in this way is called an **expletive.**

Just as nouns may be used as adjectives to modify other nouns, so infinitives with *to* may be used to modify nouns:

Harry was pleased by our offer *to help.*
Janet has the costumes *to be returned to the store.*

The infinitive *to help* modifies the noun *offer* by telling which one. The infinitive phrase in the second sentence modifies *costumes.*

Nouns may be used as adverbial modifiers of verbs, as shown in Chapter 4. Infinitives with *to* are often used in a similar way to modify not only verbs, but adjectives and adverbs as well:

Our friends waited *to see it again.*
The movie was pleasant *to watch* and not difficult *to understand.*
They stayed long enough *to miss the last bus.*

In the first sentence the infinitive phrase modifies the verb by telling why our friends waited. In the second sentence *to watch* and *to understand* modify the predicate adjectives *pleasant* and *difficult.* And in the last sentence the infinitive phrase modifies the adverb *enough* by telling how much.

These modifying infinitives are like prepositional phrases with the simple form of the verb as object of the word *to,* and modify in ways much like adjective and adverb phrases. These modifying uses are very common.

EXERCISE 3. Each of the sentences contains one or more infinitives or infinitive phrases. Find each infinitive or infinitive phrase, and decide how it is used in the sentence. Then divide a sheet of paper into two columns. In the first column, write each infinitive or phrase. In the second, tell how the infinitive is used. Number your answers with the numbers of the sentences. For the first sentence you should write:

| *1. to argue . . . semester* | *subject of "is"* |
| *to leave . . . semester* | *modifies "decision"* |

1. It is a complete waste of time to argue with Helen about her decision to leave school at the end of the semester.
2. His first thought — to pour water on the flaming stove — was quickly discarded.
3. Several people wrote to thank him for his kindness.
4. More than anything else Lola wanted to become a dancer.
5. All his questions had one purpose — to confuse us.
6. Our biggest problem was to keep Dad from discovering our plan to buy the motorcycle.
7. It would be better to wait here until time to eat.
8. I stayed after school an hour to help Miss Jameson with the chemistry exhibit to be held on Friday.
9. Hank's attitude soon became apparent — to do the least work and to claim the most credit.
10. We came early enough to get good seats.

Improving sentences

9. Use an infinitive

One of the important ways of improving sentences is to combine those that are related in meaning. When this is done to make important ideas stand out clearly, the reader can understand the sentences more easily.

Students who do not know about using infinitives for sentence improvement are likely to write sentences like these:

A person shouldn't hunt for a gas leak with a lighted match. It is dangerous.

David refused a second piece of chocolate cake. This was unusual.

Cecelie had an idea for raising money. That was to sponsor a tag day.

Diamonds can't be cut with ordinary tools. They are too hard.

What is dangerous? What was unusual? What was to sponsor a tag day? What are too hard? The pronouns that begin the second sentence of each pair make it difficult for the reader to know exactly what is meant. Notice how infinitives can be used to make such sentences clearer:

To hunt for a gas leak with a lighted match is dangerous.

For David *to refuse a second piece of chocolate cake* was unusual.

Cecelie's idea for raising money was *to sponsor a tag day*.

Diamonds are too hard *to be cut with ordinary tools*.

In the first sentence an infinitive phrase is used as the subject of *is;* in the second, as the subject of *was*. In the third an infinitive phrase is used as a predicate nominative. And in the fourth an infinitive phrase is used to modify the adverb *too*. Combining the sentences gets rid of the vague pronouns — *It, This, That,* and *They* — and makes the important ideas stand out more clearly.

Expressing closely related ideas in separate sentences often results in annoying wordiness:

Nell wanted to keep her grades up. She also wanted to be president of her class.

Nick had a regular job at practice. He would watch for violations of the rules. Then he would write down the violators' names. Later he would give them to the coach. This job made him unpopular with the players.

Using infinitives for the related ideas is one way of improving such sentences:

Nell wanted *to keep her grades up* and *to be president of her class*.

Nick's regular job at practice — *to watch for violations of the rules, write down the violators' names,* and *later give them to the coach* — made him unpopular with the players.

In the first sentence a pair of infinitive phrases tells what Nell wanted. The *and* between the phrases shows that they are closely related. In the second sentence the three infinitive phrases in apposition explain Nick's job and show why it made him unpopular.

46

Because the relationships of the ideas are easier to see, the revised sentences are easier to understand. And they are no longer wordy.

EXERCISE 4. Each of the numbered groups consists of two or three sentences. Read the groups of sentences, and decide how they can be combined by using infinitive phrases. Be prepared to read your revised sentences aloud. For the first group you might say: *Thornhill had only one object in life — to earn a million dollars and then retire.*

1. Thornhill had only one object in life. He wanted to earn a million dollars. Then he would retire.
2. Rob started a fight with the neighborhood bully. This was both foolish and brave.
3. Louise, unfortunately, couldn't say a word. She was too angry.
4. Dad's recommendation was turned down. He had recommended buying the old Turner place for a community center.
5. Emma crosses over to the other side of the street rather than speak to George. In my opinion this is silly.
6. The second step is easy and won't take much time. It is organizing the details in the order of their occurrence.
7. Barbara suggested a more practical solution. We could get part-time jobs. Then the damaged fenders could be paid for from our wages.
8. Bud would not accept the clothes that Mrs. Chalmers offered him. He was too proud.
9. Dr. Mitchell's plan was a surprise to everyone. He planned on giving up his practice to do cancer research.
10. Leonard had a proposal. He suggested using the bazaar money for playground equipment. His proposal brought a storm of protest from some of the members.

Active and passive participles

Notice the italicized words in the following sentences:

The *wailing* siren woke Martha from a sound sleep.
The one *grinning* at us is Hal's cousin.
The driver's responsibility seems almost *frightening.*

These *ing* forms of the verbs *wail, grin,* and *frighten* are used as adjectives. *Wailing* modifies the noun *siren,* describing the siren that woke Martha. *Grinning* modifies the pronoun *one,* telling which one is Hal's cousin. *Frightening* modifies the noun *responsibility,* telling what it seems to be. When *ing* forms are used in this way, they are called **active participles.** They do not state actions, but merely suggest that the modified words are performing an action.

A verb form that ends in *ing* and is used as an adjective is called an active participle.

Now look at the italicized words in the following sentences:

There were many *broken* windows in the *deserted* house.
The sheriff found the telephone wires *cut*.
The carpet in the front hall looks *worn*.

The italicized words in these sentences are also participles, since they are forms of verbs used as adjectives to modify nouns. But these participles suggest that the modified words have received or are receiving an action. The windows had been broken, the house has been deserted, the wires had been cut, and the carpet seems to have been worn. Such participles are called **passive participles.** Like active participles, they may come before or after the words they modify, or may follow the verb.

A participle which shows that the word it modifies has received or is receiving an action is called a passive participle.

Participles do not have subjects, and they cannot make statements. But they are like verbs in other ways. They may take objects and predicate nominatives and predicate adjectives. And they may be modified by adverbs and adverb phrases. Together with a participle, such words form a **participial phrase.**

verb form +
$\left\{\begin{array}{l}\text{object} \\ \text{predicate nom.} \\ \text{adverb} \\ \text{predicate adj.}\end{array}\right\}$
replacing
an adjective
= participial
phrase

In the following sentences the participial phrases are in italics:

The man *shoveling snow* started work yesterday.
We could hear you *practicing your violin lesson.*
Being the oldest boy in the group, Dick felt responsible.
Donna is the only one *becoming impatient.*
Two points will be deducted for each word *spelled incorrectly.*
Mary's gift, a lace tablecloth *imported from France,* was lovely.

In the first two sentences the participles *shoveling* and *practicing* take the objects *snow* and *lesson.* In the next two sentences *Being* is followed by the predicate nominative *boy,* and *becoming* by the predicate adjective *impatient.* In the last two sentences *spelled* and *imported* are modified by the adverb *incorrectly* and the adverb phrase *from France.*

To find the word a participle modifies, ask "Who or what is _____?" putting the participle in place of the blank. For the six sentences shown above, the participles modify *man, you, Dick, one, word,* and *tablecloth* — nouns and pronouns that are not part of the italicized phrases.

Participles sometimes modify a word in the phrase itself:

Today being a legal holiday, the bank is closed.
Mike returned home, *his left arm encased in a plaster cast.*

Asking "Who or what is *being?*" shows that the participle in the first sentence modifies a word that is in the phrase itself — *Today.* And "Who or what is *encased?*" shows that the participle in the second sentence modifies *arm,* a word that is part of the phrase and that has no other use in the sentence. Such a phrase, containing a participle and the word it modifies, is called a **nominative absolute.** A nominative absolute does not modify any word in the sentence. It merely gives added information.

Participles, like verbs, may be more than one word. For example:

Having run all the way home, Susan was out of breath.
The walls *being washed* today will be painted tomorrow.
Having been kept in the refrigerator, the butter softened only slightly during the meal.

In the first sentence *Having run* makes clear that Susan was out of breath after — not while — running home. In the second *being washed* makes clear that the washing is still going on, that the action suggested is not yet completed. In the third *Having been kept* makes clear that the butter had been in the refrigerator before — not during — the meal, that the action suggested had been completed before the time expressed by the verb in the sentence. Because they call attention to the time of the action suggested, two-word and three-word participles are sometimes needed to make sentences more exact in meaning.

EXERCISE 5. Each of the sentences contains one or more participles or participial phrases. Divide a sheet of paper into two columns. In the first column, list each participle or participial phrase. In the second, write the noun or pronoun that each participle or phrase modifies. Use a separate line for each participle. Number your answers with the numbers of the sentences. For the first sentence you should write:

1. Having heard
Mr. Wayne's lectures before   *I*
                    rambling   *sentences*
                    droning   *voice*

1. Having heard Mr. Wayne's lectures before, I didn't mind his rambling sentences and droning voice.
2. I snapped a picture of Marcia posing beside the stuffed grizzly bear.
3. He told us that leather treated with natural rubber will wear longer.
4. The two smallest children, shivering with cold, huddled together in the back of the stalled truck.
5. Migrating birds travel staggering distances and exhibit amazing endurance.
6. The next minute the cigar exploded, startling Uncle Will out of his wits.
7. Because of a tip received a week ago, the police were able to foil the attempted robbery.
8. Every week Gloria spent several fascinating hours in the laboratory, looking through a microscope.
9. Reminded of his promise to fix the broken clock, Al just grinned.
10. Having finished her homework, Karen rushed out to join her friends gathered at the drug store.

Improving sentences

10. Use a participle

Which sentence in each of the following pairs expresses the more important idea?

Tommy wanted to impress the little girls at the next table. So he ate three of the giant Clown-and-Circus sundaes.

Polly was encouraged by Miss Denby's praise. So she offered to type several more letters.

The second sentence in each pair expresses the important idea. The two first sentences merely give the reasons for Tommy's strange appetite and Polly's unusual offer. The relationship between the two ideas in each pair can be made clearer if participal phrases are used to give the reasons:

Wanting to impress the little girls at the next table, Tommy ate three of the giant Clown-and-Circus sundaes.

Encouraged by Miss Denby's praise, Polly offered to type several more letters.

Sentences related in meaning often have subjects that mean different persons or things:

In his excitement Tim scarcely even noticed the dog. It was crouched on the window seat in the corner of the room.

On his way home Peter saw Joan. She was gazing longingly at a pink giraffe. It was displayed in one of the shop windows.

In each group the first sentence states an important fact. The others merely give a descriptive detail about a word in a preceding sentence. A writer can call attention to the important fact by expressing the descriptive details in participial phrases:

In his excitement Tim scarcely even noticed the dog *crouched on the window seat in the corner of the room.*

On his way home Peter saw Joan *gazing longingly at a pink giraffe displayed in one of the shop windows.*

Now look at the following pairs of sentences:

Samantha came strolling in an hour or so before dinner. Little Jimmie was tagging along behind her as usual.

My curiosity was aroused by his remarks. So I decided to ask my algebra teacher to solve the problem.

The second sentence in the first pair merely adds an interesting bit of information and the first sentence in the second pair merely explains the cause for the decision. Both of these sentences give explanatory details about persons or things not mentioned in the other sentences. Nominative absolutes can be used for such details:

Samantha came strolling in an hour or so before dinner, *little Jimmie tagging along behind her as usual.*

My curiosity aroused by his remarks, I decided to ask my algebra teacher to solve the problem.

In revising written work, make sure that any participial phrase modifies a word in the sentence and that it is the word intended for it to modify. Watch especially for sentences like these:

Having worked all afternoon in the hot sun, the pitcher of lemonade was most welcome.

Excited at the thought of going to the party, her headache was soon forgotten.

Since a participle at the beginning generally modifies the subject, these sentences seem to mean that the pitcher of lemonade had been working and that the headache was excited at the thought of the party. The writers, intent on getting on with their stories, have carelessly omitted the words the participles were intended to modify. The participles are said to be **dangling** participles, because they have no words to modify. Such dangling modifiers are easily corrected. Simply supply the missing words, changing the sentences to make the words the subjects:

> Having worked all afternoon in the hot sun, *we welcomed the pitcher of lemonade.*
>
> Excited at the thought of going to the party, *she soon forgot her headache.*

Watch, also, for howlers like these:

> We saw many bears driving through Yellowstone Park.
>
> Suspended from the ceiling by a single hair, Damocles saw a shining sword.
>
> He ran outside and chased after the cat with a broomstick wearing just his underwear.

Each of these sentences contains the word the participle is intended to modify. But the writers of the first two sentences have carelessly placed the phrase last, where they seem to modify *bears* and *broomstick,* while the writer of the third sentence has misplaced the phrase first, where it seems to modify Damocles. These misplaced participles, also, are easily corrected. Simply move the phrases closer to the words they are intended to modify:

> *Driving through Yellowstone Park,* we saw many bears.
>
> Damocles saw a shining sword *suspended from the ceiling by a single hair.*
>
> *Wearing just his underwear,* he ran outside and chased after the cat with a broomstick.

EXERCISE 6. Read each of the pairs of sentences, and decide which sentence is the more important. Then revise the sentences, using participial phrases or nominative absolutes in place of the less important sentences. Be ready to read your revised sentences aloud. For the first sentence you might say: *Linda, thrilled by the prospect of her first visit to New York, slept hardly a wink all night.*

1. Linda was thrilled by the prospect of her first visit to New York. She slept hardly a wink all night.
2. The penguin swims very fast. He uses his wings as flippers.
3. Two burly guards walked at his side. They protected him from the mobs of autograph hunters.
4. Mrs. Watkins was impressed by Clifford's great skill. So she offered him a job in the ceramics plant.
5. The director paced back and forth on the stage. She ranted and raved at everyone in sight.

52

6. Native American chestnut trees may soon reappear. They were almost wiped out by a blight. *After almost being wiped out by w*
7. Carrie was seated in the back of the room near an open window, So she did not hear her name being called.
8. Fearfully they groped their way through the dark passage. They were trying desperately to find the mouth of the cave. *Desperately trying w*
9. Mike was frightened by these mysterious warnings. So he reported the matter to the foreman of his department. *Frightened by them w*
10. Dad was poring over the latest issue of *Fish and Stream*. He hardly heard a word of my story. *Poring over the latest issue w*

Chapter 6

Clauses

What a subordinate clause is

Groups of words that have subjects and verbs may stand alone as independent sentences. But there are also groups of words that have subjects and verbs and that are used as parts of sentences.

Mr. Cole likes *fast* automobiles.
Mr. Cole likes automobiles *that have powerful engines.*

The word *fast* in the first sentence is an adjective that tells what kind of automobiles Mr. Cole likes. In the second sentence a group of words is used to tell what kind of automobiles Mr. Cole likes. Although there is a verb *have* and a subject *that,* the group of words is not a sentence but only a part of a sentence — a modifier of the noun *automobiles.* Because the italicized words do the work of a single word in the sentence, they are called a **subordinate clause.** The rest of the sentence is called the **main clause.**

A group of words that contains a subject and a verb and that is used as a single word in a sentence is called a subordinate clause.

Subordinate clauses are used as adjectives, as nouns, or as adverbs. One that does the work of an adjective is called an **adjective clause:**

An *angry* man usually lacks judgment.
A man *who is angry* usually lacks judgment.

One that does the work of a noun is called a **noun clause:**

I don't understand your *attitude.*
I don't understand *what you mean.*

One that does the work of an adverb is called an **adverb clause:**

She wrote the letter *afterwards.*
She wrote the letter *after she saw him.*

Adjective clauses

Adjective clauses may be attached to the nouns or pronouns they modify by pronouns or adverbs:

Jim should have teachers *who would make him work.*
Harriet is the only one *whose sense of humor never fails.*
Myra hasn't a friend *whom she can trust.*

Dave has a golf club *which once belonged to Bobby Jones.*
By mistake I got on a train *that makes all the local stops.*

The phone never rings at a time *when I'm not busy.*
Do you remember the store *where we bought our raincoats?*
Is that the reason *why he failed?*

The pronouns *who, whose, whom, which,* and *that* are called **relative pronouns.** The adverbs *when, where,* and *why* are called **relative adverbs.** A relative pronoun or adverb refers, or "relates," to some noun or pronoun, called the **antecedent,** which is the word modified by the clause. In the example sentences the antecedents are *teachers, one, friend, club, train, time, store,* and *reason.* Since adjective clauses are generally introduced by a relative pronoun or adverb, they are also called **relative clauses.**

Relative pronouns and adverbs are sometimes omitted. For example, the following sentences have the same meaning, whether or not the relatives in parentheses are expressed:

His story reminded me of the summer (that) I spent in Europe with Aunt Imogene.
The people (whom) we met on shipboard were very good-natured and friendly.
I will never forget the day (when) we got our new car.
Surely that isn't the reason (why) they left!

You will find that a relative pronoun usually has one of three uses. It may be the subject of the clause:

We talked to a man *who had witnessed the collision between the truck and the bus.*

It may be the object of a verb, of a verbal, or of a preposition in the clause:

The candidate *whom the newspapers supported* was defeated.
We couldn't get tickets for the play *that we wanted to see.*
The woman *to whom he dedicated the novel* is his sister.

It may be a possessive modifier:

The man *whose lawn I mowed* gave me a big tip.

EXERCISE 1. Each of the sentences contains one or more adjective clauses. Find each clause, and decide what the antecedent of each relative pronoun or relative adverb is. Decide also how each relative pronoun is used. Then divide a sheet of paper into three columns. In the first column, write the first and last words of each clause. In the second, write the antecedent of each relative pronoun or adverb. In the third, tell how each relative pronoun is used. Use a separate line for each clause, and number your answers with the numbers of the sentences. For the first sentence you should write:

> 1. *when finish* | *night* |
> *that finish* | *lecture* | *subject of "bored"*

1. I will never forget the night when Aunt Edna insisted on taking us to a lecture that bored us from start to finish.
2. Jean Miles, whose clothes are the envy of every girl in school, designs and makes them herself.
3. The radio that was delivered is not the one that we ordered.
4. Old Mr. Whittlesey, who was the guest of honor, came late and left before ten o'clock.
5. Everyone whom the district attorney talked to told a different story about the tragic accident that had horrified the town.
6. Tom has evidently forgotten the many times when he borrowed money from you.
7. The garage was the only place where we could practice our skit without annoying interruptions.
8. The children whose parents owned the castle were not allowed to play with Terry, who worked in the kitchen.
9. The company that my sister works for has a profit-sharing plan which benefits all the workers.
10. The movie which I least enjoyed seeing was the one that I had wanted most to see.

Improving sentences

11. Use an adjective clause

Adjective clauses are useful in combining related sentences like the following:

> Gloria was one of those spoiled, self-centered girls. Such girls always insist on having their own way.
> Jim Tilson works for Mr. Hale every day after school to help support the family. Jim's father is an invalid.
> Years ago Mike Daly used to impress our old gang with his motorcycle tricks. Now Mike is terrorizing the neighborhood with an old racing car. He bought the car from a junk dealer.

The important facts and explanatory details are expressed in separate sentences. Using adjective clauses for details that are merely explanatory or descriptive makes the important ideas stand out more clearly:

> Gloria was one of those spoiled, self-centered girls *who always insist on having their own way.*
>
> Jim Tilson, *whose father is an invalid,* works for Mr. Hale every night after school to help support the family.
>
> Mike Daly, *who years ago used to impress our old gang with his motorcycle tricks,* is now terrorizing the neighborhood with an old racing car *that he bought from a junk dealer.*

EXERCISE 2. Read the groups of sentences, and decide which sentence in each is the important one. Then change the groups into good sentences, using adjective clauses in place of weak explanatory sentences. For the first group you might say: *We are planning to hold the celebration at Brant Park, where there are outdoor fireplaces and a shady picnic grove.*

1. We are planning to hold the celebration at Brant Park. There are outdoor fireplaces at the park. There is also a shady picnic grove.
2. A tall, dignified old man was seated next to Mrs. Bruce at the speakers' table. His face seemed rather familiar.
3. Mrs. Gibson is one of those jittery drivers. Such drivers consider the horn the most important part of a car.
4. In reply Ruth merely groaned loudly and pointed to her left foot. It was encased in a heavy plaster cast.
5. Larry was completely bewildered by the many pieces of silverware spread before him. He had never eaten in a swanky restaurant before.
6. Under the giant oak tree in the corner of the yard was a playhouse. Uncle Will had built it for Miriam.
7. I don't suppose I'll see Elizabeth again until a year from June. Our class will hold its fifth reunion banquet then.
8. Mr. Norton was late for work as usual. He crashed into our privet hedge. It was Dad's pride and joy.
9. Louise was annoyed by the incessant chatter around her. She gathered up her papers and moved to the office at the end of the hall. In this office she could have some peace and quiet.
10. At the party tonight we must try to keep Max away from old Mrs. Carson. Max is always saying the wrong thing. Mrs. Carson always goes around looking for opportunities to take offense.

Noun clauses

A subordinate clause that does the work of a noun is called a **noun clause.** Noun clauses may be used as objects:

I doubt *if she has enough money for both tickets.*
Dad refused to tell *who had dented the fender.*
For an hour they argued about *which movie was the best.*

They may be used as subjects, either before the verb or — in sentences beginning with *It* — after the verb:

What he does with his time after school is his own business.
It makes no difference to me *whether or not she knows Bill.*
It is not known *how he acquired that large sum of money.*

They may be used as predicate nominatives:

The most exciting moment was *when the elevator stalled.*
Home for him is *where he hangs his hat.*

Or they may be used as appositives:

John's suggestion, *that we leave without him,* made us suspicious.
She could no longer hide the fact *that she had lost the necklace.*

The introductory words may be adjectives like *which,* pronouns like *who* and *what,* adverbs like *how* and *when* and *where* — each of which has a use in its clause. Or they may be words like *if* and *whether* and *that,* which have no use except to introduce their clauses.

Students sometimes confuse the relative pronoun *that* with a *that* introducing a noun clause. For example, which of the following sentences contains a noun clause?

Years ago people laughed at the theory *that Columbus suggested.*
Years ago people laughed at the theory *that the world is round.*

In the first sentence *that* is a relative pronoun. It has an antecedent — the noun *theory.* The clause is an adjective clause modifying the antecedent *theory* by telling which theory was laughed at. In the second sentence *that* is merely an introductory word. It is not a relative pronoun and has no antecedent. The clause is a noun clause in apposition with *theory,* telling what the theory was. A simple test for such clauses is to substitute a *which* for the *that.* If the sentence still makes sense, the clause is probably an adjective clause.

In Chapter 5 an example sentence showed that infinitives can be used like adverbs to modify predicate adjectives *(pleasant* and *difficult):*

The movie was pleasant to *watch* and not difficult to *understand.*

Noun clauses may be used in a similar way:

Be careful *how you act at the party.*
The director is afraid *that you will forget your lines.*
I was sure *Linda had started the rumor.*

The italicized noun clauses tell in what way you should be *careful,* in what way the director is *afraid,* and in what way I was *sure.* Notice that the noun clause in the third sentence is not introduced by the word *that.* Noun clauses without an introductory word are common in speech and writing:

Didn't he realize *she was angry?*
Be sure *you call before seven.*
I had a hunch *the billfold would be found.*

EXERCISE 3. Each of the sentences contains one or more noun clauses. Find each noun clause, and decide how it is used in the sentence. Then divide a sheet of paper into two columns. In the first column, write the first and last words of each noun clause. In the second, tell how the clause is used. Number your answers with the numbers of the sentences. Use a separate line for each clause. For the first sentence you should write:

1. where you | object of "to ask"

1. Jane called to ask where she should meet you.
2. Nancy's usual excuse is that she left her notebook at home.
3. What you see is what you get.
4. There was a violent dispute over whose name should appear first.
5. Dad's only comment was that we got exactly the treatment we deserved for interfering in other people's business.
6. Hannah's proposal, that we raise money by sponsoring a series of dances, was rejected.
7. Don't let yourself be fooled by what you read in the ads.
8. Dave finally began to understand why he had been benched.
9. What really bothered me was your insistence that no one could help.
10. Seth's explanation will probably be that he was busy working and forgot to check on what time it was getting to be.

12. Use a noun clause

Sometimes writers will use two sentences to express what is really one idea, using *this* or *that* to show that the first sentence is closely related to the second one:

The Crandall High players didn't even offer to shake hands. *This* seemed strange to us.
Will Ted do his share of the work? *That* is the real question.
Frankness is not always a virtue. Few people seem to realize *this*.
Bonnie will get the lead in the operetta. I'm sure of *that*.

The sentences have a choppy, almost childish effect. In addition, they force the reader to decide for himself what the important ideas are. When noun clauses are used to combine the two sentences in each pair, the reader has no difficulty:

It seemed strange to us *that the Crandall High players didn't even offer to shake hands.*
The real question is *whether Ted will do his share of the work.*
Few people seem to realize *that frankness is not always a virtue.*
I'm sure *that Bonnie will get the lead in the operetta.*

The revised sentences are easier to understand because the important ideas stand out more clearly.

Even when one sentence has a noun clause, further revision may be needed to show how it is related to another sentence:

The real question is *whether Ted will do his share of the work.* It can be answered only by him.
Everybody cheered the announcement. It was *that the final game of the series would be played at home.*

Using the noun clauses as appositives and combining the sentences would make the meaning clearer:

The real question, *whether Ted will do his share of the work,* only he can answer.
Everybody cheered the announcement *that the final game of the series would be played at home.*

Occasionally a writer puts sentences next to each other without showing what relationship he or she has in mind:

She might not pass the course. The fear haunted her constantly.
One man's evidence convicted the men. He had seen them enter the building together.

Such sentences may often be improved by using noun clauses in apposition:

The fear *that she might not pass the course* haunted her constantly.
One man's evidence, *that he had seen them enter the building together,* convicted the men accused.

EXERCISE 4. Each of the groups consists of two sentences. Change each group into one effective sentence by using a noun clause. Be ready to read your revised sentences aloud. For the first group you might say: *The fact that they appear in unpredictable cycles makes locusts hard to control.*

1. Locusts appear in unpredictable cycles. This fact makes them hard to control.
2. Jim's ankle may improve enough for him to play in Friday's game. That is our only hope.
3. Most of the weather in the United States travels from west to east. Did you know this?
4. The boys would not wear tuxedos to the dance. I was positive of that.
5. War makes more problems than it solves. Will men ever learn that?
6. Al's mother could not afford to pay for the broken display window. That was Don's real reason for taking the blame.
7. Miss Kimball added an interesting comment. She said that *Oklahoma* was a Choctaw word for "red people."
8. Larry's uncle did not mention the accident. That seemed queer to me.
9. Caroline had reached the cottage before us and had taken the rowboat. We were sure of that.
10. Sue had reported seeing Henry at Dober's Hardware Store at six o'clock the day of the accident. This fact made me realize how unfair the accusations were.

Adverb clauses

A subordinate clause that does the work of an adverb is called an **adverb clause.** Most adverb clauses that modify verbs or verbals tell where, when, how, for what reason, or for what purpose:

Jane wins friends *wherever she goes.*
While I go to the store, you can peel the potatoes.
I tried to pronounce the words *as Miss Cardozo did.*
Bob cut his vacation short *because he ran out of money.*
Be sure to come early *so that we can get good seats.*

Adverb clauses may also tell under what condition a statement is meant:

We would have been thoroughly soaked *if it had rained.*
Although Bob missed several cues, he played his part well.
The team is leaving promptly at noon, *whether Tim is ready or not.*

In each sentence the adverb clause gives the circumstances under which the thought expressed by the main clause is true.

The verb or verbal modified by an adverb clause may be in another subordinate clause:

There was an usher who checked our tickets *as we entered.*
Jack said that he doesn't approve of hitting a man *when he's down.*
Mother is annoyed if we interrupt her *after a program has started.*

The italicized clause in the first sentence modifies the verb *checked* in the adjective clause beginning with *who.* The one in the second sentence modifies the gerund *hitting* in the noun clause introduced by *that.* And the one in the third sentence modifies the verb *interrupt* in the adverb clause introduced by *if.*

The words that introduce adverb clauses — such as *while, although, as if, so that, until, since* — are called **subordinating conjunctions.** A subordinating conjunction joins the clause to the word it modifies:

Ed will call *after* they leave.   Ed will call *if* they leave.
Ed will call *before* they leave.   Ed will call *when* they leave.

In these sentences the subordinating conjunctions show different relationships between "they leave" and *will call,* the verb the clauses modify. Subordinating conjunctions do not have antecedents, as the relatives that introduce adjective clauses do.

Adverb clauses of comparison

Adverb clauses, like adverbs, may modify adjectives and adverbs:

The grown-ups seemed noisier *than the children had been.*
Martha Wilkins spoke longer *than she had intended.*

The clause in the first sentence modifies the predicate adjective *noisier* by telling how much noisier the grown-ups seemed. The clause in the second modifies the adverb *longer* by telling how much longer Martha Wilkins spoke. Adverb clauses that modify adjectives and adverbs used in making comparisons (like *noisier, longer, easier, worse*) are called **adverb clauses of comparison.**

Some clauses of comparison are introduced by *as* or *that:*

> The test was not so hard *as we had feared.*
> It was so cold *(that) we built a fire.*
> He eats as much food in one day *as I eat in a week.*
> Dad made such a fuss about the bills *that I returned the hat.*

In the first and second sentences the clause modifies the adverb *so.* In the third the clause modifies the adverb *as.* And in the fourth the clause modifies the adjective *such.* The subordinating conjunction *that* in the second sentence may be omitted without changing the meaning.

Adverb clauses are not always grammatically complete:

> Joan studies more *than Mary* (studies).
> Carl worked as hard *as Tom* (worked).
> Mrs. Ryan scolds Terry more often *than I* (do).
> Mrs. Ryan scolds Terry more often *than* (she scolds) me.

The verbs and subject in parentheses are not ordinarily expressed, since the meaning is clear without them. When words not necessary to the meaning are omitted, the clause is called an **elliptical clause.**

EXERCISE 5. Each of the sentences contains one or more adverb clauses, some of which are elliptical. Find the adverb clauses, and decide what words they modify. On a sheet of paper, write the first and last words of each clause and, after them, the word or words the clause modifies. Use a separate line for each clause, and put parentheses around the modified words. Number your answers with the numbers of the sentences. For the first sentence you should write:

> *1. Though out (left)*
> *where out (to hang)*

1. Though I was careful to hang his hat where he would see it on his way out, he left without it.
2. Velma is a fine actress, though you may dislike her personally.
3. While her mother was away, Jane's room looked as if a tornado had struck it.
4. Scientists have found that brain workers require more sleep than physical laborers.
5. Real gold does not dissolve when it is placed in diluted nitric acid, as does "fool's gold."

6. Just before the broadcast began, we were instructed to applaud when the announcer gave the signal.
7. Alice's brother is as noisy as Larry.
8. Taking off my shoes, I tiptoed in slowly so that I wouldn't wake Dad.
9. Isn't Mildred taller than Eldon?
10. When the dachshund saw the collie approaching, he ran for the porch as fast as his little crooked legs could carry him.

Improving sentences

13. Use an adverb clause

Inexperienced writers are likely to use separate sentences for related ideas, often relying on such words as *and, but,* and *so* to show a relationship in meaning between the ideas:

Emily was talking on the telephone. And the soup boiled over.
Dick is over six feet tall. But he weighs only one hundred twenty.
Anna sings loudly. So she can be heard above everyone else.
Bob and I set out for the cabin at daybreak. It was cold and rainy. We wore our raincoats.

A writer who knows about adverb clauses can improve such sentences. Using subordinate clauses for less important ideas can make important ideas stand out clearly. By selecting suitable subordinating conjunctions, a writer can show the exact relationships. Notice some of the ways in which the sentences above may be combined:

While Emily was talking on the telephone, the soup boiled over.
The soup boiled over *because Emily was talking on the telephone.*
Although Dick is over six feet tall, he weighs only one hundred twenty.
Dick is over six feet tall, *though he weighs only one hundred twenty.*
Anna sings loudly *so that she can be heard above everyone else.*
Anna sings so loudly *that she can be heard above everyone else.*
Since Anna sings so loudly, she can be heard above everyone else.
When Bob and I set out for the cabin at daybreak, we wore our raincoats *because it was cold and rainy.*
Because it was cold and rainy when we set out for the cabin at daybreak, Bob and I wore our raincoats.

In experimenting with adverb clauses, there are three cautions to keep in mind. One of these is to be sure that the important idea is in the main clause. Otherwise sentences like these are created:

I was quietly reading a book, when suddenly the tornado struck.
Although Dad delivered a stern lecture to the boys next door, he
seldom gets angry.

Such sentences seem topsy-turvy. They imply that the tornado and
Dad's unusual display of temper are matter-of-fact occurrences,
while the meaning of the sentences is just the opposite. Each
sentence is more forceful when the important idea is put in the
main clause:

As I was quietly reading a book, the tornado suddenly struck.
Although Dad seldom gets angry, he delivered a stern lecture to the
boys next door.

A second caution is to be sure that each adverb clause clearly
modifies what it should modify. Compare these two sentences:

Mary decided to eat her breakfast at the cafeteria on the corner *before she got up.*
Before she got up, Mary decided to eat her breakfast at the cafeteria
on the corner.

The first sentence seems to mean that Mary was going to eat her
breakfast before getting up. In the second sentence the clause has
been put first to show the reader that it modifies the verb *decided.*
Shifting an adverb clause in this way often makes the meaning
clearer.

The third caution is to avoid elliptical clauses that may have
two meanings:

The older players taught me more *than the coach.*
Is the sun ever closer to the moon *than the earth?*

The first sentence might mean:

The older players taught me more *than the coach did.*
than they taught the coach.

The second sentence might mean:

Is the sun ever closer to the moon *than the earth is?*
than it is to the earth?

Always supply the words necessary to make meaning clear.

66

EXERCISE 6. Read the sentences in each group, and decide how they are related. Then change each group into one good sentence, using adverb clauses in place of the less important sentences. Be sure that you place each adverb clause so that it clearly modifies the right word. Be prepared to read your revised sentences aloud. For the first group you might say: *Al and I agreed to work until nine o'clock so that we could have Saturday off to go fishing.*

1. Al and I agreed to work until nine o'clock. And then we could have Saturday off to go fishing.
2. The steel frames of tall buildings act as conductors. So city people are in less danger from lightning.
3. Usually Bob speaks. Then he thinks.
4. My sister was teaching me to drive last summer. We had many long and loud arguments during the process.
5. Philip stepped up to receive his medal. The crowd roared its approval.
6. I was cleaning the top shelf with its valuable collection of crystal. The dust cloth caught on a nail, upsetting two vases.
7. Nicholas was very eager to make a good impression on Ellen's mother. He didn't notice the rest of us giggling at his elegant manners.
8. Philip had been driving a car for years. But these narrow mountain passes frightened him.
9. I was rechecking the day's sales slips in the little office at the back of the store. I heard the bell of the cash register ring.
10. The minutes of the last meeting were read and approved. Michael then announced his decision to resign from the presidency.

EXERCISE 7. Write a "super sentence" — a single sentence that contains (in any order you wish) a prepositional, participial, gerund, and infinitive phrase and adjective, noun, and adverb clause.

Chapter 7

Review of Grammar

The Kinds of Sentences

What a simple sentence is

Compare these two sentences:

Bob yawned.

About a mile or so from the northern edge of the city, partly hidden from sight by tall trees and dense foliage, stands the old Raynor mansion, now crumbling with age and neglect, the home of two elderly impoverished spinster sisters, the only living descendants of a once proud and aristocratic family known throughout the state during most of the last century, hated, feared, yet respected for the power and wealth then represented by the Raynor name.

The first sentence consists of two words and has no modifiers. The second sentence consists of seventy-seven words and has many modifiers. Yet the two sentences are alike in one important respect: Each has only one subject and one verb. (To be sure, the second sentence is far too long. It could be called a *tour de force:* an illustration of how many modifiers can be joined to one subject and one verb. In most writing such a sentence would more effectively be made into three. "About a mile . . . Raynor mansion. Although now crumbling with age and neglect, it is the home . . . last century. It was a family hated, feared, . . . Raynor name.")

Subjects and verbs may be compound:

Thelma, Sally and *Madge* planned a surprise party for my sister and me.

Dick *caught* the pass and *ran* twenty yards.

He and *I* then *collected* the money and *turned* it in.

Each of these sentences is of medium length. And unlike the two example sentences in the first paragraph, each contains a direct object. Yet in spite of the differences, all five sentences are alike in one important respect: Each has only one subject and one verb.

A sentence that has only one subject and one verb, either or both of which may be compound, is called a simple sentence.

In grammar the words *simple sentence* do not mean a short sentence or an uncomplicated one. Long or medium or short, with or without objects, complements, appositives, or modifiers, a sentence that has only one subject and one verb is — grammatically — a simple sentence.

Parts of the simple sentence

Earlier chapters have discussed and illustrated verbs of one or more words, nouns and pronouns, adjectives and adverbs, prepositions and conjunctions, verbals and verbal phrases. These have been used as subjects and predicates and modifiers and appositives to make simple sentences. Now review the ways in which words and phrases are used as parts of simple sentences.

Verbs and their subjects are the framework of simple sentences. The verb in each sentence is a word or a group of words that makes a statement or asks a question or gives a command. It may consist of one, two, three, or four words; and these words may be separated from each other. The subject of the verb may be a noun or a pronoun, a verbal or a verbal phrase; and it may be compound. In the first ten sentences the verbs are in italic type. Who or what is the subject of each verb?

1. What *did* your mother and father *say* about the scraped fender?
2. Either Bob or the regular relief pitcher *should have been sent* in long before the fifth inning.
3. *Could* the rest of the Scouts *have missed* the last trail marker?
4. This *can't* possibly *be* the road to the lake.
5. There *have* always *been* too many candidates for the cheerleading squad at our school.
6. Behind the school *are* a football field and two tennis courts.
7. Being chosen May Queen *will be* an unexpected honor for Alice.
8. It *would be* foolish to ignore the parking ticket.
9. No sliding down banisters or drumming on the piano *would have been tolerated* in Billy's own home.
10. To run for governor again or to go into private business *is* the decision facing my uncle.

Predicate words are used in various ways to help verbs tell about their subjects: Predicate adjectives modify subjects. Predicate nominatives explain subjects. Objects of verbs tell who or what receives the actions expressed by verbs. Indirect objects tell to whom or for whom actions are done. Objective predicates modify or explain the objects of verbs. These predicate words are italicized in the next nineteen sentences. In sentences 11-15 predicate adjectives are in italics. Identify the verb in each sentence and the word that is modified by the predicate adjective:

11. The woman in the apartment across the hall has acted somewhat more *friendly* lately.
12. Seward's desire to purchase Alaska was considered *foolish* by many of his contemporaries.

13. Doesn't mink fur feel *soft* and *silky?*
14. Boiled coffee often tastes quite *bitter.*
15. The completely informal classes must have seemed *strange* to you.

In sentences 16-19 predicate nominatives are in italics. Name the verb in each sentence and the word that is explained by the predicate nominative:

16. The gift in the huge box will probably be a tiny *pair* of earrings.
17. Either Walter or Harold should have been the *master of ceremonies* at the athletic banquet.
18. Jane's favorite pastimes are *reading mystery stories* and *eating potato chips.*
19. Her main reason for studying so hard is *to beat everyone else.*

In sentences 20-23 objects of verbs are italicized. Pick out each verb and tell its subject:

20. Only after a great deal of study can you understand the *meaning* of the essay at the end of the chapter.
21. My father and brother enjoy *playing checkers* and *arguing loudly over each move.*
22. Would you mind *mailing my letters on your way downtown?*
23. Each of the bus drivers tries *to be friendly and courteous at all times.*

In sentences 24-29 indirect objects and objective predicates are italicized. What are the verbs and the direct objects in each of the sentences?

24. My aunt brought *me* four beautiful sweaters from Canada.
25. Who gave *you* permission to put posters up in the library?
26. The school should have given *Bob* and *Jim* some recognition for their work on the Community Fund drive.
27. Why did you call Marie a *coward?*
28. The new curtains have made the room more *attractive.*
29. Did the class elect Tim or Veronica *president?*

Modifiers are words and phrases used to make clear the exact meaning of other words. Nouns and pronouns may be modified by adjectives and adjective phrases, possessive nouns and pronouns, and verbals. Verbs, verbals, adjectives, and their modifiers may be modified by adverbs and adverb phrases, adverbial nouns, and verbals. Modifiers of these kinds are italicized in the next twenty-three sentences. In sentences 30-39, identify the noun or pronoun that is modified by each word or phrase in italics:

30. Flashes *of light* were glimpsed *in the deserted old ramshackle* house.

31. *Several* sailboats and *cabin* cruisers were lying at anchor in *the smooth, glassy, blue* bay.
32. Can you suggest *a good* way *to earn some extra spending* money?
33. Did you see *those* fish *playing leapfrog* with *floating* sticks?
34. *Puffing and chugging, Keith's old* car finally reached *the* top *of the first hill.*
35. For *many* years Mother has packed *Dad's* lunch in *that old tin* pail.
36. *Being an expert tennis player,* he can certainly land *a coaching* job without *any* trouble.
37. *Having had the last word,* Phyllis marched majestically past *the gossipy old* women *in the room.*
38. *All* year Joe had unusually *bad* luck, *almost losing his farm at one time.*
39. *Having graduated with honors,* Nancy was offered *generous* scholarships by *several good* schools.

In sentences 40-49, name the verb that is modified by each word or phrase in italics:

40. *Suddenly* the angry man broke *away from the two policemen* and ran *toward the alley.*
41. Lola has *always* played the piano *brilliantly* and *with enjoyment.*
42. Do *not* go *back there for several months.*
43. Bill has *never* gone *to the opera with Mother and me.*
44. Mother *actually* drove the car *downtown* last *night by herself* and parked it *without help.*
45. *Since its publication* several people have written *in to complain.*
46. *Slowly* but *surely* the settlers moved *westward to find new homes.*
47. *Maybe* we should have practiced *more before entering the contest.*
48. Joe stopped *for a moment to consider* and *then* began to protest.
49. *With a joyous shout* the child *quickly* ran *to the Christmas tree* and *eagerly* pointed *to the lights.*

In sentences 50-52, what is the adjective or adverb modified by each word or phrase in italics?

50. This system is *just too* expensive *to be practical.*
51. Sing the second stanza *more* slowly and *very* softly.
52. The judges are *about* ready *to announce their decision.*

Appositives are set alongside other words to explain or add to the meaning of those words. Appositives do not modify anything, and they are not essential parts of sentences. In sentences 53-61, show what words are explained by the italicized appositives:

53. We stopped for a few minutes to admire Nita's paintings, a *group* of colorful landscapes.

54. Two qualities you must cultivate — *cheerfulness* and *determination.*
55. The higher-priced coats, *those* with inner linings, are really far more practical for us.
56. My uncle is a recognized expert in philately, the *collection* and *study* of postage stamps.
57. The young comedian, *Denny Dense,* should be a great success in show business.
58. Flora's main enthusiasms — *sailing* and *fishing* — are not shared by her twin brother.
59. Mother's idea — *to redecorate* Bob's bedroom in chartreuse and black — brought howls of protest.
60. Some professions — such as *law* and *medicine* — require a lengthy and expensive education.
61. Marion's favorite daydream — *to write* a great novel, *make* a million dollars or so from it, and *live* in leisure the rest of her life — certainly has little chance of coming true.

Just knowing the parts of simple sentences is not, by itself, of much value to you. Only by putting this knowledge to work, by using it constantly to help you make better sentences, can you come to know its true worth. Most writing offers opportunities for revising sentences to make them clearer, more forceful, and more interesting. To take advantage of these opportunities — moving sentence parts around to sharpen meaning and to avoid monotony, combining sentences to make important ideas stand out clearly — is to understand and appreciate the practical values of studying grammar for sentence improvement.

Compound sentences with conjunctions

What are the words in the following sentences that show how the sentences in each pair are related in meaning?

The walls had been newly papered. The floor had been carpeted, too.
Ed has a good chance of winning. However, he mustn't count on it.
The bus was an hour late. Therefore I missed my appointment.
Everyone knew I was wrong. Nevertheless, no one said a word.
Tell Diana to bring a compass. Otherwise we may have trouble following the map that Dick gave us.
Dave wouldn't admit that his scheme was impractical. He wouldn't take the advice we offered him, either.

The relationship between the sentences in each pair is shown by the adverbs *too, However, Therefore, Nevertheless, Otherwise,* and *either.* Similar relationships can be shown by joining the sentences with appropriate coordinating conjunctions:

> The walls had been newly papered, *and* the floor had been carpeted.
> Ed has a good chance of winning, *but* he mustn't count on it.
> I missed my appointment, *for* the bus was an hour late.
> Everyone knew I was wrong, *yet* no one said a word.
> Tell Diana to bring a compass, *or* we may have trouble following the map that Dick gave us.
> Dave wouldn't admit that his scheme was impractical, *nor* would he take the advice we offered him.

In the first three examples the coordinating conjunctions *and, but,* and *for* join simple sentences. Notice that the order of the statements in the third example has been changed. In the last three examples the coordinating conjunctions *yet, or,* and *nor* join simple and complex sentences. In comparing the last examples in each group, be aware of the order of words after *nor.* Joining two or more sentences with coordinating conjunctions makes a compound sentence. Since the sentences that make up a compound sentence are of equal importance grammatically, they are called **coordinate** clauses.

A sentence that consists of two or more coordinate clauses is called a compound sentence.

EXERCISE 1. Read each pair of sentences carefully to see how they are related in meaning. Then combine each pair, using *and, but, for, yet, or,* or *nor* to show the relationship. Be prepared to read your compound sentences aloud. For the first one you might say: *We didn't stop to talk to Ruth, for we had only five minutes to get to the station.*

1. We had only five minutes to get to the station. Therefore we didn't stop to talk to Ruth.
2. Sam's assistant was a thin and bent old man. However, the muscles of his arms and back were strong.
3. By noon the temperature was twenty degrees below zero. The sidewalks were a glare of ice, too.
4. Dorothy insisted that Jim had been at the library all evening. However, I was sure I had seen him at the carnival.
5. Ten minutes before curtain time the main floor seats were filled. People were standing in the aisles, too.
6. All of the trains were running late. Therefore crowds of impatient commuters were milling about in the small station.
7. Macy's had swimming suits of every color and style imaginable. Nevertheless, Clara couldn't find one that she liked.

8. On her return the ambassador would not answer any of the questions the reporters asked. She would not pose for newspaper pictures, either.
9. What he says sounds logical. Nevertheless, I have a feeling he's wrong.
10. Hide your packages in the hall closet. Otherwise Clara will suspect that something special is going on.

Compound sentences without conjunctions

Are the sentences in each pair that follow related in meaning?

Mr. Hansen gave the orders. We had to do the work.
Bob stayed home. He had some work to finish.
There were twenty questions. I got all of them right.

Although there is no word to show the relationship between the two statements in each example, the sentences in each pair are clearly related in meaning. In the first pair the second sentence expresses a contrast. In the next pair the second sentence gives a reason. In the last pair the second sentence adds an important idea. When a writer wants to emphasize the obvious relationship in meaning, he makes a compound sentence of the two statements simply by putting a semicolon between them:

Mrs. Hansen gave the orders; we had to do the work.
Bob stayed home; he had some work to finish.
There were twenty questions; I got all of them right.

Because the relationship between the coordinate clauses in each compound sentence is obvious, no conjunction is needed. Each semicolon shows clearly where one clause ends and the next begins.
Now look at the following examples:

Sam earned only twenty dollars a week. *Nevertheless,* he managed to save enough money for a motorcycle.
The boys waited until Reilly turned his back. *Then* they sneaked out of the room.
Laura is rather noisy. She is, *however,* a good worker.

In each of these examples there is a word to show how the two statements are related. Without the adverbs *Nevertheless, Then,* and *however* the relationship between the two sentences in each pair would not be clear. To emphasize the relationship expressed by the adverb, make a compound sentence of the two statements simply by putting a semicolon between them:

Sam earned only twenty dollars a week; *nevertheless,* he managed to save enough money for a motorcycle.

The boys waited until Reilly turned his back; *then* they sneaked out of the room.

Laura is rather noisy; she is, *however,* a good worker.

Because the relationship between the coordinate clauses in each compound sentence is shown by an adverb, no conjunction is needed. Each semicolon shows clearly where one clause ends and the next begins.

Adverbs that are often used to show relationships between sentences can be classified roughly into six groups, meaning

1) "for that reason": *accordingly, consequently, therefore, hence*

2) "in spite of that": *however, nevertheless, still*

3) "in addition to that": *also, besides, furthermore, likewise, moreover, too*

4) "in fact": *indeed, really, truly*

5) "of course": *certainly, surely*

6) "after that": *later, next, then;* "at last": *finally;* "at the present time": *now*

Use an adverb that expresses clearly the relationship in meaning intended.

EXERCISE 2. Read each pair of sentences, and decide how they are related in meaning. From the list of adverbs on this page, select one that shows clearly the relationship you think is intended. Then change each pair of sentences into a compound sentence, beginning the second clause with the adverb you have chosen. Do not use any coordinating conjunctions. Be prepared to read your revised sentences aloud. For the first one you might say: *The car was a real bargain; indeed, the dealer sold it to us for almost nothing.*

1. The car was a real bargain. The dealer sold it to us for almost nothing.
2. Frank was rude, outspoken, and selfish. He had few friends.
3. Joanna knew her mother would be angry if she were late for dinner. She stayed to see the movie twice.
4. A few minutes later the sounds grew fainter. They stopped entirely.
5. The house was ugly, old-fashioned, and in bad repair. The living room was much too small for the eight Johnsons.
6. Gorton's record in Congress speaks for itself. You would not want to see such a man returned to office.
7. Henry searched carefully through every file in the office. He found what he was looking for.
8. Mabel used to be the fattest, most awkward girl in our class. She is a model for an advertising agency.

9. Fred was quitting at the end of the week. He didn't care what new rules the boss announced.
10. The stranger's story sounded plausible enough. There was something about him that made my mother suspicious.

What a complex sentence is

In what way are these three sentences alike?

I'll call *before we leave.*
If Dale comes, give him the money *that I collected from the freshmen and sophomores.*
When we rushed into the lobby, the woman *who was taking tickets* told us *the concert was half over.*

The first sentence has one subordinate clause. The second has two. The third has three. But all three sentences are alike in one respect: each has only one main clause.

A sentence that consists of one main clause and one or more subordinate clauses is called a complex sentence.

In grammar the words "complex sentence" do not mean a complicated sentence. Long or short, easy or difficult to understand, a sentence that has only one main clause and one or more subordinate clauses is a complex sentence.

Chapter 6 discussed subordinate clauses that modify nouns and pronouns:

A person *who weighs 150 pounds on the earth* would weigh only 24 pounds on the moon.
The anonymous letter, which was evidently written by someone *whose mind was slightly unbalanced,* arrived in the morning mail.
The post is still vacant, since the Senate refused to appoint the man *whom the President named.*
Clara has suggested that we go to some resort *where we can rent boats and fishing equipment.*

The italicized clauses are used as adjectives. They modify the words *person, someone, man,* and *resort.* The word modified may be part of the main clause, as in the first sentence, or part of an adjective, adverb, or noun clause, as in the other sentences.

Chapter 6 also discussed subordinate clauses that are used as nouns:

What I don't understand is *why he accepted the job in the first place.*
My sister is the sort of person who thinks *that money grows on trees.*

When Jill finally realized *that she was not going to get her own way,* her whole attitude changed.

What makes you think that Jim knows *who put the book on Mr. Anderson's chair?*

Noun clauses may be important parts of a main clause, as in the first sentence, or part of an adjective clause, an adverb clause, or another noun clause, as in the other sentences.

Finally, Chapter 6 discussed subordinate clauses that modify verbs, adjectives, and adverbs:

Even if you finish your test in a short time, you must remain in the examination room *until the bell rings.*

We were all laughing at Marva, who was making horrible faces *as she tried to type the exercise.*

Mr. Thompson doesn't realize that we spend more time on math *than we do on all the rest of our subjects together.*

You can always tell when old Mr. Bronson is in the audience, because he laughs louder and longer *than anyone else.*

The italicized clauses are used as adverbs. Notice that the verbs, adjectives, and adverbs that they modify may be part of the main clause, as in the first sentence, or part of an adjective clause, a noun clause, or another adverb clause, as in the other sentences.

The important thing about complex sentences is that every subordinate clause does the work of a single word — an adjective, a noun, or an adverb. To realize that subordinate clauses are never separate, independent sentences, but only parts of sentences, is another step toward sentence sense.

EXERCISE 3. Find the subordinate clauses in the sentences, and decide how each one is used. Then divide a sheet of paper into three columns. In the first column, write the first and last words of each adjective clause and, in parentheses, the word modified. In the second, do the same for adverb clauses. In the third, write the first and last words of each noun clause and, in parentheses, tell how the clause is used. Number your answers with the numbers of the sentences. For the first sentence you should write:

| *1. who inconvenienced* | *Whenever down* | *that problems* |
| *(people)* | *(register)* | *(object of "realizing")* |

1. Whenever the city transportation system bogs down, many of the people who are inconvenienced register vigorous protests with the Mayor, not realizing that he lacks authority to deal with such problems.
2. Captain Andy explained that the age of fur seals can be told from their teeth, which have growth layers around the roots.

3. The house we moved to was so small that my sisters had to share a room.
4. Have you noticed how charming he can be whenever he wants to?
5. However hard she tried, Mildred couldn't rid herself of the feeling that the woman who was in charge of the office didn't like her.
6. Frightened because she had never before applied for a job, Alice forgot all that she had planned to say.
7. Scientists have found that grasshoppers, which were a favorite food among the American Indians, are actually more nutritious than fish and have a taste similar to that of lobster.
8. The hat Mother bought to wear to the reception was so extreme that Dad said he wouldn't go with her if she insisted on wearing it.
9. If Jimmy should be hurt while he is riding the tricycle I gave him, his mother will say that it is my fault.
10. As I walked up the stairs, trying to decide what excuse I could give for being late, I realized that I had left my purse in the taxi.

Improving sentences

14. Use a complex sentence

Here are four related sentences that seem equally important:

Someone had been tampering with the school clocks. Mr. Fulton heard about it. He immediately sent for Bud Andrews. Bud is always the chief suspect on such occasions.

The sentences may be combined by using all three kinds of subordinate clauses. Now it is easy to determine which idea the writer considers most important:

When Mr. Fulton heard that someone had been tampering with the school clocks, he immediately sent for Bud Andrews, *who is always the chief suspect on such occasions.*

Although the revised sentence has the same number of words as the four separate sentences, it is easier to understand because the relationships of the various ideas are clearly shown.

Sentences may, of course, be combined in more than one way. Here is a group of three related sentences:

Tom was the team's most valuable player. But his marks were low. The principal ordered him off the basketball squad for a full month.

The group might be combined in either of these ways:

Because Tom's marks were low, the principal ordered him off the basketball squad for a full month, *even though he was the team's most valuable player.*

Tom, *who was the team's most valuable player,* had such low marks *that the principal ordered him off the basketball squad for a full month.*

The sentences differ in meaning because they have different main clauses. In the first sentence the principal's action stands out as most important. In the second sentence the emphasis is on Tom's low grades. Where two or more revisions are possible, always choose the one that most clearly expresses the meaning intended.

Two cautions: In using complex sentences, avoid repeating the same conjunction too often in one sentence. For example:

As Dick sat out in front honking the horn, Marge threw things into the picnic hamper as fast *as* she could, *as* she knew he hated to be kept waiting.

Barbara reported sadly *that* the only fish *that* she had caught all day was a trout *that* was so small *that* she had to throw it back into the lake.

Such sentences can be improved by using more exact conjunctions and by omitting unnecessary conjunctions:

While Dick sat out in front honking the horn, Marge threw things into the picnic hamper as fast *as* she could, *since* she knew he hated to be kept waiting.

Barbara reported sadly *that* the only fish she had caught all day was a trout *which* was so small she had to throw it back into the lake.

Subordinate clauses are only one of the means for combining related sentences. Used too often, they produce a condition called *excessive predication,* discussed in the Glossary (Chapter 11).

EXERCISE 4. Read the sentences in each group, and decide how they are related. Then combine them, using one or more subordinate clauses and any of the other ways you have learned. Be prepared to read your revised sentences aloud. For the first group you might say: *While Mother hurried from room to room, closing all the windows, I pulled the sheets off the clothesline and dragged the lawn furniture into the garage.*

1. Mother hurried from room to room. She closed all the windows. Meanwhile I pulled the sheets off the clothesline. I also dragged the lawn furniture into the garage.
2. A narrow dirt road leads to my grandfather's farm. In the spring it becomes impassable. Then he has to park his car along the state highway. It is a mile from his house.

3. Many immigrants came to America with high hopes. They would make tremendous fortunes. Most of them were soon disillusioned.
4. Mr. Atkins worked day and night for years. He finally managed to pay off his debts. He had accumulated them during the depression.
5. My invention would be successful. I was sure of that. But I could not sell the idea to Mr. Wilkins. He hated to risk his precious money.
6. Neil heard his father's voice in the hall. He hid the comic books. He had borrowed them from Van. Then he quickly started to work on some algebra problems. Mr. Wilson had assigned them for the next day.
7. Harold has no musical talent. But Mrs. Ames insists on his taking piano lessons. She forces him to practice long hours each day. He might better be out-of-doors with the other fellows.
8. I was coming up the stairs from the basement. My face and hands were smeared with green paint. Just then Martha Cole walked into the kitchen. She sat in a chair. It was right opposite the basement door.
9. Marguerite hates the noise and dirt and confusion of the city. So she spends every weekend at her parent's home in Martin's Corners. This village is very small. It doesn't even have a movie theater.
10. Marge and Helen waited for more than an hour on the corner. Mary was supposed to meet them there. They finally decided to go on to the game without her.

Improving sentences

15. Avoid the tiresome "and"

When writers use too many compound sentences with *and,* their writing takes on a monotonous, seesaw quality. The tiresome repetition of *and* can often be avoided by using other kinds of sentences.

Not all compound sentences with *and* need to be changed. Those in which *and* is used to join coordinate clauses of equal importance are useful and effective. For example:

Dorothy prepared the meal, and her sister washed the dishes.
In the last two seconds of play Tom shot the ball through the hoop, and Cleveland High won the game.

In these sentences the *and* is appropriate, since it shows clearly the relationship between the clauses. But notice the following sentences:

Bob and Dick had promised to pay for the broken window, and they had to find some way to earn the money.
Agnes studied all night before the test, and she managed to pass.

In these sentences the conjunction *and* is not appropriate, since it does not show the exact relationship in meaning between the clauses. The sentences can be improved by using an adverb clause in the first example and a gerund phrase in the second:

Since Bob and Dick had promised to pay for the broken window, they had to find some way to earn the money.
By studying all night before the test, Agnes managed to pass.

Compound sentences with *and* often seem clumsy when the coordinate clauses are not of equal importance:

Rain or shine, Mrs. Blair always carries an umbrella, and it looks like an old black tent.
Tabby watched us playing with her kittens, and her eyes were shining with motherly pride.
The drum major was a tall, thin fellow, and he was a clever twirler.
Nick and I cautiously entered the cellar of the deserted house, and we hardly dared to speak above a whisper.

One clause in each of the sentences states an important fact; the other one merely gives an explanatory detail. By using an adjective clause, a nominative absolute, an appositive, and a participial phrase for the explanatory details, a writer not only avoids the tiresome *and*'s, but also makes the important facts stand out more clearly:

Rain or shine, Mrs. Blair always carries an umbrella *that looks like an old black tent.*
Tabby watched us playing with her kittens, *her eyes shining with motherly pride.*
The drum major — a tall, thin fellow — was a clever twirler.
Hardly daring to speak above a whisper, Nick and I cautiously entered the cellar of the deserted house.

Consider these compound sentences:

The club is being organized for only one purpose, and that is to promote social activities for teen-agers.
Silas's life was built around one conviction, and this was that gold is more important than friends.

The second clause in each example merely explains a word in the first clause. The same meaning can be expressed more effectively by using an infinitive phrase in the first sentence, a noun clause in the second:

> The club is being organized for only one purpose — *to promote social activities for teen-agers.*
> Silas's life was built around a conviction *that gold is more important than friends.*

Notice the subjects of the coordinate clauses in the following sentences:

> Mr. Hill opened the safe, and he pulled out a large metal box.
> The walls were washed on Monday, and they were painted on Friday.

An overuse of compound sentences like these, in which the co-ordinate clauses have subjects meaning the same person or thing, makes compositions sound childish. It is a simple matter to improve such sentences by dropping one of the subjects and using a compound verb:

> Mr. Hill *opened* the safe and *pulled* out a large metal box.
> The walls *were washed* on Monday and *painted* on Friday.

EXERCISE 5. Read the sentences, and decide how they can be improved by changing them to effective simple or complex sentences. Use as many ways as you can to show the different relationships between the ideas in the sentences. Be prepared to read your revised sentences aloud. For the first sentence you might say: *The Tyrells had a large guest room, which Mrs. Tyrell let us use for our weaving and leather tooling.*

1. The Tyrells had a large guest room, and Mrs. Tyrell let us use it for our weaving and leather tooling.
2. Clifford decided that his bowling was costing him too much money, and he withdrew from the league.
3. Ted and Roby were perched out of sight in the hayloft, and they were listening to every word that we said.
4. The Simmons warehouse was a large brown frame structure that had been built twenty years before, and it was destroyed by the fire.
5. The painters worked until ten every evening for a week, and they finished the decorating in time for the first day of classes.
6. Seth is constructing a fan, and it can be used for either heating or cooling.
7. You should do all of your assignments in study halls, and then you won't have to carry books back and forth every day.
8. Margaret had eaten a huge lunch, and she could hardly keep her eyes open during her afternoon classes.

9. Nella, it seems, had a better suggestion, and that was to package the apples in perforated cellophane bags.
10. Hannah could not possibly do all the work herself, and I thought we ought to help her.

EXERCISE 6. Write a coherent paragraph that contains the following sentence order: 1. simple sentence 2. compound sentence 3. complex sentence 4. compound-complex sentence 5. complex sentence 6. compound sentence 7. simple sentence. You are invited to make this paragraph (known as a *seven-carat diamond*) as readable as you can.

Improving sentences: Fifteen ways

1. **Use an active verb. (Chapter 1)**
2. **Choose exact modifiers (Chapter 2)**
3. **Begin with an adverb (Chapter 2)**
4. **Begin with a preposition (Chapter 3)**
5. **Use a compound verb (Chapter 3)**
6. **Begin with an object (Chapter 4)**
7. **Use an appositive (Chapter 4)**
8. **Use a gerund (Chapter 5)**
9. **Use an infinitive (Chapter 5)**
10. **Use a participle (Chapter 5)**
11. **Use an adjective clause (Chapter 6)**
12. **Use a noun clause (Chapter 6)**
13. **Use an adverb clause (Chapter 6)**
14. **Using complex sentences (Chapter 7)**
15. **Avoid the tiresome "and" (Chapter 7)**

These are fifteen ways you have learned — and used — to improve your sentences. Each of the fifteen devices serves one of three main purposes — to help avoid the monotony of too many subject-first sentences, to help get rid of weak explanatory sentences, or to help make expression as clear, forceful, and interesting as possible through the use of effective words.

EXERCISE 7. The numbered sentences tell a story about an accident at sea.* As you can see, almost all the sentences begin with subject and verb. Review the various ways of improving sentences and then rewrite the story, revising the sentences in the ways you have learned.

*Adapted from "The Most Dangerous Game," copyright, 1924, by Richard Connell. Copyright, 1952, by Louise Fox Connell.

And group related sentences into paragraphs that will help the reader know where there is a shift in time or place or action. You will probably need four or five or six paragraphs. The first one might begin in this way: *Rainsford lay in his chair on the deck of the yacht, puffing at his favorite pipe and thinking over the events of the past week.*

(1) Rainsford lay in his chair on the deck of the yacht. (2) He was puffing at his favorite pipe. (3) He was thinking over the events of the past week. (4) He grew drowsy soon. (5) A sharp sound startled him. (6) It was off to the right. (7) His ears were trained to that sort of sound. (8) They could not be mistaken. (9) He heard the sound again. (10) Someone had fired a gun twice somewhere off in the darkness of the night. (11) Rainsford sprang up. (12) He moved quickly to the rail. (13) He was mystified. (14) He strained his eyes. (15) He could not see at all through the dense blackness, however. (16) He jumped up on the rail. (17) He thought he might see better from there. (18) His pipe struck a rope. (19) It was knocked out of his mouth. (20) He lunged for it. (21) He stretched too far. (22) He lost his balance. (23) The warm waters of the Caribbean Sea closed over his head. (24) He struggled to the surface. (25) He shouted wildly. (26) The wash of the yacht slapped against his face. (27) It made him gag and strangle. (28) He struck out in desperation after the lights of the yacht. (29) They were rapidly receding. (30) He swam frantically for about fifty feet. (31) He stopped then. (32) He had to calm his excited nerves. (33) He knew this. (34) This was not the first time he had been in a tight place. (35) He regained his self-possession quickly. (36) He had to decide then what to do next. (37) He realized one thing. (38) There was a slight chance that someone on the yacht was still on deck. (39) This person might hear his cries. (40) He shouted with all his power for several minutes. (41) No one heard him. (42) The lights of the yacht grew fainter. (43) They were blotted out by the night soon.

EXERCISE 8. The numbered sentences tell of some of the unusual foods prized in various parts of the world. Most of the sentences begin with subject and verb. After reviewing the fifteen ways of improving sentences, rewrite the account, revising the sentences to make them more clear, forceful, and interesting. Be sure to group related sentences into paragraphs that show a shift from one phase of the subject to another. You will need five paragraphs.

(1) There are many strange foreign foods. (2) We consider these foods unappetizing. (3) We shudder at the thought of eating such foods. (4) They are considered rare delicacies by native connoisseurs. (5) Such exotic dishes as shark-fin soup and snails in vinegar are among these unusual foods. (6) Another is African black ants. (7) These ants are deep

fried. (8) Another exotic dish is sea-slugs. (9) We are particular about one thing in America. (10) We must have our eggs fresh. (11) Fermented eggs are highly esteemed in China. (12) These eggs are buried for long periods of time. (13) They become green then. (14) They become cheeselike. (15) The older the eggs are, the more flavorful they are considered. (16) They are considered more valuable, too. (17) There are eggs one hundred years old. (18) These might be served in the homes of the very wealthy. (19) Another Chinese luxury is bird's-nest soup. (20) This soup is made from the nests of a species of swifts. (21) These swifts build their homes high on the faces of cliffs. (22) They build their homes at the mouths of caves, also. (23) The nests are made of twigs and seaweed. (24) The birds glue the twigs and seaweed together with their saliva. (25) The twigs and seaweed are strained out and discarded. (26) The saliva is used in bird's-nest soup. (27) The nests are very hard to get. (28) The cost of them is extremely great, therefore. (29) None except the rich can afford this rare delicacy for this reason. (30) We Americans like our tea with lemon. (31) We may like cream instead. (32) The Tartars of central Asia prefer butter in their tea. (33) The Tibetans prefer this, too. (34) They are also of central Asia. (35) They use a reeking, rancid butter for this purpose. (36) It is made from yak's milk. (37) The Oriental uses this butter on his cigarettes, also. (38) This causes the cigarettes to splutter in burning. (39) It makes them emit a choking and pungent smoke, also. (40) These strange habits and these strange foods are revolting to us. (41) They disgust us. (42) Many Americans eat raw clams, rattlesnake meat, and sweetbreads, however. (43) They consider them treats. (44) Such treats would delight the palate of a gourmet. (45) Taste is just a matter of geography maybe.

Chapter 8

Punctuation: Commas mostly

A speaker helps listeners understand meaning by raising and lowering his or her voice, by increasing its force, and by pausing for various lengths of time. The manner of speaking lets listeners know where sentences begin and end, and whether they are statements, questions, or exclamations; which words are important, and which are merely side remarks; where clauses and phrases begin and end, and whether they are restrictive or nonrestrictive.

A writer must rely on punctuation to help the reader make sense of the many words on paper. For this reason the eighteen rules of this chapter and the next show the ways in which periods, commas, dashes, quotations marks, semicolons, colons, and parentheses help to make intended meaning clear.

1. Punctuating sentences accurately

Here is a basic rule of punctuation, one every writer has seen many times and undoubtedly knows:

Rule 1. **A sentence begins with a capital letter and ends with a period, a question mark, or an exclamation mark.**

This rule is given here as a reminder that readers expect to be shown clearly where sentences begin and end. When a writer fails to do so, readers may decide that "translation" into sentences is not worth the trouble. What has been learned about recognizing and improving sentences will be of little value in writing unless careful punctuation enables readers to tell where each sentence ends and the next one begins.

Even though it may seem like a game, Exercise 1 is intended to help clarify the reader's point of view and bring realization of the importance of punctuating sentences accurately.

EXERCISE 1. Read the paragraphs, and decide where the sentences begin and end. On a sheet of paper, write the number of each paragraph and, after it, the first word and the last word of each sentence it contains. Capitalize each first word. Put a period, a question mark, or an exclamation mark after each last word. For the first paragraph you should write: *1. Go away! We do. These today. Can't while?*

1. Go away we have a great deal of work to do these cards must be mailed today can't you play with your electric train for a while
2. Jim cares nothing at all about his appearance he doesn't wear a white shirt from one year to the next the very thought of a tie makes him miserable to him, the ideal all-purpose costume consists of a wrinkled pair of jeans and a plaid shirt
3. Marge is a thoroughly absent-minded cook she salts everything either several times or not at all almost everything is charred there are always ingredients missing from her concoctions she ruins untold quantities of good food
4. Everyone makes at least one comment a day about the weather on the bus each morning I hear long discussions on this subject every day at least three of my teachers mention the weather it is the starting point of many conversations
5. For three hours every evening Joan practices her violin lesson in the room directly beneath our kitchen we honestly enjoy these practice sessions her violin has a beautiful tone it is a very valuable instrument someday she will undoubtedly be a successful concert violinist within the next few years she is going to Europe to study

2. Comma for series

Here is a puzzle: How many people voted for Henry?

Mary Ellen Mitchell James Harvey Allen Alfred May and Cora voted for Henry.

Was it nine? Or seven? Or five? Who can tell for sure? The sentence gives a series of names, but no clue as to how many people are in the series. By using commas to separate the various names, the writer can make his meaning clear:

Mary Ellen Mitchell, James, Harvey Allen, Alfred May, and Cora voted for Henry.

Now you can tell that there are five distinct items in this series — the names of five people. Punctuate that sentence in another way and make it eight voters:

Mary Ellen, Mitchell, James, Harvey, Allen, Alfred, May, and Cora voted for Henry.

And if Mary and Ellen are two people, make it — with one more comma — nine!

Rule 2. **Words used as distinct items in a series are separated by commas.**

The items in the series may be one word or several. And they may be words of any kind that might be joined by *and* or *or:*

88

The most popular subjects were *biology, history, art, typing,* and
shorthand.
Nancy is *kind, friendly,* and *courteous* to everyone.
The car *stopped, turned,* and *disappeared* down the lane.
Did you look *behind the table, under the bed,* or *in the desk?*
For breakfast we could order *ham and eggs, sausage and waffles,*
or *pancakes and maple syrup.*

A comma is not used after the last item in a series. But notice that
in each of the sentences a comma is used before the final *and* or *or.*
Without this comma a three-part series looks like a + (b + c). We
want it to look like a + b + c, to show at a glance the number of
items. Often this comma is needed for clearness. If there were no
comma after the word *typing* in the first sentence, for example,
you would not know whether to think of *typing* and *shorthand* as
one subject or two. In periodicals and books this comma is often
omitted, but many writers and teachers prefer a comma before the
final *and* or *or* in a series.

A comma is not used before *and* and *or* when they connect
only two items:

He always complains about the *food* and the *weather.*
Freda doesn't *skate* or *ski.*

Nor are commas ordinarily used when all the items of a series are
connected by *and* or *or:*

Our principal is *kind* and *cheerful* and always *ready* to help.
I can't stand *Mr. Jones* or his *son* or his *grandson.*

Sometimes a series is written without *and* or *or:*

He crept *slowly, cautiously, silently* toward the guard.
The messenger was *tall, dark, handsome.*
A *tall, dark, handsome* man delivered the message.
The beach was covered with *small, thin, round, flat* stones.

In these examples equal stress is given to the items in each series,
just as if they were joined by *and*'s and *or*'s. The commas show
that the items are distinct and of equal importance.

When adjectives preceding a noun are closely connected with
it in meaning, no commas are needed. For example:

A *pretty little French* girl met us at the station.
The table was made of *three dirty old knotty-pine* boards.

In the first sentence the writer wants you to think of the little

French girl as pretty. In the second sentence he wants you to notice the number of dirty old knotty-pine boards.

When two or more adjectives precede a noun, the first one is usually most prominent and so seems most important. Putting a comma after it indicates to the reader that the next one is equally important, and so on. Each comma calls attention to the importance of the adjective that follows it. For example:

> many long, wide stretches of soft, velvety grass
> a single tough, thin black, elastic, noncorrosive covering

The commas show which adjectives are distinct items in a series and so are of equal importance.

> a few quick glimpses of clear blue water
> many smart new white linen summer dresses.

Notice that commas are not used between adjectives that are not distinct items in a series. Without commas, the important adjectives are *few, clear,* and *many.*

Use commas with two or more adjectives before a noun or a pronoun only between those that are distinct items in a series. Reading the sentence aloud can show whether two or more of the adjectives receive the same stress.

EXERCISE 2. Most of the sentences below need commas to separate words in series. All need end marks. Decide what punctuation is needed for each sentence. Then write the numbers of the sentences. After each number, put the punctuation marks needed in that sentence and the word preceding each mark. For the first sentence you should write: *1. pen, ruler, compass.*

1. For geometry class you will need a pen a ruler and a compass.
2. Are you fellows going to the zoo to the fair or to the hockey game
3. Old Mrs. James is stingy and mean and vicious
4. Dr. Smith Mr. Hanley Professor White and you will be our guests
5. Are we supposed to send a check a money order or cash
6. My uncle recently bought five little Boxer pups
7. Olga's father is a doctor a musician and the best fisherman in town
8. Harry's careless indifferent attitude will get him into trouble
9. Slowly gracefully reluctantly she walked to the front of the auditorium
10. Rubber-surfaced playgrounds save shoe leather and cut down on the danger of skinned arms legs and faces

3. Commas with coordinating conjunctions

To omit commas often leads to confusion, to misunderstanding, to ambiguity:

Dick and I had to do the dishes for Mother had cut her hand.

Does the writer mean "do the dishes for Mother"? Surely not, yet that reading is natural enough — until the reader comes to "had cut her hand," which then makes no sense. Meaning and understanding are immediate with the proper comma before the coordinating conjunction *for:*

Dick and I had to do the dishes, for Mother had cut her hand.

Rule 3. A comma is ordinarily used before a conjunction joining coordinate clauses in a compound sentence.

Can you tell where commas should be used in the following sentences?

Pass the news on to Larry or Jane will feel hurt.
No one knew the answer but Sophia pretended that she did.
Sam hasn't offered to help yet I feel sure he will soon.
The coach sent in Ed and Jim and Carl protested angrily.

In the first three examples commas before *or, but,* and *yet* would make the sentences easier to read by showing where one coordinate clause ends and the next one begins. The last sentence has two meanings. The writer can show which of the two meanings he intends by using a comma before the *and* that joins the clauses:

The coach sent in Ed and Jim, *and* Carl protested angrily.
The coach sent in Ed, *ar.d* Jim and Carl protested angrily.

Many newspapers and magazines do not use the comma before coordinating conjunctions when the clauses are short. But most writers prefer a comma before each conjunction that joins coordinate clauses.

Rule 3 has to do only with coordinate clauses. Commas are not used before conjunctions joining words, phrases, or subordinate clauses:

Marcia gave a *brief* but *interesting* report.
Jerry swept the dirt *behind the door* and *under the carpet.*
He refused to tell *when she left* or *where she went.*

Remember that *but* and *for* and *yet* are not always used as conjunctions. When they are used in other ways — as prepositions or adverbs — they are not preceded by commas:

There seems to be nothing *but* trouble when he is around.
She typed a letter *for* Dad before she left.
The third time she spoke *yet* more firmly.

EXERCISE 3. Read the sentences, and decide where commas are needed before conjunctions that join coordinate clauses. On a sheet of paper, write the numbers of the sentences. After each number, write the last word of the first coordinate clause, following it with a comma and the conjunction. For the first sentence you should write: *1. antiques, for*

1. She will not sell any of her treasured antiques for money is not important to her.
2. The sea was stormy and gray and dark clouds added to the gloom.
3. Kenneth promised to do all the algebra problems but the third one was too hard for him.
4. You had better call Bill or Aunt May will start complaining again.
5. At Farrell's scream Clara jumped up and down crashed the figurine.
6. Tim had to borrow a dollar from Sarah for the tickets were more expensive than he had expected.
7. Old Mr. Zahn approved of all his grandchildren but Harriet was his pride and joy.
8. I'll send the money to you and Mary can get her share from you.
9. On the way home they met Karl and Ed and Mike told him the news.
10. Sue is going with Lee and Bert and I will walk over by myself later.

4. Setting off introductory adverb clauses and verbal phrases
Consider this sentence:

If Jake runs the election will be a close contest.

The sentence begins with an adverb clause. Where does the clause end? If the writer had used a comma to set off the clause from the rest of the sentence, a reader would have no trouble:

If Jake runs, the election will be a close contest.

The comma that sets off an introductory clause shows the reader where the adverb clause ends and the main clause begins. Where should there be a comma in each of the following sentences?

Whenever I offered to help Dad pretended there was nothing to do.
As Dr. Henderson walked through the angry mob grew quiet.
When I had finished eating the plates and platters were empty.
Although the organdy dresses are dainty and lovely women seem to prefer the more colorful linens.

Commas after *help, through, eating,* and *lovely* would make the sentences easier to read. While some newspapers and magazines do not use commas after introductory clauses, most writers prefer them because they make reading easier.

Rule 4. **An introductory adverb clause is set off from the rest of the sentence by a comma. A modifying verbal phrase at the beginning of a sentence is generally set off by a comma.**

Here are some examples of the second sentence in Rule 4:

> Having been warned about Mr. Allen's surly disposition, we didn't let his remarks discourage us. (Participial phrase)
> After reading each question, mark one of the squares with an X. (Gerund phrase within a prepositional phrase)
> To understand the principles of radio, you need to know something about electricity. (Infinitive phrase)

EXERCISE 4. The sentences below contain introductory adverb clauses and modifying phrases that should be set off.

On a sheet of paper, write the numbers of the sentences. After each number, write the marks you think are needed, giving the word preceding each mark. For the first sentence you should write: *1. ironing, clothesline.*

1. While Sarah was ironing, a sheet blew off the clothesline.
2. Before Nicholas could finish counting, the boys had left their seats and were swarming around the pony.
3. To play tennis, racquet work is essential.
4. Gasping for breath, the exhausted runner staggered over the finish line.
5. Although the hats were uncomfortable, and ugly, women wore them.
6. Whenever Mother leaves, the children become unmanageable.
7. After dancing twice with Elizabeth, Thomas returned to his seat.
8. Noting Jerry's laziness, we shook our heads and continued working.
9. After the twins joined, the club became more active.
10. Before Philip could finish reading, the letter was snatched from him.

5. Setting off nonrestrictive participial phrases

The italicized phrases in the following sentences are necessary to identify particulars of the words they modify:

> The boy *wearing a storm coat* is Dorothy's brother.
> Movies *made in 1915* look rather ridiculous to us now.

If the phrase in the first sentence were omitted, a reader would not know exactly which boy was meant. The phrase restricts the meaning to one particular boy — the one wearing the storm coat. If the phrase in the second sentence were omitted, a reader would find the sentence absurd. The meaning intended is not that all movies look ridiculous, but only those made in 1915. Phrases that are necessary to identify the words they modify are called **restrictive**. Because they are closely connected in meaning with the modified words, restrictive phrases are not set off.

Now look at these sentences:

Bob Gray, *wearing a storm coat,* wanted the bus window left open.
"Citizen Kane," *made in 1941,* was first on his list of the ten best movies ever produced.

The italicized phrases in these sentences are not essential to the meaning. They add interesting, but not necessary, details. Even without the phrases a reader would know which person wanted the bus window left open and which movie was first on the list. The names *Bob Gray* and *"Citizen Kane"* clearly identify them. Phrases that do not restrict the meaning of the words they modify are called **nonrestrictive.** Nonrestrictive phrases are set off to show that they are not closely connected in meaning with the other words in a sentence.

Rule 5. **Nonrestrictive participial phrases are set off from the rest of the sentence.**

Since nominative absolutes are not closely connected in meaning with the other words in the sentence, they are always set off:

Kay walked slowly toward the door and then turned, her eyes blazing with anger.
This point settled, further argument seemed foolish.

In many sentences the participial phrases may be either restrictive or nonrestrictive. The reader knows by the way the phrases are punctuated whether they are explanatory details or modifiers that restrict the meaning. Compare the following sentences:

The guards, crouched behind the barricade, did not see the signal.
The guards crouched behind the barricade did not see the signal.

The first sentence means that all the guards, who — incidentally — were crouched behind the barricade, missed the signal. The second sentence means that of all the guards around the place only those crouched behind the barricade missed the signal.

EXERCISE 5. Read the groups of words, and decide whether each numbered group is one sentence or two sentences. Decide also where commas should be used to set off nonrestrictive phrases. On a sheet of paper, write the first and last words of each sentence. Capitalize each first word, and put a period after each last word. Always give the word preceding each comma. Arrange your answers in a column, and number them with the numbers of the sentences. For the first group you should write: *1. A post. The driver, impact, road, fall.*

1. A truck,loaded with five-gallon drums of white lead,had crashed into the telephone post the driver thrown from the cab by the terrific impact lay on the road stunned by his fall
2. She examined the gadget thoughtfully,trying to guess its purpose
3. Hoping to get an exclusive interview with the famous pianist,Tom stationed himself in the hotel lobby early in the morning
4. A man standing beside the bridge flagged us to a stop,Dad pulled over and got out of the car grumbling at the delay
5. The first prize was awarded to Kenneth's picture of the Landorf twins,taken with an old box camera
6. Embarrassed by her sarcasm,Jim slumped lower in his chair determined never again to ask a question
7. The photographs entered in the contest were displayed in the art room,grouped according to subjects,clipped to each picture was an identifying number
8. The hotel is a two-story frame building standing on a narrow strip of land,extending far into the bay
9. Sarah Davis,running through the alley on her way to the bus stop,saw us and warned Maurice,advising him to go out the front door
10. Jane had not bothered to read the directions,printed in small type on the back of the package

6. Setting off nonrestrictive clauses

Adjective clauses are often used to identify, to make more specific, more exact, the words they modify. For example:

The children are fond of a policeman *who directs traffic near their school.*

At any restaurant *where prices are reasonable* you can get a full meal for less than a dollar.

The italicized clause in the first sentence limits the meaning of the word *policeman* by telling which one is meant. Obviously, there are many policemen, but the children are fond of a certain one — that particular one "who directs traffic near their school." The italicized clause in the second sentence limits the meaning of the word *restaurant* by telling what kind is meant — that particular kind "where prices are reasonable." Clauses that identify, or restrict, the words they modify are called **restrictive.** Not setting off such clauses shows the reader that they are closely connected in meaning with the words they modify, that without them sentences do not have the meaning intended.

Sometimes, however, adjective clauses merely add explanatory information:

The children are fond of Officer Reilly, *who directs traffic near their school.*

At our school cafeteria, *where prices are reasonable,* you can get a full meal for less than a dollar.

The italicized clauses in these sentences are not needed to limit the meaning of the words they modify. The name *Officer Reilly* tells which policeman is meant. The modifiers *our* and *school* tell which cafeteria is meant. The clause in the first sentence merely adds a bit of interesting information. It means about the same thing as "and, by the way, he directs traffic near their school." The clause in the second sentence adds an explanation. It means about the same thing as "and, incidentally, the prices there are reasonable." Clauses that merely add information in this way are called **nonrestrictive.** By setting them off, a writer shows that they are not closely connected in meaning with the words they modify.

Rule 6. **Nonrestrictive adjective clauses are set off from the rest of the sentence.**

Adverb clauses, like adjective clauses, may be restrictive or nonrestrictive.

Jane and I left the house *before Uncle Bill arrived.*
Don't leave the presents *where the children will see them.*
Nancy was angry *because Steve had not called her.*
We talked in whispers *so that we wouldn't wake Dad.*
Why don't you do *as you were told?*
She always calls on us *if she wants to borrow something.*

Without the italicized clause in each sentence to tell the one particular time, place, reason, purpose, manner, or condition that is meant, the sentences would have different meanings. Since the clauses are closely connected in meaning with the other words in the sentence, they are restrictive and are not set off.

Now notice the adverb clauses in these sentences:

Jane and I got there at five, *before the box office opened.*
Hal stood right behind me, *where he could not be seen.*
We didn't stay for the last act, *because it was getting late.*
The letter was written in ink, *so that I couldn't erase the mistake.*
Why don't you stand in line, *as you were told to do?*
She will get her own way, *if I know Helen.*

The adverb clauses in these sentences merely add explanatory details or comments. Since the clauses are not closely connected in meaning with the other words in the sentence, they are nonrestrictive and are set off by commas.

Clauses of comparison are always restrictive and are never set off, even if they are far from the modified words:

Vera spends more time translating a single line of Cicero *than Jack does on the whole assignment.*

Eleanor was so annoyed by the gossip and foolish chatter she heard at last night's meeting *that she left early.*

Clauses introduced by *though, although, whether, no matter, however,* and *whatever* are usually nonrestrictive:

Dick managed to get home in time, *though he missed the first bus.*

We didn't dare contradict him, *no matter how wrong he might be.*

Jerry, *however stupid he pretends to be,* is extremely shrewd.

You can count on our cooperation, *whatever you decide to do.*

When clauses introduced by *as* and *since* tell the particular time that is meant, they are restrictive:

I bumped right into Mrs. Snyder *as I turned the corner.*

Bob hasn't driven the car at all *since he ran over Ed's dog.*

When they tell a reason, they are nonrestrictive and are set off:

Laura took charge of the ticket sale, *as everyone else was busy.*

Hattie prefers skis made of glass fiber, *since it does not twist or*

Clauses introduced by *when* and *while* are restrictive when they tell the particular time that is meant:

Mr. Evans didn't even look up *when Sam came in.*

A baby walrus clings to its mother's neck *while she dives and swims.*

But when they give an opposing or contrasting fact, they are nonrestrictive and are set off:

She blamed me for the accident, *when it was actually her fault.*

To please his parents, Dave studied law, *while he really wanted to become a professional baseball player.*

EXERCISE 6. Read each of the groups of words, and decide whether it is one sentence or two sentences. Then look for adverb clauses that need to be set off. On a sheet of paper, write the numbers of the groups and, after them, the first and last words of each sentence. If the sentence has an introductory or nonrestrictive clause, be sure to include the word preceding each comma that is needed to set it off. Capitalize each first word. Put a period or question mark after each last word.

If you think a clause could be interpreted as either restrictive or non-restrictive, write both sets of punctuation, and be prepared to explain the difference in meaning. For the first group you should write:

> 1. *The waitress, customers.*
>   *The customers.*

1. The manager fired the waitress who had accidentally spilled a bowl of hot soup over one of the customers
2. I can remember the time when Boyd did not dare say two words before an audience.the assurance that he now has was achieved by hard work and perseverance
3. It takes forever to go downtown on the local buses which stop at every corner
4. Thanksgiving Day was sheer torture for Mother, who is desperately trying to lose weight she ate only a small portion of the dinner that she had prepared
5. The potato salad which Joanna had ordered from the corner delicatessen for the picnic made a big hit with the gang
6. Since we knew that Mr. Burton had a rather shaky sense of honor we read the contract carefully when we were satisfied that even the fine print contained no tricky clauses we signed the paper.
7. The flowers of the witch-hazel shrub do not appear until its leaves have turned to a golden yellow
8. You must learn to accept criticism gratefully, although it is only human to feel resentment when your work is being attacked
9. Sue didn't answer the doorbell because she thought a magazine salesman was ringing.when she discovered later that it was Uncle Will, she was greatly embarrassed as you can imagine
10. Mrs. Jones spends as much money in a year on hats alone as I spend on my complete wardrobe

7. Setting off appositives

Appositives (studied in Chapter 4) merely explain or add to the meaning of some other word or words in a sentence. Because they are not an essential part of the sentence, the appositive and its modifiers — an **appositive phrase** — are set off from the other words.

Rule 7. **An appositive, together with its modifiers, is usually set off from the rest of the sentence.**

Ordinarily commas are used to set off an appositive:

Number 17 is Fred Smith, *captain of the team this year.*
A gangster by instinct, the bluejay is hated by other birds.
Even the nurse, *a sour-faced old lady of few smiles and fewer laughs,* was amused by Joe's outrageous antics.

When the appositive phrase is last in the sentence, one comma precedes it. When it is first in the sentence, one comma follows it. Otherwise *two* commas are needed, one before the phrase and one after. Appositives, then, are set off on both sides.

Frequently dashes are used to set off an appositive:

Then the dry ingredients — *flour, salt, and baking powder* — are sifted together several times.

Some of these activities — *for example, the school newspaper and the safety patrol* — keep students busy every day.

Ten members of the class — *seven girls and three boys* — are on the honor roll this month.

One trait made him hard to work with — *his extreme stubbornness.*

In the first sentence dashes are needed to show where the series of appositives begins and ends. In the second sentence dashes are needed to set off the appositive phrase and to show that "for example" is part of the appositive phrase. In the third and fourth sentences dashes are used to call attention to the appositive phrases. Because dashes are conspicuous marks, they are generally used only (1) when the appositive phrase itself has commas in it and (2) to emphasize an appositive that would ordinarily be set off with commas.

Appositives explain or add to the meaning of another word. There are other appositives that help identify a word by limiting, or restricting, its meaning. For example, notice the following sentence:

My cousin Ed pronounces the word *rodeo* one way, while my cousin Jenny pronounces it another way.

Since the writer of this sentence has more than one cousin, he or she uses the appositives *Ed* and *Jenny* to show which cousins are meant. The appositive *rodeo* tells which word they pronounce differently. Here are other examples:

the composer Beethoven   Frederick the Great
the liner *Queen Elizabeth*   John the Baptist
the poem "Mending Wall"   Henry the Eighth
his friend Melanie   her sister Alice

In each example the appositive limits the meaning of the word to the only one of its kind. Appositives that help identify other words in this way are called **restrictive appositives.** They are not set off by commas, since they are closely connected in meaning with the other words.

Appositive adjectives are sometimes used to explain or add to the meaning of other words in much the same way as appositive nouns are:

The baby, *hungry* and *restless,* began to wail loudly.
Tall, wiry, and *fast* on his feet, Ned Hopkins made a good forward.
The little fellow strolled through the crowd, quite *unconscious* of his ridiculous appearance.

Such adjectives are called **appositive adjectives.** They may be placed after or before or at some distance from the words they explain, and they are set off just as appositive nouns are.

EXERCISE 7. Read each of the groups of words, and decide whether it is one sentence or two sentences. Then look for appositives, appositive adjectives, items in series, and parenthetical words that need to be punctuated. On a sheet of paper, write the numbers of the groups and, after them, the first and last words of each sentence. Capitalize each first word. Put a period after each last word. Write the word preceding each punctuation mark needed in the sentences. For the first group you should write: *That load — blankets, jug, chair, percolator. Strapped pan.*

1. That morning John carried the heaviest load two blankets the thermos, jug a camp chair and a percolator strapped to his back was a frying pan

2. Dolls and moving puppets the delight of millions of children throughout the world today were popular toys back in the days of ancient Egypt

3. The sheriff found the first important clue to the robber's identity a small leather address book it contained just three names Henry Lawrence Mason Long and Clarence Abbott

4. Later that evening we drove out to see the Prestons' new home a large attractive ranch-type house with a bright red roof Mr. Preston a New York architect had designed it himself

5. Evening after evening I had to stay home with my cousins and play fan-tan a childish and stupid card game bridge my idea of a good game didn't interest them at all

6. Jill politely listened to Mr. Dean talk about his favorite subject the need for vocational guidance in the schools

7. Joe Allen the captain of the Blue Hornets got into a bitter argument with the umpire a tough and rather stubborn old man and was thrown out of the game

8. Mr. Rankin came right to the important point Mitchell's salary he offered Mitch seventy-five dollars a week a considerable sum for a sixteen-year-old

9. The night of the Glee Club broadcast my little sister was allowed to stay up until midnight an unheard-of privilege in my younger days
10. Neither of us Catherine or I ever dared talk back to Grandpa or stamp our feet or slam doors to show our anger such outbursts of temper would have been punished immediately

8. Commas for parenthetical words

Notice the commas that set off the italicized words in the following sentences:

For example, she absolutely refused to help with the dishes.
Dr. Werner will stay, *I suppose,* until the research is completed.
Sheila won the first prize, *of course.*

The italicized words are not essential parts of the sentences. In each example they merely add an explanatory comment or side remark that could be omitted without changing the meaning of the rest of the sentence. Such words are called **parenthetical.** They are set off to show the reader that they are not closely connected in meaning with the other words in the sentence.

Rule 8. **Parenthetical words are set off by commas.**
Adverbs like *however, though, indeed, then, nevertheless, consequently,* and *moreover* are often parenthetical — and are therefore set off by commas:

They always contribute, *though,* in spite of their poverty.
Let me know, *then,* about your vacation plans.
Nevertheless, I admire her sincerity.

Such expressions as *in the first place, in fact, after all, to be sure, by the way, it seems, I hope,* and *you should realize* are also frequently parenthetical:

After all, you haven't even seen the play.
He has written some excellent short stories, *to be sure.*
She is, *you should realize,* far from stupid.

And so forth, and so on, and *etc.* are usually parenthetical. But always remember that no word or expression is in itself parenthetical. No rule can say, for example, that the words *perhaps* and *surely* are always set off from the rest of the sentence. A rule can only say that *perhaps* and *surely* are set off when they are used parenthetically. When closely connected in meaning with other words in a sentence, they are not set off. Read the following pairs of examples,

noticing the difference between a word or phrase that is parenthetical and one that is not:

> You may, *perhaps,* be able to get the information from Vera.
> *Perhaps* the butler really did commit the murder.

> He is, *however,* very angry about the delay.
> *However* angry he is, he will cooperate.

> The director, *of course,* will make the final decision.
> *Of course* you may join us for lunch.

> I shall apologize, *then.*
> I shall apologize *then.*

Never use commas blindly. Always consider the effect they will have
on meaning. Commas, like all punctuation marks, are used only to
make written sentences clear to the reader.

EXERCISE 8. All punctuation marks have been omitted from the
sentences. Decide where the necessary commas, periods, and question
marks should go. Then write the numbers of the sentences. After each
number, put the punctuation marks needed in that sentence and the word
preceding each mark. For the first sentence you should write: *1. Why,
then, now?*

1. Why then should you expect me to help you now
2. The living-room furniture will last for another year or two I hope
3. In the first place a job would take too much time away from your
   studies
4. The average housewife on the other hand seems to enjoy soap operas
5. Mr. Quarles she noticed was sound asleep before the end of the first
   act
6. However Connie Mack never showed favoritism to any player on his
   baseball teams
7. Loretta at least should have known better
8. The librarian had it seems locked up all the Zane Grey books
9. Work out the minor details however you like of course
10. Uncle Will fortunately was not in the store then

9. Setting off words with commas

In speech, meaning is made clear by changes in the tone or
pitch of voice. In writing, punctuation marks show what words
mean. Notice how important the commas are in these sentences:

> Mary, Ann wants to borrow your notebook.
> Who can tell, my friends, what will happen next?
> I think the radiator has frozen, Dad.

The commas show the reader that the words *Mary, my friends,* and *Dad* merely name the persons to whom the remarks are addressed. Such words are called **nouns of address.** In writing, they are set off by commas to show the reader that they are not closely connected in meaning with the other words in the sentence. Notice that a word beginning a sentence is set off by putting a comma after it. A word ending a sentence is set off by putting a comma before it. Elsewhere in the sentence, words are set off by using two commas — one before and one after.

Similar to nouns of address are words such as *Yes, No, Oh, Well,* and *Why* that are often used at the beginning of a sentence to show the speaker's attitude. In writing, such words are set off to show that they are not closely connected in meaning with the other words in the sentence:

No, members of the cast are to be excused early.
Yes, men are at work on the problem right now.
Well, people are always getting sick.

Without commas the meaning of each sentence would be quite different. The commas help the reader know what meaning is intended.

Rule 9. **Nouns of direct address,** *yes* and *no,* **and introductory words like,** *oh, well, why* **are set off by commas.**

When two or more introductory words are used, each is set off:

Why, yes, I think I can go with you tomorrow.
Oh, no, Jane, we didn't mean your committee.

EXERCISE 9. All punctuation marks have been omitted from the sentences. Decide where the necessary commas, periods, question marks, and exclamation marks should go. Then copy the numbers of the sentences. After each number, put the punctuation marks needed in that sentence and the word preceding each mark. Do not use any commas except for the definite reasons given in this lesson. For the first sentence you should write:

1. Why, Mary, waiting?

1. Why Mary how long have you been waiting
2. Oh does your watch lose Nan
3. Well when are you leaving George
4. Did you know that the door is sticking Mr. Willis
5. Oh what a beautiful voice she has
6. Margaret Phil will call for you and the other girls at eight
7. What Mother needs is a new coat that will fit her Father

8. Did anyone call me, Sally, while I was away ⸎
9. Yes, I saw the light change, Mr. Wilson.
10. No, Laura, the rehearsal is Friday night.

10. Commas for addresses and dates

Omitting the commas in *$3,476,372,101,558* would not change the amount, but it would make the number harder to read — $3476372101558. The same thing is true of addresses and dates; omitting the commas would not change the meaning, but would make reading more difficult.

Rule 10. **The second and all following items in addresses and dates are set off by commas.**

My brother's new address is 422 Maple Street, Riverview, New Jersey.

After June 8, 1952, send all contributions to Juniper, Dalton County, Pa., unless you receive other instructions in the meantime.

My grandfather was born at Jamaica, Long Island, New York, in April, 1923.

There is no comma between *422* and *Maple,* or *June* and *8,* because the numbers and the names together are thought of as single items. Notice the commas after *1952* and *Pa.* in the second sentence and after *New York* in the last sentence. Remember that two commas are needed to set off an item, unless it comes at the end of the sentence. Notice also that the period after the abbreviation *Pa.* precedes the comma. When an abbreviation comes at the end of a sentence, only one mark is used, except in a question or exclamation:

They have moved to 243 River Street, Lawrence, Me.
Will you please write me from St. Louis, Mo.?

EXERCISE 10. Some of the groups of words contain one sentence; some contain two sentences. Except for periods after abbreviations all punctuation marks have been omitted from the sentences. Decide where the necessary commas, periods, question marks, and capital letters should go. Copy the numbers of the groups. After each number, put all the punctuation marks needed in the group and the word preceding each mark. Capitalize and include in your answers any words that begin a second sentence in a group. For the first group you should write: *1. Ogden, Utah. Between Diego, California.*

1. On June 14, Dick and Rod arrived in Ogden, Utah, between, them, they had only seven dollars to last until their arrival in San Diego, California

104

2. Reverend James Murray will be sent either to Dallas, Texas, or to Denver, Colorado, to build a new church
3. Major Andre was captured on September 23, 1780. from him the Americans learned of Arnold's treachery
4. Should the address read Rochester, N. Y. or Rochester, Minn.?
5. The company's biggest branch offices are in Havana, Cuba, and San Juan, Puerto Rico, through them we get many orders for our products

11. Comma for clearness

An introductory adverb phrase is not usually set off. For example, a comma is not needed in this sentence:

To me he is the only player on the team.

But suppose that proper nouns were used instead of pronouns:

To Betty Spencer is the only player on the team.

Now the sentence is rather puzzling. In fact, it may have to be read twice before a reader realizes that the introductory phrase is *To Betty* — not *To Betty Spencer*. Using a comma after the name *Betty* would prevent confusion:

To Betty, Spencer is the only player on the team.

Rule 11. **A comma is used to keep the thought clear wherever parts that are not closely connected in meaning appear to join.**

In each of the following sentences there are parts not closely connected in meaning that seem to join. Where should commas be used to make the meaning clear?

Far below the people on the sidewalk looked like insects.
To the poor old age brings many other problems.
Why don't you call Hazel now and then write to George?
Aunt Liza wants a real mink coat not a muskrat dyed to look like mink.
Tell those who want to leave to leave quietly.
Mother prefers curtains made of cotton for several reasons.

The first two sentences are easier to read when a comma is used after *below* and after *poor:*

Far below, the people on the sidewalk looked like insects.
To the poor, old age brings many other problems.

The next two sentences are easier to read when a comma is used before *and* and before *not:*

Why don't you call Hazel now, and then write to George?

Aunt Liza wants a real mink coat, not a muskrat dyed to look like mink.

The last two sentences are easier to read when a comma is used after the first *to leave* and after the phrase *made of cotton:*

Tell those who want to leave, to leave quietly.
Mother prefers curtains made of cotton, for several reasons.

In sentences like these, commas are needed to keep the thought clear. But remember that Rule 11 does not justify a careless use of commas. Only when punctuation marks are used intelligently, to make meaning clear, do they have any importance to readers.

EXERCISE 11. Read the sentences, and decide where commas are needed for clearness. On a sheet of paper, write the numbers of the sentences and, after them, the words preceding each comma. For the first sentence you should write: *1. before,*

1. Just two weeks before Clara had decided to take the job in Newton.
2. Inside the house was clean and rather attractive.
3. The children who came came because their parents had insisted on it.
4. To Mary Jane seemed kind and helpful.
5. Mother may agree now and then change her mind when the time comes for us to leave.

Chapter 9

Punctuation: Other than commas

12. The "half-period" semicolon

Compound sentences can be made in two ways — with co-ordinating conjunctions and without. When a compound sentence is made by putting two related sentences together without a conjunction, a semicolon is used to show clearly where the first coordinate clause ends and the next one begins:

> The waitress didn't answer; she was too angry to talk.
> Two of the questions no one could get; the rest were easy.
> Jim had little chance of winning; nevertheless, he did his best.
> The cashmere coats were expensive; in fact, they cost twice as much.

If the two clauses in each of these examples were written as separate sentences, a period would be needed to keep the sentences from running together. A semicolon used for the same purpose — to separate coordinate clauses in a compound sentence — can be called a "half-period" semicolon.

Rule 12. A semicolon is used between coordinate clauses that are not joined by a coordinating conjunction.

Newspapers and periodicals usually use commas to separate three or more short coordinate clauses in a series, and sometimes even to separate two that are very closely connected in meaning. But many writers prefer semicolons between all coordinate clauses, even when the clauses are short and in a series:

> Richard pleaded with his mother; he argued with her; he made extravagant promises; but she would not give him permission to drive to the Rushville game.

Notice that a semicolon is used even before the conjunction *but,* to show that the four clauses are of equal importance.

Between the coordinate clauses of a compound sentence there must be either: (1) a semicolon or (2) a comma **and** a conjunction. Using a comma alone is a serious sentence error — a "comma blunder."

EXERCISE 12.. Decide where a semicolon is needed to make a compound sentence of each group of words. On a sheet of paper, write the numbers of the word groups. After each number, write the word preceding the semicolon, then the semicolon and the word following it. For the first group you should write: *1. opposition; Jane*

1. Mr. Smith would tolerate no opposition Jane received notice of her dismissal the very next morning.
2. Ryan clattered up the staircase two steps at a time then he stopped and looked warily around.
3. Mother approved of Jerry in fact she even invited him to dinner.
4. We told Mac the road was impassable however, he insisted on starting.
5. Two years ago, Miriam had to skimp to get along now she earns three hundred dollars a week.
6. Don't take the green umbrella it belongs to Harriet.
7. Joe bravely offered to lead the way however, he was frightened.
8. Rip Van Winkle moved toward his home reluctantly he was, of course, not anxious to hear what his wife would have to say.
9. The brown bear is common in the temperate regions the polar bear, however, prefers a much colder climate.
10. After several more unsuccessful attempts to get a part in a radio show, Thelma became rather discouraged nevertheless, she refused to give up.

13. The "double-comma" semicolon

In each of the following compound sentences the coordinate clauses are joined by a coordinating conjunction. And in each sentence a semicolon is used before the conjunction:

When Paul gave his report, he was nervous, embarrassed, and miserable; *and* his hands shook so much he could hardly hold his notes.

The city engineer, who had studied the problem from every angle, said that the scheme was impractical; *yet* Mr. Donovan, the Council president, seemed determined to go on with it.

Harold won't be able to start at three, since he can't leave work early; *but* knowing how fast he drives, I predict that he'll arrive at camp before we do.

Ordinarily, a comma is used to separate coordinate clauses joined by *and, or, nor, but, yet, for*. It would not be wrong to use a comma in these sentences; but it might be confusing, since there are commas used for other purposes in one or both of the coordinate clauses. Using a semicolon instead of a comma before the conjunction shows clearly where one clause ends and the next one begins. Because the semicolon takes the place of an important comma, it can be called a "double-comma" semicolon.

Now notice how the semicolons are used in the two following sentences:

The Robertsons have a large house in Summit, New Jersey; a summer cottage near Danbury, Connecticut; and a hunting lodge somewhere in the Adirondacks.

The three main characters are Willy, a henpecked husband; his wife Maude, a disagreeable old woman; and Jim, their slow-moving, slow-talking hired man.

Each of these sentences consists of only one clause. The groups of words separated by semicolons are merely items in a series. Ordinarily, commas are used between the items in a series. But since the items themselves contain commas, there is a need for a stronger mark to show clearly where one item ends and the next one begins. Using double-comma semicolons to separate the items avoids confusing the reader.

Rule 13. A semicolon may be used in place of a comma before a coordinating conjunction or between items of a series to avoid confusion with other commas in the sentence.

EXERCISE 13. All punctuation marks have been omitted from the sentences. Read each sentence, and decide where the necessary commas, semicolons, and periods should go. Then write the numbers of the sentences. After each number, put the punctuation marks needed in that sentence and the word preceding each mark. For the first sentence you should write: *1. course, fool; passed, teacher.*

1. When Laura began the course she was sure that the professor was a fool but before many weeks had passed she realized he was a truly wise and good teacher
2. The child had filthy bedraggled hair a tear-stained dirty face ragged untidy clothes and a thoroughly woebegone expression.
3. Tippy ran toward us barking menacingly but when he saw who we were the ugly barks turned into whimpers of delight
4. Brad received letters in track baseball and football a medal for his work in public speaking and a cash award for his high grade in the science comprehensive exam
5. Although Uncle Will grumbles constantly about spending money he is very generous and if you explain how necessary a new hospital wing is I'm sure he will send you a large contribution
6. During the tour Martha played Babette the maid who appears briefly in Act One Lizzie the nosey neighbor of Act Two and one of the extras in the ballroom scene in Act Three

Chapter 9 The "Double-Comma" Semicolon 109

7. If Peter gets a job at Smith's Grocery we will have to give up our trip for he is the only one in our group who has a car

8. The main building has a utility room with washing machines dryers mangles and ironing boards a kitchen with a dishwasher a large refrigerator two stoves and a long work table a dining hall for fifty guests and a huge recreation room

9. Centuries ago the chicken was a wily elusive resourceful hard-to-capture wild animal but since it has become domesticated those qualities have vanished

10. Aunt Millicent who never could keep things straight sent a box of cigars to Dad who never smokes a bottle of Chantilly my favorite perfume to Jane an elaborate rhinestone pin to Mother who dislikes costume jewelry and a box of building blocks to Ted who is old enough now for a grown-up bicycle.

14. Colons that introduce

A colon is most frequently used to direct the reader's attention to what follows. In this book you have seen colons a great many times, usually after words that introduce examples:

Now look at the following sentences:
Here are examples:

And you have probably seen a colon used after the salutation in a business letter, to introduce the body of the letter:

Dear Sir: Gentlemen: Dear Mrs. Orwell:

A colon is also used to introduce a quotation that is formal or rather long:

As we stood there in the hot sun, the orator droned on and on: "We owe a tremendous debt of gratitude to our glorious forefathers. We must match their stirring deeds by bravery and fortitude . . ."

A colon is also used in this way when the introductory words are formal or contain a definite reference to what follows. "She spoke as follows:" or "He answered this way:" are examples.

A colon is regularly used to introduce a list of appositives that ends a sentence:

I have known several strange pairs of friends from the animal world:
a *goat* and a *rhinoceros,* a *cat* and a *deer,* a *cat* and a *rat.*
The list of nominations has finally been narrowed down to three names: *Milton Morrow, Sylvia Clarke,* and *Ronald Harris.*

Sam Stewart has these invaluable assets as a comedian: a *face* that can be twisted into a thousand shapes, a *flair* for speaking in dialects, and a remarkable *memory* for gags.

Our coach expects each player to do these things: *to play* the game to the best of his ability, *to be* a good loser, and *to be* an equally good winner.

The italicized words in the first example are in apposition with the word *pairs.* Those in the next three sentences are in apposition with *names, assets,* and *things.*

Rule 14. **A colon is used to introduce a formal quotation or a list of appositives that ends a sentence.**

A colon is not used to introduce a list of items unless they are in apposition with a preceding word in the sentence. For example:

Claudia excels in *golf, tennis, bowling,* and *archery.*

The italicized words are not appositives; they are parallel objects of the preposition *in.* Because they are essential parts of the sentence, a colon is not used. But look at this sentence:

Claudia excels in four sports: *golf, tennis, bowling,* and *archery.*

In this sentence the colon is used to call the reader's attention to the italicized words, which are in apposition with *sports.*

EXERCISE 14. Read the sentences, and decide where colons and commas are needed. Then write the numbers of the sentences. After each number, write the marks that are needed in the sentence, giving the word preceding each mark. For the first sentence you should write: *1. simple, pieces: front, back, collar,*

1. The pattern is simple consisting of only four pieces front back collar and tie sash.
2. On a silver plaque below the statue was engraved this sentence: "A plowman on his legs is higher than a gentleman on his knees."
3. Laurie has been in every state in the Union but three: Washington Oregon and Idaho.
4. The Nobel Prize for literature has been won by five American writers: Sinclair Lewis Eugene O'Neill Pearl Buck William Faulkner and John Steinbeck.
5. Each camper is expected to provide himself with soap toothbrush toothpaste towels swimming suit tennis shoes and stamps.

15. Dashes that interrupt

Dashes set off appositives like these:

Marcia's outfit combined some rather startling colors — fuchsia, lime green, and orchid — but the effect was flattering.

An ambitious group of upperclassmen — mostly seniors, I believe — is directing a thorough clean-up campaign.

Finally Sue made up her mind to go to Ohio with her aunt — a decision that was to change the course of her life.

In the first two examples the dashes are used to set off appositive phrases that contain commas, and in the last the dash is used to call attention to an appositive that sums up the meaning of a whole group of words. Now look at these sentences:

Fresh air, good food, beautiful scenery, interesting companions — these things make Blakewell Inn a perfect vacation spot.

Lack of sleep, poor dietary habits, and a hatred for work — all help to explain Lawrence's miserable grades.

In each sentence a dash is used before a word that sums up a preceding list of items. The dash shows clearly where the list ends.

Dashes are also used to set off explanatory comments or remarks that interrupt a sentence. Here are examples:

Mr. Wallingford's recent novel — his first attempt at fiction, you know — has been praised by most of the leading critics.

You'll enjoy the antics of Puff and Fluff — if you happen to like cats, that is.

Everyone heard Mrs. Thompson — her voice carries entirely too well — offering her opinions at the end of each act.

Robert's ventriloquist act — how clever he is! — was the hit of the evening.

Some of the comments set off by dashes are explanatory, as in the first sentence. Others show an abrupt change in thought, as in the fourth sentence. But in each sentence the dashes call special attention to the remark. Commas are used within the comments, but a remark in the form of a statement (as in the third and fourth sentences) does not begin with a capital letter or end with a period. The dashes set it off clearly enough from the rest of the sentence. Exclamation marks and question marks are used before a dash, but commas and periods are not.

Rule 15. **Dashes are used to call attention to explanations or comments that are not closely connected with the rest of the sentence.**

Dashes are conspicuous marks that usually indicate an abrupt change in the thought of the sentence. Use them only when you want to call the reader's attention to a remark or comment.

EXERCISE 15. Read the sentences, and decide where dashes should be used to set off appositives or other explanatory matter. Then copy the sentences, putting in the dashes and all other punctuation marks that are needed. Number each sentence. For the first sentence you should write: *1. The miserable, cold, rainy weather made Martha — ordinarily a cheerful, ambitious girl — unhappy and even lazy.*

1. The miserable cold rainy weather made Martha ordinarily a cheerful ambitious girl unhappy and even lazy
2. A great many of her early books the detective novels in particular were best sellers
3. The routine details of the work filing typing and checking orders are handled by Mrs. Ford's niece
4. Tim ran an errand for Mrs. Kernan once and she paid him a quarter thirty cents in fact
5. The use of heat to clear fog over airports a system developed in England during the war has been adopted for commercial use
6. Mona is polite and obliging when she knows she's being watched
7. Whenever he wanted something he couldn't have Jimmy used to hold his breath until his face turned blue a habit that always frightened his mother into giving him his way
8. I sent copies of the story how stupid it sounds to me now to several magazine editors
9. Sarcasm meanness stinginess these are what John thought of when Si Coogan's name was mentioned
10. Mabel insisted and you know how insistent she can be that we stay for dinner

16. Parentheses

To show the reader that a part of a sentence is intended merely as an added explanation or an incidental comment, writers often use parentheses. For example:

> Walking from our apartment to theirs (a distance of eight blocks), we passed six antique shops.
> Since Kay was angry at Bill (incredible as that may seem), she went to the movies with us.

In the first sentence the explanation in parentheses is part of the introductory phrase. In the second the comment in parentheses is part of the introductory clause. Notice that the commas used to set off the phrase and the clause come after the parentheses.

Parentheses are often used to enclose appositives that are merely reminders:

The use of laughing gas (nitrous oxide) as an anesthetic sometimes produces amusing effects.

One of our local papers (the *Star-Tribune)* has been discontinued because of financial difficulties.

I plan to spend part of my vacation with Uncle Larry (my mother's only brother).

The words enclosed in parentheses may be sentences, as in these examples:

Tom's excuse for being late (by the way, he has yet to arrive at a meeting on time) was that he missed his bus.

No matter what Aunt Grace says (she'll say plenty; she always does), we're going on our bicycle trip around the lake.

Statements enclosed by parentheses do not begin with capital letters or end with periods. The parentheses set them off from the other words in the sentences. But inside the parentheses the usual punctuation is used. In the first sentence the phrase *by the way* is set off by a comma, and in the second the two coordinate clauses are separated by a semicolon.

Though periods are not used at the ends of sentences in parentheses, question marks and exclamation marks are:

The next day I ran into Jean Larsen (do you remember her?) at Field's, buying a hat.

Horace Coulter (how he hated his name!) is now a successful Broadway producer.

Rule 16. Parentheses are used to enclose an explanation or a comment that is not closely connected with the rest of the sentence.

Parentheses offer a convenient way of inconspicuously adding a brief remark to help the reader better understand your full meaning. But used frequently, they cause the reader to detour for one explanatory comment after another, until he may lose all track of what the writer is trying to say. Several sets of parentheses on one page are usually a sign that further revision is needed.

EXERCISE 16. Read the sentences, and decide which words should be enclosed in parentheses. Then write the numbers of the sentences and, after each number, the words that should be in parentheses. Add all necessary commas, semicolons, question marks, and exclamation marks,

114

placing them within the parentheses or after them as needed. For the first sentence you should write: *1. (it cost forty cents a sheet),*

1. Knowing how expensive the drawing paper was (it cost forty cents a sheet) Herb took special pains with his work.
2. America's only marsupial (an animal that carries its young in a pouch) is the opossum.
3. Paul Douglas (the senator not the actor) was once a professor.
4. In handling sodium hydroxide (more commonly known as lye) be careful not to spill any of it.
5. Realizing that he couldn't study at home (Jimmy and Terry his young nephews were visiting George) started off for the library.
6. Jo's dress was inexpensive (she had made it herself, of course) but it brought her many compliments.
7. When I complained about paying ten dollars for a velveteen beret (do you blame me) the clerk just shrugged and walked away.
8. "Stonewall" Jackson (many times confused with Andrew Jackson) who fought in the War of 1812) was a Confederate general in the Civil War.
9. Just before I had my interview with Mr. Smithers (what a crab he was) I talked with Mrs. Davis about a job at the store.
10. Although Sally was an orphan (her father had been killed in a plane crash her mother had died of pneumonia) she had had every advantage.

17. Direct quotations

In reporting what other people have said, writers often want to use the exact words spoken. For example:

Ellen rounded the corner and called back, "Where's the car?"
"It's in the next block and across the street," replied Peggy.
"We'll never be able to find it," Ellen complained, "before the rain starts."

In writing about what Ellen and Peggy said, the writer gives their exact words, enclosing them in quotation marks to show that these words are not his own. Words so enclosed are called **direct quotations.** In the first sentence the quotation comes at the end and is set off from the rest of the sentence by a comma. Ellen's question begins with a capital letter and ends with a question mark. In the second sentence the quotation comes at the first of the sentence and ends with a comma to show that the rest of the sentence follows it. In the third sentence the quotation is divided, part of it coming before the subject *Ellen* and part of it coming after the verb *complained.* Two commas are used to set off Ellen's words from the rest of the sentence. The commas and the period precede the quotation marks.

Rule 17. **A direct quotation begins with a capital letter and is enclosed in quotation marks. When it is in a sentence, it is set off from the rest of the sentence.**

When a quoted exclamation or question comes at the beginning, no comma is used, since the exclamation mark or question mark sets off the quotation from the rest of the sentence:

"Stop playing that infernal record!" shouted Mr. Owen.

"What's the matter, Dad?" asked Mary. "You must not appreciate good music."

The exclamation mark and the question mark come before the quotation marks to show the reader that Mr. Owen's command is an exclamation and that Mary's first remark is a question.

Mary's second remark is a statement. It begins with a capital letter and ends with a period to show that it is a separate sentence, that it is not part of the first remark. See what happens when Mary's statement comes at the end of an exclamation or a question:

How impolite it was for Mary to say, "You must not appreciate good music"!

Did Mary really say, "You must not appreciate good music"?

In the first sentence the exclamation mark comes after the quotation marks to show that the whole sentence — not Mary's remark — is an exclamation. In the second the question mark comes after the quotation marks for the same reason — to show that the whole sentence is a question. There is no period after Mary's statement, since the other punctuation marks show where the sentences end.

When a quotation consists of two or more sentences, only one set of quotation marks is needed if the quoted sentences come together:

"Why don't you enter the contest? You might win," said Ed.

Mother called, "Hurry up! Breakfast is ready. You'll be late for school."

The quotation marks enclose all the words spoken at one time. When the writer adds words of his own to one of the sentences, he must be careful to show where the sentence ends:

"Why don't you enter the contest?" asked Ed. "You might win."

"Hurry up!" Mother ordered. "Breakfast is ready. You'll be late for school."

"Hurry up! Breakfast is ready," called Mother. "You'll be late for school."

The periods after *Ed* and *ordered* and *Mother* show where sen-

116

tences end. The sentences following these periods begin with capital letters.

A quotation that comes within another quotation is enclosed in single marks:

> "Only last week Mr. Wilson asked, 'Is your class having a party this term?'" Tom reported.
> Then Jean added, "But didn't Mr. Wilson also say, 'Be careful not to schedule it during exam week'?"

Each quotation begins with a capital letter and is set off from the rest of the sentence. The position of the question mark, shows to which quotation it belongs.

Improving sentences

Use a direct quotation

By giving the exact words of the people he or she is telling about, a writer often can make an incident come to life. Compare these two accounts:

Jim went out to the kitchen, reached for a towel, and announced to his mother that he would dry the dishes for her. Mrs. Burton, startled by this strange offer, asked him what the matter was. She wanted to know if his conscience was bothering him. He replied in an injured tone that it wasn't. He said that he just wanted to help her get away from the kitchen a little earlier. Then, after drying two or three glasses, he casually mentioned that the family needed a dog. He promised that if they got one he would take care of it all by himself.

His mother reminded him that she had heard him say those same words several times before and that each time his caretaking efforts had lasted about three days. Jim argued that this time he really meant to keep his promise and reminded his mother that she liked dogs, too. Mrs. Burton thought a

Jim went out to the kitchen, reached for a towel, and announced, "I'll dry the dishes for you, Mom."

"What's the matter, Jimmy?" asked Mrs. Burton, startled by this strange offer. "Is your conscience bothering you about something?"

"Of course not," he replied in an injured tone. "I just wanted to help you get away from the kitchen a little earlier." Then, after drying two or three glasses, he remarked casually, "Mom, this family needs a dog. If we get one, I'll take care of it all by myself."

"I've heard you say those same words several times before," his mother reminded him. "And each time your caretaking lasted about three days."

"This time I really mean it, Mom," argued Jim. "I'll keep my promise. You'll see. And don't forget, Mom, you like dogs, too."

moment. She finally agreed to give Jim another chance. Then she said she would have Mr. Burton look for a puppy the next day.

Grinning broadly, Jim said that she wouldn't have to bother his father. He said he already had the dog he wanted. It was in the garage. He explained that Dave Parks had given him the dog after school that evening. He asked if she would like to see the dog.

"All right, Jim," agreed Mrs. Burton, after thinking a moment. "I'll give you another chance. I'll have Dad look for a puppy tomorrow."

"Oh, you won't have to bother Dad," remarked Jim, grinning broadly. "I already have the dog I want. He's in the garage right now. Dave Parks gave him to me tonight after school. Want to see him?"

The account at the right is easier and more interesting to read. By using direct quotations, the writer makes the people that he is telling about seem more alive and the incident seem more real.

Seldom does a composition have as much conversation as there is in the incident above. But often there are places where direct quotations can vary sentences and make writing more effective. In revising, look for sentences like these:

Mother glared at Buddy. She told him to eat his spinach and stop fussing.

Mary Ann hesitated for a moment. Then she said she would take the job on a trial basis.

Max told us he had just bought a new car. He pointed toward the driveway. He said that is was far from beautiful but seemed to be in good mechanical condition.

The related sentences in each group can be combined by using verbal phrases or compound verbs. And by substituting direct quotations to give the actual words of the speakers, the combined sentences become more forceful:

Mother glared at Buddy and said, "Eat your spinach and stop fussing."

After hesitating for a moment, Mary Ann said, "I'll take the job on a trial basis."

"I've just bought a new car," Max told us, pointing toward the driveway. "It's far from beautiful, but seems to be in good mechanical condition."

Sometimes direct quotations are necessary to make the meaning clear:

Kurt grinned broadly. He told Dave that he would get all of his money back within a week.

118

Because the pronouns *he* and *his* in the second sentence could refer to either Kurt or Dave, the sentence can have two meanings. A direct quotation would clearly show one meaning or the other:

Grinning broadly, Kurt said to Dave, "I'll get all of my money back within a week."
Grinning broadly, Kurt said, "You'll get all of your money back within a week, Dave."

EXERCISE 17. Read each of the numbered groups of sentences. Decide how to combine related sentences and how to improve the sentences by using direct quotations. Then write the revised sentences, punctuating them correctly. Remember that each direct quotation should begin with a capital letter. Number your answers. For the first one you might write: *1. The bank teller turned the check over and said with a scowl, "You haven't endorsed it."*

1. The bank teller turned the check over. He told me that I hadn't endorsed it. He spoke with a scowl.
2. Hank showed me a picture of the cabin. He asked me if I would like to go up there with them sometime during the hunting season.
3. Frank paid no attention to Miss Hale's frown. He whispered that he could have the car Friday night.
4. Dad pounded his fist on the table. He asked who had cut a section out of the editorial page.
5. The clerk shoved Betty's package on a scale. He inquired if there was anything breakable in the box.
6. Miss Dexter blushed with embarrassment. She insisted that she was sure she had given the clerk a five-dollar bill.
7. Keith groaned ruefully. He told Jim that his father had been asked to see the principal Tuesday afternoon also.
8. Mrs. Jackson tried on almost every pair of shoes in the store. Then she announced that she didn't really need new shoes until summer.
9. Larry slammed down the receiver. He turned to us. Then he said that Bill was planning to skip play rehearsal again.
10. Mr. Hixon stopped us at the door. He wanted to know which of us three fellows had been tampering with the water bubbler.

18. More uses for quotation marks

Quotation marks have other uses besides enclosing the exact words of a speaker. They are used to enclose the titles of chapters of books, magazine articles, essays, short stories, short poems, songs, and plays not published as books:

The only chapter the boys enjoyed was "Beaver Society."
Be sure to read "Our Changing Weather" in next month's issue.

Hetty Green, the heroine of "The Third Ingredient," is lovable.
Poems like "Chicago" sound almost like essays.
Isn't "America" sung to the tune of "God Save the King"?
We have been acting out "Mr. Barton's Blues" in English class.

Commas and periods come before the final quotation marks. Questions marks do not, unless the title is a question:

I wasted fully an hour reading the article "Why Waste Time?"

Quotation marks are also used to call the reader's attention to a word or a group of words that is used in a special way:

Paul will some day have to realize that there are other adjectives besides "swell" and "lousy."
These untroubled years in America's political history are known as "the era of good feeling."

Notice that the words in quotation marks are not set off by commas. But writers who know they haven't yet found the exact word should not retreat into using a less effective word and excusing it by putting it in quotation marks.

Members of Congress worked "hard" to pass the bill.
Members of Congress worked diligently to pass the bill.

Rule 18. **Quotation marks may be used to enclose titles of items that are not themselves entire volumes. Quotation marks may also be used to call attention to words used as words or to special expressions.**

EXERCISE 18. All punctuation marks have been omitted from the sentences. Each of the sentences contains one or more titles or expressions that are usually enclosed in quotation marks. Copy each sentence on a sheet of paper, adding quotation marks and other needed punctuation marks. Number the sentences. For the first answer you should write:
1. The article "Hi-Jinks" offers the usual analysis of teen-age problems.

1. The article Hi-Jinks offers the usual analysis of teen-age problems
2. She referred us to Farm Boy a good article in last month's issue
3. Can you remember the first line of Old Ironsides
4. Try to avoid this here and that there as you would the plague
5. Is the Little Theater giving Pandora's Box or A Game of Chess
6. After his triumph in the class play John's friends referred to him as the poor man's Lawrence Olivier
7. We became annoyed at Jim for using old chap in every other sentence

120

8. Did Christine say that the most exciting short story she had ever read was Jack London's The Madness of John Harned

9. Many people who use the expression feel badly think they are being grammatically precise

10. Martha outlined the first chapter A Point of View and summarized the eighth Certain Matters of Importance

Summary review of all marks

In Chapters 8 and 9 are eighteen rules of punctuation. These rules discuss several uses of the comma: to separate items of equal importance (Rules 2, 3, 10), to set off words not closely connected in meaning with the rest of the sentence (Rules 4, 5, 6, 7, 8, 9), and to avoid possible misreading (Rules 10, 11). What are the uses of the commas in the following sentences?

1. Maggie made a dirndl skirt, a blouse, and a kerchief out of the parachute silk Don brought home.

2. The frightened stagecoach passengers closed their eyes and prayed during their wild, fast, reckless ride through the mountain pass.

3. On May 29, 1897, the rebels staged their long-delayed march on the capital city.

4. Mr. Cole draws sketches of the proposed articles of furniture, and Mr. Adams supervises their construction.

5. I am positive, Your Honor, that the witness has mistaken me for someone else.

6. No, I am not in a position to judge Stella's character.

7. The back left fender has a huge dent in it, too.

8. To tell the truth, I can't remember where I put the keys.

9. Francis Bacon, for example, has been both honored and scorned in the pages of history.

10. Mr. Winters seemed pleased with his going-away present, a large leather suitcase.

11. Joan spends most of her time on her hobby, designing ski clothes.

12. Marilyn's suggestion, to dispense with decorations at the next dance, was unanimously vetoed by the other girls.

13. The though uppermost in Lee's mind, that she must lead the class in scholarship, is the result of her mother's prodding.

14. Sarah, annoyed by their silly jokes, picked up her books and left the living room.

15. Her facing showing a mixture of pride and modesty, Sally walked slowly up to the stage to receive the award.

16. "You'd better pick out a book some time today," Nick warned, "if you expect to have a report ready by Friday."

17. We went to old Mr. Noble, who had been a newspaperman for over fifty years, for some practical advice.

18. I pretended to be surprised, though Mary Ann had told me about the party weeks in advance.
19. Since Keith refused to help, Jerry had to work an hour longer.
20. Because of the cold, people are staying home much more nowadays.

A semicolon may be used as a kind of "half period" (Rule 12) or as a sort of "double comma" (Rule 13). Colons can introduce (Rule 14). Explain the uses of the semicolons and colons in the next five sentences:

21. We shall have to prepare something simple for dinner; Jud is going to pick us up at six-thirty.
22. When the hamburgers were finally served, they were burned, hard, and tasteless; but we ate them with great gusto.
23. The Wilson chain has restaurants in Augusta, Maine; Boston, Massachusetts; and Newport, Rhode Island.
24. Under Aunt Em's guidance we each made samplers bearing this motto: "Beauty is as beauty does."
25. The coach will insist that you follow three general training rules: eat well, sleep a lot, and never miss a practice.

Certain words not closely connected with the rest of the sentence may be set off by parentheses (Rule 16) or by dashes (Rule 15). Consider the uses of the dashes and parentheses in the next five sentences:

26. For the table top a close-grained wood (mahogany, for example, or birch) should be used.
27. The main advantages of the smaller English cars are that they use very little gasoline (an Englishman would say "petrol," of course) and are easier to park.
28. In many countries of the world the basic farm work — plowing, planting, and cultivating — is done with implements that would seem almost primitive to most American farmers.
29. Patience, kindness, perseverance — these qualities you must develop.
30. The view of the mountains from our back porch — such a breath-taking sight! — always fascinated our guests.

Quotation marks in combination with other punctuation marks are discussed in Rules 17 and 18. Explain the use and place-ment of the punctuation marks in each of the next five sentences:

31. Frank called downstairs, "Where did you put my argyle socks, Mother?"
32. Did you hear her say, "It's going to rain before night"?

33. "Why didn't you let me know you were bringing Julie to dinner?" Rose asked. "I bought only four pork chops."
34. "Stay out there with that old rat!" Mother yelled to Fluffy.
35. Four of the "barber-shoppers" sang their favorite, "Sweet Adeline."

Writing will appear to its best advantage if it is punctuated correctly. Knowing when punctuation is needed, which marks to use, and where to place them will do much to keep meaning clear and to make writing effective.

Chapter 10

A Glossary of Troublesome Words

Adapt and *adopt*

Adapt is a verb that means "to adjust" or "to make suitable." Unlike *adopt, adapt* is usually followed by the prepositions *to, for,* or *from:*

Her eyes soon *adapted to* the harsh light.
Have you heard that *The Scarlet Letter* has been *adapted for* television?

Adopt means "to take as one's own":

Late in life the Warrens *adopted* a child.
Many students *adopt* the air of world-weary old men.

Affect and *effect*

Affect, beginning with an *a,* is always a verb, meaning "to influence": "The new ruling did not affect the freshmen." "She was greatly affected by the poverty of their home." *Affect* is sometimes confused with another verb, *effect,* which means "to bring about": "The arbitrator effected a settlement to the strike."

Effect may also be used as a noun, meaning "an influence": "The effect of the stock market crash is still being felt."

EXERCISE 1. On your own sheet of paper, write *affect* or *effect* where the blanks occur:
1. The medicine had a beneficial _____ on her.
2. The music of Beethoven always seems to _____ me powerfully.
3. His speech had quite an _____ on the audience.
4. Let's see how seriously the closing down of the factory will _____ the economy of the town.
5. Dean Smith plans to _____ many changes in the College's disciplinary system.

Compounds of *all*

All right, meaning "satisfactorily" or "very well," is spelled as two words in formal English:

Emily does all right in school.
All right, I'll stay home and babysit.

All ready means "everybody or everything ready," while *already* is an adverb of time meaning "previously." If you could use the word *ready* alone, without changing the meaning of the sentence, *all ready* is the correct choice.

All together and *altogether* are quite similar to *all ready* and *already*. If the word *together* could be used by itself, write *all together*. If the meaning you seek is "thoroughly," write *altogether*.

EXERCISE 2. On your own sheet of paper, write *all ready, already, all together,* or *altogether* where the blanks occur.
1. John was _____ to take the bus to camp.
2. Norma had _____ been to overnight camp for three weeks.
3. The members of the team pulled _____ on the rope.
4. It was an _____ satisfying experience.
5. Kevin has _____ done the dishes.

Allusion and *illusion*

Since *allusion* and *illusion* are similar in sound, they are sometimes carelessly confused. *Allusion* means "an indirect or implied reference"; *illusion* means "a misleading appearance" or "a false impression":

The title *The Little Foxes* is an *allusion* to a passage in the Bible.
A skillful arrangement of mirrors created an *illusion* of spaciousness.

Amount and *number*

In formal English, people use *number* in writing of persons or things that can be counted; they use *amount* in writing of quantities:

Ralph sold a large *number* of tickets at school.
A small *amount* of cotton was stored in the warehouse.

EXERCISE 3. On your own sheet of paper use *amount* or *number* where the blanks occur.
1. Have you noticed the great _____ of traffic accidents reported lately?
2. The _____ of high school students increases every year.
3. Mrs. Kirby spent a considerable _____ of money for the antique table in her living room.
4. The greatest _____ of mistakes came in answering the algebra questions in the test.
5. Are you surprised at the large _____ of gullible people there are in the world?

Beside and *besides*

In formal English, the word *beside* is most commonly used as a preposition meaning "by the side of." *Besides* is generally used as a preposition meaning "in addition to" or "except," or as an adverb meaning "moreover":

> She ate nothing *besides* a piece of toast.
> There is really only enough for two; *besides,* Sally doesn't like eggs.
> Louise is standing *beside* Harold.
> His last remark was *beside* the point.

EXERCISE 4. On your own sheet of paper, use *beside* or *besides* where the blanks occur:
1. _____ all that, I just don't want to go to a movie tonight.
2. Several others _____ Mrs. Lacey insist they saw the ghost.
3. He has no one to turn to _____ you.
4. I hadn't realized that the man standing _____ the coach was Dad.
5. Kay is a better worker than Oscar; _____, she needs the money.

Between and *among*

In formal English, people use *between* when writing about two persons or things; they use *among* when writing of more than two:

> Uncle Alfred distributed the toys *among* the five boys.
> She divided the sandwich *between* Sam and me.

However, when they are writing of more than two persons or things, but are considering each one in relation to each of the others, they generally use *between:*

> What is the difference *between* football, soccer, and Rugby?
> The treaty *between* the four powers was signed the next day.

EXERCISE 5. On your own sheet of paper, use *between* or *among* where the blanks occur:
1. Who knows the difference _____ a phrase, a clause, and a sentence?
2. Why didn't he divide the reward _____ the three girls?
3. The morning edition carries the complete text of the treaty _____ the five powers.
4. He announced that the work would be divided _____ the members who had volunteered to help.
5. The estate will probably be divided _____ her many relatives.

Borrow and *lend*

We use *borrow* when we mean "get something from another with the understanding that it must be returned"; we use *lend* when we mean "let another have or use for a time":

Please *lend* me your eraser.
He *lent* me fifty cents.
Jim *borrowed* my eraser and forgot to return it.

The preposition *from* is used with *borrow.*

Frank borrowed a dollar *from* Bob.
Did Jane borrow that umbrella *from* you?

Bring and *take*

The verb *bring* suggests motion toward the speaker; the verb *take* suggests motion away from the speaker:

Take this note to Mr. Evans.
Bring me his answer this afternoon.

EXERCISE 6. On your own sheet of paper use *bring* or *take* where the blanks occur:
1. _____ these books to Mr. Scott on your way downstairs.
2. _____ me another cup of coffee, please.
3. Why don't you _____ Bill to the cafeteria across the street?
4. Louise promised that she would _____ me a copy.
5. Did Dad say he would_____ us to the movies tonight?

Childish and *childlike*

In describing a grown person, we use *childish* when we want to suggest that he is like a child in what we consider an undesirable way. When we want to suggest that he is like a child in a way we think desirable, we use *childlike:*

Mr. Wade pounded on the table in a *childish* outburst of temper.
Mrs. Elson had a *childlike* faith in people.

Compliment and *complement*

A *compliment* is an expression of admiration, while a *complement* is something that completes:

Her precision of speech drew many *compliments.*
The dessert was a perfect *complement* to a fine meal.

Conscience, conscientious, and conscious

A *conscience* is one's sense of obligation to do right. When one is *conscientious,* he or she is conforming to the dictates of conscience. When one is *conscious,* he or she is aware:

Our *conscience* distinguishes us from the animals.
Through *conscientious* study Marty became an honor student.
The injured man remained *conscious.*

EXERCISE 7. On your own sheet of paper, write *conscience, conscientious,* or *conscious* where the blanks occur:
1. Although rich, she was often bothered by the promptings of her
_____ .
2. I am quite _____ of your objections to my proposal.
3. Because Dick was so _____, we knew we could depend on him.
4. Benson was self-_____ about his weight.
5. A strong _____ is a defense against selfishness.

Convince and persuade

Convince means "to get someone to believe something." *Persuade* means "to get someone to do something." *Convince* is followed by *of* or *that. Persuade* is followed by an infinitive:

I am *convinced of* your integrity.
I am *convinced that* you are right.
I hope to *persuade* you *to* preserve the distinction between *convince* and *persuade.*

Detect, discover, and invent

We use *detect* when we mean "uncover something that exists but is not obvious." We use *discover* when we mean "see or learn or find *for the first* time." We use *invent* when we mean "make or think out something new":

Frank *detected* a note of sarcasm in Mary's reply.
The Curies *discovered* radium in 1898.
Steele MacKaye, an American playwright and actor, *invented* the folding theater chair.

Different than and different from

Although *different than* is commonly used in informal speech, many careful writers prefer *different from:*

His answer is different *from* mine.
Her new clothes are different *from* those her aunt used to make.

Different than is the most common form that introduces an adverbial clause of comparison:

> Returning many years later, she found that her home town was *different than* she remembered it.

Except and *accept*

Except can be a verb that means "to take or leave out from a whole" or a preposition that means "with the exception of":

> One day women may no longer be *excepted* from the draft.
> The museum is open daily, *except* Sundays.

Accept, a verb that sounds much like *except,* means "to receive with approval":

> She proudly *accepted* her diploma.
> Seniors will be *excepted* from the work duty.

Farther and *further*

Farther indicates concrete distance:

> Don't go one step *farther.*
> The airport is *farther* away than the train station.

Further describes abstract ideas and means "additional" or "additionally":

> The committee requested *further* details.
> The defendant was scheduled to testify *further* in the trial.

Flaunt and *flout*

Flaunt is a verb that means "to make a display of"; *flout* is another verb that means "to treat with contempt":

> Henry *flaunted* his prodigious intelligence.
> She *flouted* the authority of the student discipline committee.

Formerly and *formally*

The adverb *formerly* has to do with time; it answers the question "When?" The adverb *formally* has to do with manner; it answers the question "How?":

> He was *formerly* secretary to the vice-president of the bank.
> In all the confusion I was never *formally* introduced to Mrs. Hill.

130

Hanged and *hung*

In formal English, people are *hanged* and things are *hung*. When we use the verb *hang* to refer to acts of execution or suicide, the principal parts are *hang, hanged, hanged*. In all other contexts the principal parts of the verb are: *hang, hung, hung*.

> They *hanged* the prisoner from the yardarm.
> She *hung* the picture over the mantel.

Have and *of*

The helping verb *have* and its contraction *'ve* sound like *of* in rapid speech. But never write *of* for *have* or *'ve*:

> He *should have notified* you sooner.
> I *might've known* he'd be late.
> You *would've enjoyed* meeting Nancy.

Imply and *infer*

Careful writers usually use *imply* when they mean "indicate without saying outright" or "express indirectly"; they use *infer* when they mean "draw a conclusion by reasoning":

> His tone *implied* that he did not really believe us.
> We *inferred* from his tone that he thought we were lying.

Incredible and *incredulous*

When something is *incredible*, it is unbelievable. When a person is *incredulous*, he or she is unbelieving, or skeptical:

> Sarah's ability to master foreign languages is *incredible*.
> We were *incredulous* when Mark told us that he had mastered Latin in a single summer of study.

Its and *it's*

Like all possessive personal pronouns, *its* has no apostrophe. *It's* is a contraction of *it is* or *it has*.

EXERCISE 8. On your own sheet of paper, use *its* or *it's* where the blanks occur:
1. _____ a beautiful day in this neighborhood.
2. _____ been a pleasure meeting all of you.
3. The cat washed _____ paws.
4. This automobile has a design that's ahead of _____ time.
5. Every dogma has _____ day.

Less and *fewer*

The adjective *less* means "not so much" and refers to amount or quantity. The adjective *fewer* means "not so many" and refers to number. Careful writers use *less* with singular nouns (things that can be measured), and *fewer* with plural nouns (things that can be counted):

The next day there were *fewer* bicycles in the stands.
Bob has *less* courage than I.

EXERCISE 9. On your own sheet of paper, write *less* or *fewer* where the blanks occur:
1. Wouldn't it be better to use _____ chairs in the kitchen scene?
2. Phyllis knows a card game that takes _____ players than this.
3. The second time we voted, Harold got still _____ votes.
4. You will have _____ trouble if you take the bus.
5. Can't you express the same idea in _____ words?

Let **and** *leave*

The verb *let* — not the verb *leave* — is used to mean "allow" or "permit":

His father *would*n't *let* him have the car.
Let me see it.
Don't leave your purse on your desk.
Have they *left* already?

Since the contraction *let's* means *let us,* a second *us* is not needed after *let's:*

Let's go to the first show.
Let's take our bicycles.

EXERCISE 10. On your own sheet of paper use a form of *let* or *leave* where the blanks occur:
1. I don't think he will _____ us change seats.
2. Won't the teacher _____ you practice your songs in her room?
3. Last year Mr. Allen _____ us use the auditorium for rehearsals.
4. Why don't you _____ your books in the car?
5. _____ Ken see how you did the first algebra problem.

Lie and lay

Since the verb *lie* means "be in or assume a flat position," it never has an object. Since the verb *lay* means "place" or "put down," it usually has an object. Most educated people do not confuse the forms *lay, laid, laid, laying* with the forms *lie, lay, lain, lying:*

Lie down, Blackie.
Tom *lay* on the cot while he waited.
She *has* just *lain* down to rest.
Laura carefully *laid* the hat on the counter.
I *had* just *laid* the books on the table, when the phone rang.
The letter *was lying* in plain sight on the desk.
Aunt Edna *is laying* the linoleum in the kitchen.

EXERCISE 11. On your own sheet of paper, use a form of *lie* or *lay* where the blanks occur:
1. Why don't you _____ down for a while?
2. While we ran the tractor, Silas _____ at his ease in the truck.
3. Why doesn't someone _____ the facts before the whole group?
4. For three days the men _____ in wait for the cattle thieves.
5. She had just _____ down to rest, when the mysterious noise sounded once more.
6. By noon of the next day all the floors had been _____.
7. Grandfather was _____ in the hammock, sound asleep.
8. Bill _____ on a rug near the fire all the while we were there.
9. His favorite saying was "Let sleeping dogs _____."
10. I'm tired and would like to _____ down.

Like and as

In informal speech and writing *like* is commonly used as a conjunction introducing an adverb clause of comparison. But careful writers prefer *as:*

I tried to pronounce the words *as* she did.
Hold your paddle *as* I do.

When a phrase is used for the comparison instead of a clause, the preposition *like,* not the conjunction *as,* is the appropriate word:

She treated me *like* a child.
She behaved *like* a rowdy.

Most careful writers do not substitute *like* for *as if:*

For a while it looked *as if* he would succeed.
Did it seem *as if* they were worried?

EXERCISE 12. On your own sheet of paper, write *like, as,* or *as if* where the blanks occur:
1. The coach smiled pleasantly and nodded, _____ she agreed with us.
2. When he returned from camp, Dave talked _____ a fugitive from a chain gang.
3. Her parents are not strict, _____ Mom and Dad are.
4. Doesn't it look _____ it will rain?
5. Why didn't you do _____ you were told?

Loose and *lose*

Loose, an adjective that means "relaxed," is occasionally confused with *lose,* a verb that means "to miss from one's possession." Try to associate the spelling of each word with its pronunciation:

Be sure not to *lose* your mittens.
The child was eager for her *loose* tooth to fall out.

Pour and *pore*

Although we occasionally encounter a carelessly written sentence in which someone pours over a book, *pour* means "to cause liquid to flow," while *pore* means "to read thoroughly":

He *poured* the syrup generously over the waffles.
Desperately seeking a job, she *pored* over the want ads.

Precede and *proceed*

We use *precede* when we mean "go or come before"; we use *proceed* when we mean "go on" or "move forward":

First translate the phrase that *precedes* the verb.
Tom answered her question and *proceeded* with his story.

EXERCISE 13. On your own sheet of paper, use a form of *precede* or *proceed* where the blanks occur:
1. When we reached the turn, we waited for the guide to _____ us.
2. Before you _____ with your plans, be sure to consult Jane Lang about the probable costs.
3. The actress, _____ by her maid and press agent, hurried out.
4. He tried to _____ with his speech, but the shouts grew louder.
5. Seven pages dressed in white _____ the princess.

Principal and *principle*

Principal may be used as a noun or as an adjective, both meaning "chief." *Principle* is a noun meaning "a fundamental law or truth":

The *principal* belief of the high school *principal* was the *principle* that every student was capable of achieving success.

Uninterested and *disinterested*

Careful writers make a distinction between *uninterested,* meaning "feeling or showing no interest," and *disinterested,* meaning "free from prejudice or selfish motives":

Louise was completely *uninterested* in Mr. Barnhill's lecture.
Both sides agreed to leave the decision to a *disinterested* judge.

EXERCISE 14. On your own sheet of paper, write *uninterested* or *disinterested* where the blanks occur:
1. He seemed rather _____, though he listened politely.
2. Why don't you agree to leave the decision to a _____ friend?
3. Anyone as _____ in his work as Mr. Anderson evidently is will never achieve success.
4. Above all, the person you choose as arbitrator must be _____.
5. The Smith Foundation was _____ in her proposal to turn mushrooms into fuel.

Unique and *unusual*

Because *unique* means "one of a kind," it is an absolute adjective that cannot be qualified by adverbs such as *very* and *most. Unusual,* on the other hand, means "distinctive" and can be qualified:

The largest of its kind in the world, the Hope Diamond is also *unique* in its beauty.
Todd's idea to rent himself out for charity was one of the most *unusual* schemes I've ever heard.

Whet and wet

Whet means "to sharpen," while its sound-alike, *wet* means "to moisten":

Beth's success in algebra served to *whet* her desire to study geometry.

During their water balloon fight, the boys managed to *wet* all the clothing hanging on the line.

EXERCISE 15. To solidify your mastery of the distinctions between and among troublesome words, try your hand at this summary exercise. Examine each pair of sentences and choose the one that answers each question correctly:

1. Which judge would you prefer?
   a. At the trial the judge was completely uninterested.
   b. At the trial the judge was completely disinterested.
2. Which request would parents be more likely to make to their children?
   a. Bring the stray dog home.
   b. Take the stray dog home.
3. Which person is more skeptical?
   a. She is an incredulous reader.
   b. She is an incredible reader.
4. In which case is Paul trying to cash in on his father's power?
   a. Paul flaunts his father's authority.
   b. Paul flouts his father's authority.
5. Which dog is in charge?
   a. A clever dog knows its master.
   b. A clever dog knows it's master.
6. Which town probably has the stronger school system?
   a. I admire the town's principals.
   b. I admire the town's principles.
7. Which student will receive the higher grade?
   a. His answers were all most accurate.
   b. His answers were almost accurate.
8. Which students received a special exemption?
   a. The draft board accepted all students.
   b. The draft board excepted all students.
9. Which speaker is smarter?
   a. In the room were four smart people beside me.
   b. In the room were four smart people besides me.

10. Which people had met previously?
    a. We were formally introduced.
    b. We were formerly introduced.
11. Which people are playing doubles?
    a. Ellen complemented Frank's tennis game.
    b. Ellen complimented Frank's tennis game.
12. Which leader is more resourceful?
    a. The mayor adapted her predecessor's policies.
    b. The mayor adopted her predecessor's policies.
13. Which speaker is more likely to be a magician?
    a. She embellished her talk with a series of allusions.
    b. She embellished her talk with a series of illusions.
14. Which Hood was careless?
    a. In tight situations, Robin Hood tended to loose arrows.
    b. In tight situations, Robin Hood tended to lose arrows.
15. Which statement definitely contains two people?
    a. Mary inferred that she was unhappy with her job.
    b. Mary implied that she was unhappy with her job.

To strengthen your mastery of troublesome words, answer the Writing Subject Test questions in Chapter 14.

Chapter 11

A Glossary of Standard English Usage

Adjectives and adverbs

In standard English writers and speakers use adjectives to modify nouns and pronouns, and adverbs to modify verbs:

This car *surely* runs *well.* I was *sure* it was a *good* car.
She spoke *rudely* to him. No one likes a *rude* person.
He can finish his work *easily* before noon. Dad gave him an *easy* job.
Helen *sadly* shook her opponent's hand. I felt *sad* about her losing the match.

Use adverbs — not adjectives — to modify adjectives or other adverbs:

Dan is *really* strong, though he is *frightfully* thin.
She played *really* well in yesterday's game.

To point out persons or things being talked about, speakers and writers use the adjectives *this, that, these, those* or the adverbs *here* and *there:*

This watch is his. *That* one is mine.
That pen scratches. The one over *here* writes smoothly.
These golf balls are new. The ones over *there* are nicked.
Those shirts on the table have plain cuffs. *These* have French cuffs.

Agreement of subject and verb

A subject that means one person or thing takes a singular verb:

Only **one** of the girls *is coming.*
The **table** next to those bookcases *is* hers.
My biggest **worry** *was* my grades.

A subject that means more than one person or thing takes a plural verb:

Three **girls** in the group from East High *have left* already.
The **tables** in front of that bookcase *are* hers.
My **grades** *were* my biggest worry.

Compound subjects joined by *and* usually take a plural verb:

Here *come* **Sally** and **Pat.**
Are the **coach** and the **manager** riding in the first car?

But when the parts of the compound subject mean only one person or are thought of as one thing, a singular verb is used:

The best **student** and **athlete** in our class *is* Harriet Brownell.
Bread and **butter** *tastes* better with jelly on it.

When the parts of a compound subject joined by *or* or *nor* are singular, the subject is considered singular, since it means only one person or thing. Though a plural verb may sometimes be used in everyday speech, especially in questions, careful writers prefer the singular:

Is **Jack** or **Bill** here?
Neither **Dad** nor **Mother** *is* in.

When the parts of a compound subject joined by *or* or *nor* are plural, or the one nearer the verb is plural, a plural verb is used:

Hot dogs or **hamburgers** *are* less bother to prepare.
Neither the **dictionary** nor the reference **books** *were* of any help.

But:

Neither the reference **books** nor the **dictionary** *was* of any help.

A singular subject takes a singular verb even when a phrase beginning with *together with, in addition to,* or *as well as* comes between the subject and the verb:

The **sheriff,** together with his deputies, *is* on the way.
The **principal,** as well as our faculty advisers, *was* there.

Collective nouns, that is, nouns that are names of groups of persons or things — like *team, crowd, herd, family, band, choir, jury* — may take a singular or plural verb, depending on the meaning intended. To show that the group is a single unit, use a singular verb:

Her **family** *is* rich.
The **jury** *has reached* a decision.

To show that the individuals are a group, use a plural verb:

The **family** upstairs *were quarreling* again.
After the meeting, the **committee** *are returning* to their homes.

Similarly, the meaning determines whether words like *all, some, none, half, more, lot, part, number, remainder* take a singular or plural verb. When one person or thing is meant, a singular verb is used; when more than one is meant, a plural verb is used:

None of the paint *is* dry yet.
None of the dresses *suit* her. OR: **None** of the dresses *suits* her.
The greatest **number** of complaints *comes* from the parents.
A great **number** of complaints *have been received.*

EXERCISE 1. On your own sheet of paper, write *is* or *are* where the blanks occur:
1. __Is__ Louise or Sally at home?
2. The reasons given in this report __are__ absurd.
3. Her biggest problem these days __is__ taxes.
4. __Are__ there any more of these sandwiches in the kitchen?
5. As usual his family __are__ arguing about what program to see.
6. __Are__ Sam and his friends coming for dinner?

In each of the next seven sentences, use *was* or *were:*
7. Neither Helen nor Jean __was__ willing to help sell the tickets.
8. Ham and eggs __was__ his favorite dish.
9. A number of valuable books __were__ destroyed in the fire.
10. Each of the members of the committee __were__ notified of the change.
11. His aunt and uncle, together with their son, __were__ at the station.
12. A large barrel filled with toys and clothes of all kinds __was__ sent.
13. All of his free time during those few weeks __was__ spent at the library.

In each of the next seven sentences, use *has* or *have:*
14. Katy, as well as her father, __has__ red hair and a quick temper.
15. The price of all foods __has__ risen sharply.
16. One of my best friends __has__ the lead in the play.
17. So far our team __has__ won four games and lost one.
18. __Have__ the boys or their adviser asked permission to give the dance?
19. Every one of these engines __has__ been carefully tested.
20. Mr. Allen or Mr. Green __have__ won the prize the last few weeks.

When a singular subject follows *there* or *here,* use a singular verb:

There *goes* the last of my money.
Here *is* a misspelled word in your very first sentence.

When a plural subject follows, use a plural verb:

There *were* several copies of the safety pamphlet on the top shelf.
Lately there *have been* fewer complaints.
Here *are* three more questions to consider.
Here *come* the elephants.

Avoiding shifts in time

In telling about something that happened, do not shift carelessly from verb forms that show past time to verb forms that show present time, or from present forms to past forms:

He *fumbled* about in his pocket and finally *pulled* out a nickel.
Every night my father *tucks* my little sister into bed and *tells* her fantastic tales.

Using forms of *be*

In writing standard English, do not use *ain't* as a substitute for *am not, isn't, aren't, hasn't,* or *haven't:*

I *am not* sure of his address.
I'*m not* going right home after school tonight.
Isn't she supposed to help, too?
Aren't you invited to the party?
He *hasn't* answered any of my letters.
Haven't you called Mother yet?

Do not use *was* with *you,* even when writing about one person:

Were you there, Helen?
You *were* asked to report yesterday, *were*n't you?
Why *were* you so worried?
Where *were* you going last night?

Comparison of adjectives and adverbs

The comparative forms of adjectives and adverbs, which are used in speaking of two persons or things, are made by adding *er* or by using *more: neater, more skillful; sooner, more seriously:*

Sue's work is *neater* than mine.
She is *more skillful* than I.
Dave gave up *sooner* than I.
I take my work *more seriously* than he.

The superlative forms, which are used in writing about more than two persons or things, are made by adding *est* or by using *most: neatest, most skillful; soonest, most seriously:*

Yesterday was the *coldest* day we've had in years.
His skit was the *most stupid* of all the acts.

Some adjectives and adverbs have irregular forms — for example: *good, better, best; bad, worse, worst; far, farther, farthest. More* and *most* are not used with these:

Jim walked *farther* than I.
She gave me the *worst* scolding I've ever had.

142

Although in everyday speech and writing the superlative is sometimes used in speaking of two persons or things, careful writers use the comparative:

Laura is the *younger* of the two sisters.
Peter and Ed weighed themselves to see who was the *heavier.*

In writing about persons or things of the same kind, use *other* or *else* after a comparative form:

Marilyn was taller than any *other* girl on the team.
Vern played better than all the *other* boys in the tournament.
Mr. Evans earns more money than anyone *else* in the shop.

But after a superlative form, do not use *other* or *else:*

That is the most interesting *of all the* stories in the book.
Mrs. Fowler was the most helpless *of the* women.

EXERCISE 2. On your own sheet of paper, use *than any other, than the other,* or *of all* where the blanks occur:
1. Bert worked harder _____ member of the club.
2. Though Bob had a motorcycle, he arrived later _____ boys.
3. Everyone agreed that Sue's sketches were the best _____ the drawings.
4. Clara, who was usually patient, complained more _____ workers.
5. Eileen could swim better _____ girl in our tent.

Forms of *do*

Do not use the form *don't* with a singular noun or with *he, she, it, this,* and *that:*

Doesn't your doorbell ring?
That *doesn't* make any difference to us.
He *doesn't* need much encouragement.
Doesn't she live on Laurel Avenue?

Double negatives

Do not use two negative words to express one negative meaning:

Bob hasn't *any* money.	**OR:**	Bob has *no* money.
He hasn't *ever* been there.		He has *never* been there.
She didn't say *anything.*		She said *nothing.*
I haven't *any* to show you.		I have *none* to show you.
He isn't *anywhere* in sight.		He is *nowhere* in sight.

It is perfectly true that listeners or readers would surely know what was meant in ''Bob hasn't no money.'' But it is clear that the second negative, "no," is better replaced by "any." Two negatives — in this sense — do not really make a positive, or an affirmative. In English long ago negatives abounded; Chaucer in the 14th century wrote of a knight: "In all his life he hasn't never yet said nothing discourteous to no sort of person." Four negatives!

Since the adverbs *hardly* and *scarcely* are negative in meaning, do not combine them with *no, not, nothing, none,* or *never:*

> There was hardly enough food for two of us.
> Frank is scarcely ever on time.
> She has done hardly anything all week.
> I have scarcely any left.

EXERCISE 3. On your own sheet of paper, use *no* or *any, nobody* or *anybody, nowhere* or *anywhere* where the blanks occur:
1. I couldn't find my gloves _anywhere_
2. Don't you have _any_ more paper clips?
3. We knew _nobody_ in Clintonville who could help us.
4. Doesn't he have _any_ golf clubs of his own?

In each of the next four sentences, use *can* or *can't, could* or *couldn't, has* or *hasn't, was* or *wasn't:*
5. Amy was so angry she _could_ scarcely say a word.
6. Jim _hasn't_ ever asked a question in class.
7. I _was_ hardly tall enough to reach the top shelf.
8. She _couldn't_ hardly refuse to help her own cousins.

Excessive Predication

When long clauses are overused in a sentence in which shorter forms, such as phrases and single words, will do the same job, the result may appear too stilted and wordy. This condition is called **excessive predication.** Here, for example, is a sentence with five subordinate clauses in it:

> Since Captain Bradley, who was the only officer left alive, knew that the Indians would attack again at daybreak, he had to decide whether he should gamble on the arrival of the cavalry before dawn or whether he should try to lead the miserable band of survivors away from the fort under cover of darkness.

The sentence can be improved by using an appositive phrase and three verbal phrases in place of four of the clauses:

> Knowing that the Indians would attack again at daybreak, Captain Bradley, the only officer left alive, had to decide whether to gamble on the arrival of the cavalry before dawn or to try to lead the miserable band of survivors away from the fort under cover of darkness.

144

Some compositions are wordy because the writer explains every little detail in a separate sentence. For example:

My uniforms are made of nylon. The nylon makes them easy to launder.

The same idea can be expressed just as well in one sentence, using clauses or phrases or modifying words:

My uniforms are made of nylon, which makes them easy to launder.
My uniforms are made of nylon to make them easy to launder.
My uniforms, which are made of nylon, are easy to launder.
My uniforms, made of nylon, are easy to launder.
My nylon uniforms are easy to launder.

See how much the writer is in control of meaning by his choosing of one of these five.

Is when and *is where* in definitions

Avoid "is when" and "is where" in defining words:

Zoology is the *study* of animals and animal life.
Hyperbole is *exaggeration* for the sake of effect.
To postpone is *to put* off until a later time.
Sizing is the *process* of stiffening the cloth by treating it with a starchy preparation.

Modifying errors

Make sure that any modifying phrase or clause used modifies a word in the sentences and that it is the word it should modify. Watch especially for sentences like these:

Dr. Ellis paid no attention to her husband busily measuring out the medicine.
Suspended from the ceiling by a single hair, Damocles saw a shining sword.

Each of these sentences contains the word the participle is intended to modify. But the writer of the first sentence has carelessly put the phrase last, where it seems to modify *husband;* and the writer of the second sentence has carelessly put the phrase first, where it seems to modify *Damocles.* Such confusing and, often, amusing errors are called **misplaced modifiers.** The confusion is easily corrected. Move the phrases closer to the words they are intended to modify:

Dr. Ellis, *busily measuring out the medicine,* paid no attention to her husband.
Damocles saw a shining sword *suspended from the ceiling by a single hair.*

Here is an example of a misplaced adjective clause:

> The tall man ducked behind the hedge that Ernie had seen prowling about the halls.

Not trying to amaze your readers with a fantastic story of wandering hedges? Place the clause right after the word it modifies:

> The tall man *that Ernie had seen prowling about the halls* ducked behind the hedge.

In using adverb clauses, be sure that each clause clearly modifies what it is intended to modify. Compare these two sentences:

> Mary decided to eat her breakfast at the cafeteria on the corner *before she got up.*
> *Before she got up,* Mary decided to eat her breakfast at the cafeteria on the corner.

The first sentence seems to mean that Mary was going to eat her breakfast before getting up. In the second sentence the clause has been put first to show the reader that it modifies the verb *decided.* Shifting an adverb clause in this way often makes the meaning clearer. And be sure to avoid elliptical clauses that may have two meanings:

> The older players taught me more *than the coach.*
> Is the sun ever closer to the moon *than the earth?*

The first sentence might mean:

> The older players taught me more *than the coach did.*
> *than they taught the coach.*

The second sentence might mean:

> Is the sun ever closer to the moon *than the earth is?*
> *than it is to the earth?*

Always supply the words necessary to make your meaning clear.

EXERCISE 4. The sentences below are confusing because modifiers have been misplaced. Revise each sentence by putting the misplaced modifier where it clearly modifies the word intended. For the first one you might say: *They used the snapshot I took of Bill standing beside the wagon.*

1. They used the snapshot of Bill standing beside the station wagon that I took.
2. Being in a rundown condition, I bought the house cheaply.

146

3. Backed up by a powerful army, no one could oppose the dictator.
4. Jim would lie on the sofa and daydream about running a four minute mile whenever he got tired.
5. Having broken all the laws of society, I feel the man should be punished.
6. She wore a new bonnet on her blonde head which had been bought in a bargain basement.
7. The little boy held his new dog in his arms, wearing a broad grin.
8. Jane had thrown the speech into the waste basket that Mr. Allan was to broadcast that evening.
9. After the fight Jimmy ran home to his mother with a bloody nose.
10. While sitting in the saddle, the horse threw the cowboy.

When the word a phrase is to modify is totally omitted, that phrase is said to be a **dangling modifier,** because it has no word to modify. In revising written work, watch out for sentences like these:

Having worked all afternoon in the hot sun, the pitcher of lemonade was most welcome. (dangling participle)
To be sure of a seat, tickets must be purchased early. (dangling infinitive)
While watching the play, her headache was soon forgotten. (dangling prepositional phrase)

These sentences seem to mean that the pitcher of lemonade had been working, that the tickets are to be sure, and that the headache was watching the play. Such dangling modifiers are easily corrected by putting the missing words back into the sentences as subjects:

Having worked all afternoon in the hot sun, *we welcomed the pitcher of lemonade.*
To be sure of a good seat, *you should purchase your tickets early.*
While watching the play, *she soon forgot her headache.*

EXERCISE 5. Undangle the dangling phrases in the sentences that follow. For the first sentence you might say: *Excited at the thought of going to the party, she soon forgot her worries.*
1. Excited at the thought of going to the party, her worries were soon forgotten.
2. While sleeping in my room, two friends came to visit.
3. To become a doctor, hard work is required.
4. Having eaten dinner, the dishes were washed and dried.
5. Running through the field, Jerry's jacket caught on a bush.

EXERCISE 6. All of the following sentences have appeared in newspaper articles or student compositions, and each contains a misplaced or dangling modifier. Identify the error in each statement as a misplaced or dangling modifier and correct the sentence.

1. Abraham Lincoln wrote the Gettysburg Address while traveling from Washington to Gettysburg on the back of an envelope.
2. Arriving at the scene, the building burst into flame.
3. Three cars were reported stolen by the Concord police yesterday.
4. After years of being lost under a pile of dust, Walter P. Stanley III found all the old records of the Bangor Lions Club at the Bangor House.
5. Using a Doppler ultra sound device, fetal heartbeats can be detected by the twelfth week of pregnancy.
6. At Heitman's, you will find a variety of fine foods expertly served by waitresses in appetizing forms.
7. While staying in a luxury hotel in Honolulu, our coats were stolen.
8. I wish to sell several very old dresses from my grandmother in beautiful condition.
9. Despite being on the scene for twenty-four hours, the fire continued to rage out of control.
10. About two years ago, a wart appeared on my left hand, which I wanted removed.

Parallel forms

How are the italicized words used in the following sentences?

The *sheriff* and his *men* reached Dalton an hour later.
Mike *lunged* past Harry, *grabbed* the picture, and *darted* out.

In the first sentence *sheriff* and *men* are used in the same way — as subjects of the verb *reached*. And in the second sentence *lunged, grabbed,* and *darted* are all used in the same way — as verbs telling three things that Mike did. Words having the same use in a sentence are called **parallel forms.** Here are other examples:

Kay's shoes are *sensible* and *sturdy,* but extremely *homely.*
Slowly and *patiently* I fitted together the pieces of the puzzle.
The squirrel scampered *up one side* and *down the other.*
Carol built a *chair* and a *bookcase* from some old packing boxes.
Keith's vacation was ruined by his fear of *bugs, bears,* and *snakes.*
Denny Brady, a four-letter *athlete* and *winner* of the Elks' scholarship award, was master of ceremonies.

The parallel forms in the first three sentences are modifiers — parallel adjectives in the first, parallel adverbs in the second, and parallel adverb phrases in the third. The parallel forms in the next two sentences are objects — of the verb *built* and of the preposition *of*. And in the last sentence the parallel forms are appositives.

Verbals and verbal phrases are often used as parallel forms:

> *Swimming* and *sailing* took most of our time.
> Is Dave planning *to write* or *to telephone?*
> I wear my glasses only *for reading* and *for sewing.*
> Bill hung around Mrs. Smith's desk for a while, *hoping to learn his test mark,* but *not daring to ask her.*

In the first sentence the italicized gerunds are parallel subjects of the verb *took*. In the second the infinitives are parallel objects of the verb *Is planning*. In the third the parallel adverb phrases both have gerund objects. And in the fourth the participial phrases are parallel modifiers of the subject *Bill*.

Subordinate clauses also may be used as parallel forms:

> Anyone *whose typing is as poor as Martha's* and *who is as sensitive as she* would have a hard time working for Mrs. Daley.
> We agreed to break the news to Dad *after he had finished eating* but *before he settled down in his easy chair for the night.*
> It was obvious *that Jane was wrong* and *that Ted was agreeing with her only to avoid a scene.*
> All of them wondered *where Jim was* and *why he hadn't written.*

In the first sentence two adjective clauses are used as parallel modifiers of the subject *Anyone*. In the second sentence two adverb clauses are used as parallel modifiers of the infinitive *to break*. In the third, two noun clauses are used as parallel subjects of the verb *was*. And in the fourth, another two are used as parallel objects of *wondered*.

EXERCISE 7. Read the sentences, and decide what the parallel forms are and how they are used. Then divide a sheet of paper into three columns. In the first column, write the parallel forms, one under the other. In the second, tell what they are. In the third, tell how they are used. Number your answers. For the first sentence you should write:

1. cutting the grass	gerund	objects of
trimming the hedge	phrases	"After"

1. After cutting the grass and trimming the hedge, Dad was exhausted.
2. I'm sure you will find George either on the golf course or in the pool.
3. The procession moved slowly and solemnly toward the altar.
4. Mike's cousin was small, blonde, and very lovely.

5. Len Dawes, chief machinist at Fenton's and manager of the Hilton Flashes, predicts a big turnout for the last game of the city series.
6. Reading mystery stories, playing golf, and going to the movies were his favorite pastimes.
7. I can't decide whether Roberta is extremely smart or unusually stupid.
8. Horrified, he pointed to the tiny red ants that streamed across the table, up the cupboard door, and over the shelves.
9. Mary offered to call for Don and to take him to the station.
10. Before you leave, see that the fire is completely out and that there are no papers lying around.

EXERCISE 8. On January 20, 1961, President John Fitzgerald Kennedy delivered one of the most memorable inaugural addresses in American history. A large part of the power of President Kennedy's speech is its striking use of parallel structure. Here are four excerpts from that address. Identify the use of the parallel forms in each passage.
1. "We observe today not a victory of party but a celebration of freedom, symbolizing an end as well as a beginning, signifying renewal as well as change."
2. "Let the word go forth from this time and place, to friend and foe alike, that the torch has been passed to a new generation of Americans, born in this century, tempered by war, disciplined by a hard and bitter peace, proud of our ancient heritage, and unwilling to witness or permit the slow undoing of those human rights to which this nation has always been committed, and to which we are committed today at home and around the world."
3. "So let us begin anew, remembering on both sides that civility is not a sign of weakness, and sincerity is always subject to proof. Let us never negotiate out of fear, but let us never fear to negotiate."
4. "And so, my fellow Americans, ask not what your country can do for you; ask what you can do for your country. My fellow citizens of the world, ask not what America will do for you, but what together we can do for the freedom of man."

Improving sentences

Use parallel forms

Writers who do not know about parallel forms often create sentences like these:

The man who lives in the apartment below ours is disagreeable, spiteful, and a gossip.

150

I finally gave up my old green coat, since both pockets were torn and the fur collar looking rather shabby.

Father is supposed to take the pink pills for colds and when his head aches.

Anne had read enough of the novel to be able to identify the important characters, for describing the historical background, and so that she could tell the main plot.

Though the meaning is clear, these sentences are awkward because ideas of equal importance have not been expressed in parallel ways. When parallel forms are used, the sentences are more effective:

The man who lives in the apartment below ours is *disagreeable, spiteful,* and *gossipy.*

I finally gave up my old green coat, since both pockets *were* torn and the fur collar *looked* rather shabby.

Father is supposed to take the pink pills for *colds* and *headaches.*

Anne had read enough of the novel to be able *to identify* the important characters, *to describe* the historical background, and *to tell* the main plot.

Often there is a choice of ways of using parallel forms to express parallel ideas. The last two sentences, for example, might be revised by using parallel subordinate clauses and parallel verbs:

Father is supposed to take the pink pills *when he has a cold* and *when his head aches.*

Anne had read enough of the novel so that she *could identify* the important characters, *describe* the historical background, and *tell* the main plot.

Now look at the following sentences:

At the end of the fight Billy had a puffy black eye, and there was a large, purplish bruise on his forehead.

Small revolutionary societies were forming throughout Italy, and the same activity was going on in France during this period.

Our new sewing machine makes neat buttonholes, and you can use it to sew on buttons, too.

They worked hard during the day, and their evenings were spent in going to the movies, or cards were played.

These compound sentences are very weak. Even though the coordinate clauses are grammatically parallel, the ideas can be more effectively expressed by other parallel forms in simple sentences:

At the end of the fight Billy had a puffy black *eye* and a large, purplish *bruise* on his forehead.

During this period small revolutionary societies were forming throughout *Italy* and *France.*

Our new sewing machine *makes* neat buttonholes and also *sews* on buttons.

They *worked* hard during the day and *spent* their evenings *going* to the movies or *playing* cards.

Look at the following groups of related sentences:

Carolyn Adams has announced her retirement from Service Club work. She founded the local branch of the Club. She has also acted as its president for the last ten years.

During Harry's concert Thelma Wilson sat in a front-row seat. She was almost bursting with pride at her son's skill. At the same time she was trying to appear calm.

You should attend the lecture to be given by Mr. Jensen. He has done a great deal of research, and historians the world over respect his opinions.

If each group of sentences is combined into a single sentence having parallel parts, the reader can more easily see which ideas are of equal importance:

Carolyn Adams, *founder* of the local branch of the Service Club and its *president* for the last ten years, has announced her retirement.

During Harry's concert Thelma Wilson sat in a front-row seat, almost *bursting* with pride at her son's skill, yet *trying* to appear calm.

You should attend the lecture to be given by Mr. Jensen, *who has done a great deal of research* and *whose opinions are respected by historians the world over.*

There are, then, several ways of using parallel forms to make better sentences. By using them to call attention to ideas that are of equal importance, a writer makes it easier for the reader to understand intended meaning.

EXERCISE 9. Read the sentences, and decide how they can be improved by using parallel forms. Be prepared to read your revised sentences aloud. For the first one you might say: *The principal complimented us for keeping the school grounds neat and for clearing the halls quickly between classes.*

1. The principal complimented us for keeping the school grounds neat and the halls being cleared quickly between classes.
2. At first Kate's only duties were to file the orders, answering the phone, and the mail had to be sorted.
3. Her cousin Sadie, I remembered, was efficient and witty, but a person who liked to boss everyone.
4. Once more Loren explained who he was and his purpose in coming.
5. Leonard Martin spent a great deal of time and money on his clothes, but never looking very well dressed.
6. No one wanted to be in his class because of his quick temper and how sarcastic his remarks were.
7. Dad hates to attend bridge parties, going to the movies, and he doesn't like to have to visit Aunt Agatha every Sunday, either.
8. The teacher told us to go to the coach's office and that we should ask him for insurance blanks to fill out.
9. At camp last summer Neil learned to carve soap figures, how to tool leather, and riding horseback.
10. Our new boarder was a tall fellow with large blue eyes, and he had a shock of red hair.

Pronoun cases

Pronouns as subjects

No careful writer uses both a noun and a pronoun meaning the same person or thing as the subject of one verb:

My *sister* went to the game.   OR: *She* went to the game.
The *bracelet* was stolen.   *It* was stolen.
The *boys* sneaked in.   *They* sneaked in.

The pronouns *I, you, he, she, it, we, they* are used as subjects; and when talking about two persons or groups of persons, writers usually mention themselves second:

She and *I* addressed the invitations this morning.
Bill and *I* have already bought our tickets.
He and *we* had an argument.
They and *we* are going to play tennis this afternoon.

Pronouns as objects

The pronouns *me, you, him, her, it, us,* and *them* are used as objects.

Mrs. Allen invited Paul and *me* to ride in her car.
Everyone except *her* enjoyed the concert.

Mother scolded Sally and *him* for being late.
He sent telegrams to *them* and *us.*

EXERCISE 10 In each of the sentences below, use *I, me, he,* or
him where the blanks occur:

1. Ryan asked if he could go to the game with Jane and _____.
2. It was _____ that I saw on Gary's porch, I'm sure.
3. I brought a surprise for everyone but you and _____.
4. The teacher sent _____ and _____ to the office.
5. I moved to the end of the bench to make room for Sally and _____.

Pronouns as predicate nominatives

The pronouns *I, he, she, we,* and *they* are used after forms of
the verb *be:*

It is *I.*	That wasn't *I.*	It could have been *he.*
Is that *she?*	It was *we.*	Might that be *they?*

Since in everyday speech and informal writing people commonly use
"It is me" or "That wasn't me" instead of "It is I" or "That
wasn't I," the form *me* is considered acceptable in all but formal
situations. But other pronoun forms after *be (her, him, us,* or *them)*
are not appropriate, even in informal speech or writing.

In a humorous poem, "The Jackdaw of Reims," Richard
Barkam (1788-1845) has this line: "Heedless of grammar, they all
cried, 'That's him!'" Barkam knew, but that is what he says
"they" said! Too bad.

Pronouns with gerunds

The possessive forms of the personal pronouns — *my, your,
his, her, its, our, their* — are used before gerunds:

She was surprised at *my* remembering her name.
Do you object to *their* joining us?

EXERCISE 11. In the sentences below, use *me, my, you, your,
him,* or *his* where the blanks occur:

1. Joe's mother objected to _____ driving so fast in traffic. .
2. I don't like _____ taking all the credit, when he did so little to
   make the dance a success.
3. "Did he mind _____ leaving before the end of class?" I asked Clifford.

154

4. I expected to find _____ working in the garden, but he wasn't anywhere in sight.
5. We had looked forward to _____ coming and were disappointed when you postponed your visit.

Pronouns as appositives

When a pronoun is in apposition with a subject, the form *I, he, she, we,* or *they* is used. When a pronoun is in apposition with an object, the form *me, him, her, us,* or *them* is used:

The whole family — Mother, Dad, Clara, and *I* — made plans to stay for a week.
Uncle Will invited the whole family — Mother, Dad, Clara, and *me* — to stay for a week.

The pronouns *myself, yourself, himself, herself, itself, ourselves, yourselves,* and *themselves* are often used as appositives for emphasis. They are not set off by commas, whether they come right after the word they emphasize or at the end of the sentence:

The manager *himself* sold us the tickets.
The manager sold us the tickets *himself*.
The candidates paid for the advertisements *themselves*.
The candidates *themselves* paid for the advertisements.

EXERCISE 12. In each of the sentences below, use *I, me, he,* or *him* where the blanks occur:
1. Our advisor asked three members of the staff — Jim, George, and _____ — to interview the mayor.
2. Those two — Laura and _____ — have won all the doubles matches.
3. Should we — Grace, Brad, and _____ — meet you at Kelley's after the game?
4. Which Phil do you want — Phil Evans or _____?
5. I was asked to notify two people — you and _____.

The forms *we* as a subject and *us* as an object are used even when an appositive noun follows the pronoun.

Should *we* girls go on without them?
All of *us* students grumbled about the assignment.
Dad agreed to take *us* boys to the golf course first.

EXERCISE 13. In the sentences below, use *we* or *us:*
1. Why does he pick on _____ girls to answer the hardest questions?
2. The gym is reserved for _____ sophomores tonight.

3. _____ boys all agreed to say nothing about the accident.
4. All of _____ boys agreed to say nothing about the accident.
5. Should _____ four start on without the other three?

Pronouns in adverb clauses of comparison

When a personal pronoun is the subject of the omitted verb in an elliptical clause of comparison, the form *I, he, she, we,* or *they* is used:

Lorraine is no wiser than *he.*
He is just as silly as *she.*

When the pronoun is the object of the omitted verb, the form *me, him, her, us,* or *them* is used:

The teacher liked Tom better than *me.*
Do you trust me as much as *him?*

EXERCISE 14. On your own sheet of paper, use *I, me, he, him, she, her, we, us, they,* or *them:*

1. Since my brother studies harder than his friends do, he always gets better grades than _____.
2. Alice is my aunt, yet I am older than _____.
3. Both Peg and Ed are friends of ours, but we like Ed better than _____.
4. Since Tom was a better salesman than Ken and I, he sold twice as much as _____.
5. Naturally Mr. Evans paid Tom more than he paid Ken and _____.

Reference of pronouns

Notice how the italicized pronouns are used in these sentences:

After school, students must wash the blackboards; otherwise *they* begin to look smudged.
Grinning broadly, Phil told Dick that *he* would get all of his money back.

In the first sentence, who or what will begin to look smudged — the students or the blackboards? In the second sentence, is it Phil or is it Dick who will be getting all of his money back? Because in each sentence the italicized pronouns can refer to either of two antecedents, the result is an **ambiguous reference.**

Every pronoun must have a single, clear antecedent. If the reference of a pronoun is not clear, the result is likely to be comic (as in the first sentence above) or puzzling (as in the second sentence). The comedy or confusion that results from ambiguous references can be cleared up by replacing the ambiguous pronoun with a noun:

After school, students must wash the blackboards; otherwise the *blackboards* begin to look smudged.

or by recasting the sentence:

Grinning broadly, Phil said to Dick, "I'll get all of my money back." or:
Grinning broadly, Phil said, "You'll get all of your money back, Dick."

Ambiguous reference exists when a pronoun might refer to two or more antecedents. **Vague reference** exists when the antecedent of a pronoun is merely implied or is not stated at all, as in the following sentences:

In Shakespeare's *Macbeth, he* creates an atmosphere of blood and blackness.
People want to strengthen their language habits, *which* explains why they study grammar and usage.
In the textbook *they* use too many childish pictures.

In the first sentence, the pronoun *he* carelessly refers to an antecedent noun, *Shakespeare's,* that is relatively subordinate in the syntax of the sentence. The sentence should be recast:

In *Macbeth,* Shakespeare creates an atmosphere of blood and blackness. Or:
In Shakespeare's *Macbeth,* the playwright creates an atmosphere of blood and blackness.

In the second sentence, the *which* clause vaguely refers to the entire main clause rather than to a specific antecedent noun. This error can be corrected by using the expression *a fact that* or by eliminating the relative pronoun:

People want to strengthen their language habits, a fact that explains why they study grammar and usage. Or (and better):
People study grammar and usage to strengthen their language habits.

In the third sentence the antecedent to *they* is neither implied nor stated. The sentence must be restructured:

In the textbook the authors use too many childish pictures. Or:
The textbook contains too many childish pictures.

EXERCISE 15. Rewrite the sentences below to eliminate ambiguous or vague reference of pronouns. For the first sentence you might say: *Walking beside the old horse, the farmer became angry and kicked him.*

1. The farmer was walking beside the old horse when he became angry and kicked him.
2. The trouble with psychology is that they think they have all the answers.
3. To be sure that her children saw her notes, Mother taped them to the refrigerator.
4. Mr. Clark was a very enthusiastic teacher, which is why I enjoyed the course.
5. An expert fisherman, Dan can do it for hours on end.
6. Joe often interrupted people in the middle of a statement, which angered everyone.
7. In the article they say that the climate is gradually becoming warmer.
8. Colorful dresses hung on the racks, but they were hidden behind a large pillar.
9. In Sally's diary she keeps her deepest secrets.
10. It says in the newspaper that they are having earth tremors out west.

EXERCISE 16. All of the following sentences have appeared in newspaper articles, and each contains a reference error. Rewrite each sentence to correct the error.
1. Great care must be exercised in tying horses to trees as they are apt to bark.
2. We do not tear your clothing with machinery; we do it carefully by hand.
3. After Governor Baldridge watched the lion perform, he was taken to Main Street and fed twenty-five pounds of red meat in front of the Fox Theater.
4. The Duchess handled the launching beautifully, confidently smashing the champagne against the prow. The crowd cheered as she majestically slid down the greasy runway into the sea.
5. Anti-nuclear protestors released live cockroaches inside the White House Friday, and these were arrested when they left and blocked a security gate.

Relative pronouns: *Who, whom,* etc.
Ordinarily the relative pronouns *who, whose, whom* are used to refer to persons, *which* to refer to things, and *that* to refer to

158

either persons or things, though many writers prefer "who" for persons, "that" for things:

The clerk *who* had sold me the shoes was gone.
The second explosion, *which* came five minutes later, was worse.
The woman *who* was standing beside me fainted.
I didn't see the car *that* hit us.

When the relative is the subject of an adjective clause, *who* is used:

Tanya interviewed the men *who* were rescued from the cave-in.
Bill is the only person *who* I think deserved a prize.

Notice that the inserted expression "I think" has no effect on the use of the relative.

When the relative is the object of the verb or preposition, *whom* is the appropriate form. Although people often use *who* in everyday speech, they generally use *whom* in writing:

The waitress *whom* he scolded blushed a fiery red.
The boys for *whom* the lecture was meant weren't there to hear it.
He finally found a governess *whom* he thought Sally would like.

When the relative shows possession, *whose* is used:

There are the boys *whose* mother is a movie star.
I have never met anyone *whose* temper is worse than Dan's.

When the antecedent is a thing rather than a person, either *whose* or *of which* is used:

They lived in a tiny cottage *whose* walls were covered with vines.
Sam wore his old tweed coat, the pockets *of which* bulged with newspapers.

When the antecedent of a relative pronoun used as a subject is singular, the verb in the relative clause and any pronoun in the clause that refers to the antecedent are singular:

Hal is the only *one* of the boys who *has written* to *his* parents for more money.
Laura is the only *one* of the girls who *has*n't paid *her* dues.

When the antecedent is plural, a plural verb and pronoun are used:

He is one of those *men* who always *grumble* about *their* bad luck.
That is another of those *schemes* that *are* practical in theory but not in practice.

EXERCISE 17. In each of the first ten sentences, use *who, which,* or *that.* Use each pronoun at least three times.

1. Frank and Ed are the ones _____ told me the news.
2. All employees _____ were interested were given tickets to the show.
3. The blue felt hat, _____ looked best on me, was too expensive.
4. My father knew the man _____ lost his life in the fire.
5. Every member _____ had not been on a committee had to help.
6. Grandfather stumbled over Jim's skates, _____ had been left on the first landing.
7. Her favorite teacher was Miss Wood, _____ taught geometry.
8. Can you see the officers _____ are standing behind General Ford?
9. Ted had to wear Dad's new coat, _____ was much too large.
10. Is that the only pen _____ holds ink?

In each of the next ten sentences, use *who, whom,* or *whose:*

11. The woman _____ was in charge of the employment office told us to come back the following Monday.
12. Dale was the only one in class _____ work showed originality.
13. I had given all my change to the boy _____ delivers our papers.
14. Most of the students to _____ we sent questionnaires filled them out carefully and sent them back within a few days.
15. Their father was a mean, short-tempered man _____ we were all afraid of.
16. Take the book to _____ ever asks for it first.
17. George Travers, _____ we thought had stolen the test questions, hadn't been on the third floor at all that afternoon.
18. The man _____ we suspected was a shoplifter was the manager.
19. Blair's Detective Agency, _____ license had been revoked, moved to another state.
20. Terry Blaine, _____ I expected Miss Hale would choose for the lead, was given the part of the maid.

In each of the next five sentences, use *is, are, has, have, his, her,* or *their:*

21. Mabel is the only one of the girls in the class who _____ finished _____ report.

160

22. All students in the class play who _____ to be excused from _____ classes tomorrow must get a permit from the office.
23. Isn't yours one of those umbrellas that _____ collapsible?
24. I'd like another of those rolls that _____ coconut icing.
25. Hand George the pencils and paper that _____ on that shelf.

Self and selves

Pronouns that end in *self* — *myself, yourself, himself, herself, itself, oneself* — refer to one person or thing. Pronouns that end in *selves* — *ourselves, yourselves, themselves* — refer to more than one person or thing. These pronouns are used as objects of prepositions or of verbs when the objects mean the same person or thing as the subject:

I glanced quickly at *myself* as I passed the shop windows.
Did you hurt *yourself* badly?
Phil ordered a steak for Ed and a hamburger for *himself*.
She bought *herself* a new hat with her birthday check.
After a current interruption the electric motor starts *itself*.
We forced *ourselves* to stay awake.
Gentlemen, ask *yourselves* one question.
Shortly after dinner they excused *themselves* and left.

The pronouns *his* and *their* are not combined with *self* and *selves:*

Frank blamed *himself* for the accident.
Tell the girls to suit *themselves*.

Careful writers avoid using these pronouns as objects when they mean persons or things different from the subject:

The next day she asked my friends and *me* to dinner.
Mrs. Karnes will send copies to Sam and *you* later.

Avoid using these pronouns as subjects.

That very evening Mr. Peters and *I* had an argument.
The only ones at the meeting were Mary and *he*.

Sentences such as "Helen and myself agreed to run the auction" and "The dean invited my roommate and myself to dinner" are incorrect in careful speech and writing. Addressing this overuse of *myself,* sports columnist Red Smith once wrote,

"*Myself* is the foxhole of ignorance where cowards take refuge because they were taught that *me* was vulgar and think *I* egotistical."

EXERCISE 18. In each of the following sentences, use *he, him, himself,* or *themselves:*

1. Jerry had always thought of _____ as unselfish and tolerant.
2. After he left, they amused _____ by telling ghost stories.
3. Why don't you ask Laura and _____ to meet us there?
4. For years Peter has supported his mother and _____.
5. It might have been Nancy and _____ in the back row.

Sentence errors: fragments and run-ons

Appositives and their modifiers do not make statements, ask questions, or give commands. They are merely substitute expressions for other words in a sentence. To begin such an expression with a capital letter and to end it with a period produces a serious error called a Sentence Fragment. A sentence fragment is just what its name implies — a piece of a sentence, but not a whole sentence.

You will need to be particularly careful about an appositive at the end of a sentence:

Mr. Scoggins hired a new secretary, a tall, thin, gray-haired woman interested only in doing her work efficiently.

Uncle Frank usually walked a mile or two before breakfast — a practice his friends never tried to imitate.

We are looking forward to our annual game with the Wildcats, the only team to be feared in either league this year.

Such appositives must remain attached to the words they explain. It is a serious error to punctuate them as separate sentences.

Another common type of sentence fragment occurs when a verbal is mistakenly written as a complete statement, masquerading as a sentence. No matter how long a verbal phrase is or how much information it gives, it is not a sentence but only a part of a sentence.

Participles are used as modifiers, not as verbs. The group of words "All through the night the snow, *falling* steadily and silently on the quiet city" is not a sentence. The participle *falling* does not state an action; it merely suggests that the modified word, *snow,* is performing an action. To make a statement of the group, other words — including a verb — must be added, or the participle must be changed to a verb.

162

All through the night the snow, falling steadily and silently on the
quiet city, *delighted* the sleepless man.
All through the night the snow *was falling* steadily and silently on
the quiet city.

Gerunds and infinitives are used as nouns, not as verbs. "By
moaning about the length of the English assignment instead of *getting to work*" is not a sentence. Neither is *"To see* these young
boys wearing fancy cowboy outfits and *to hear* them trying to *talk*
like the hero of a Western movie." Each of these groups contains
verbal nouns that name actions. But the verbal nouns do not state
actions. To make sentences of the groups, other words — including verbs — must be added:

I *made* her angry by moaning about the length of the English assignment instead of getting to work.
To see these young boys wearing fancy cowboy outfits and to hear
them trying to talk like the hero of a Western movie *amused* us
all greatly.

Like verbal phrases, subordinate clauses may also end up as
sentence fragments. Although subordinate clauses have subjects
and verbs of their own, they are not sentences but only parts of
sentences — modifiers or nouns. To detach such a clause from its
sentence by beginning it with a capital letter and by ending it with a
period is a serious error.

We finally managed to get a call through to Dad, *who wired us the
money immediately.*
One of the boys came up with a plan *that pleased everybody greatly.*

Even though the adjective clauses are not closely connected in
meaning with the other words in their sentences, they are still parts
of those sentences and must not be detached from the words they
modify.
Do not punctuate a noun clause as a separate sentence, even
though it does have its own subject and verb. But a noun clause at
the end of a sentence sometimes seems almost like a separate explanation:

The very first day the teacher made the statement *that no one in any
of his classes ever got by without working.*
It certainly was lucky for us *that George had saved the receipt.*
Ernest constantly complained about his mother's demand *that he
should be home by midnight.*
The group reached only one major decision — *that student council
officers would serve for two semesters.*

A nonrestrictive adverb clause adds an explanatory detail or comment that is not closely connected in meaning with the rest of the sentence. An adverb clause is just a modifier, as a single adverb is. In writing "Our rural mailman always manages to get through regardless," no one would detach the adverb *regardless* from its sentence. Nor should a writer detach adverb clauses like these:

Our rural mailman always manages to get through, *whatever the condition of the roads or the weather may be.*

The farmers and fishermen of northern Norway do not sleep much during June and July, *because the sun never sets then.*

We patiently typed several copies of the petition and got four hundred signatures, *although we were sure our work would be a waste of time.*

EXERCISE 19. Read each of the groups of words, and decide what other words you will add to make it a sentence. Then write the sentences on a sheet of paper. Capitalize the first word of each sentence. Put a period or question mark after each last word. Put in any commas that are necessary. For the first group of words you might write: *1. Herb turned wearily back to his typewriter, muttering to himself about the impossibility of pleasing people.*

1. muttering to himself about the impossibility of pleasing people
2. to sneak out of the house at that hour without being seen
3. after threatening to tell his mother about his having broken the window
4. swinging lazily in the bright green hammock stretched between two large maples in the back yard
5. a huge, many-colored painting, set in an ornate, gold frame
6. an accomplished athlete and violinist
7. right where she had left them
8. that people might actually enjoy the play
9. who enjoyed playing chess for six hours every day
10. because such an adjustment will dislodge other parts of the machine

Two sentences written as one, with only a comma (or no mark at all) between them, are called a *run-on* sentence. Run-on sentences are most likely to occur when the second sentence is closely related in thought with the preceding sentence, especially when the second sentence begins an adverb or prepositional phrase. The adverb most commonly used in this way in school compositions is *then:*

Mr. Thomas took a sip of water and pushed back his chair. *Then* he began to talk.

164

Though the group of words beginning with *Then* is closely related in thought with the preceding sentence, it is grammatically an independent sentence. Therefore it is separated from the preceding sentence by a period and begins with a capital letter. Following are more examples of sentences closely related in meaning, but independent grammatically. Notice the italicized adverb that begins the second sentence of each pair:

We argued with Dad all during dinner. *Finally* he agreed.
The next day Sue looked in the attic for the album. *There* it was.
Dale used to be sarcastic and grouchy. *Now* he is quite pleasant.
Mr. Kenton offered Neil seventy cents an hour. *Still* he refused.
Martha used every conceivable argument to persuade us. *However,* we would not be swayed.

Using a comma instead of a period between any of the above pairs of sentences would create a run-on sentence.

Notice the prepositional phrases in the following examples:

The medicine did her no good. *In fact* it made her feel worse.
He honked the horn a fourth time. *At last* he caught her attention.
Dad had a severe headache. *Because of it* he was rather grouchy.

The italicized phrases are like the adverbs *therefore* and *furthermore* and *then*. Each phrase shows a relationship in meaning between two sentences. It also modifies the verb that follows. No matter how closely related the two sentences are in meaning, they are independent grammatically. Each must begin with a capital letter and end with a period.

EXERCISE 20. In each group of words there is a serious sentence error — the use of a comma before an adverb or prepositional phrase that begins a grammatically independent sentence. Write the number of each group on a sheet of paper. After each number, write the first and last words of the two sentences in that group. Capitalize each first word. Put a period after each last word. For the first group you should write: *1. The up. Still return.*

1. The townspeople had long since given him up, still Irma was certain that he would return.
2. Robert Burns was not always a great man, however, he was a truly great poet.
3. She must have had many fears and forebodings during her long stay at Pinehurst, on the contrary, she radiated only cheer and confidence.
4. You are supposed to rub the piece of amber briskly, then it will attract the bits of paper.

5. The refugee child came into a home that was filled with love and laughter, finally he forgot the terrors of his former life.
6. She is a talented writer, in fact, she is a genius.
7. The weary travelers stopped beside a clear spring, there they camped for the night.
8. The flowers there are beautiful, however, they bloom only in the month of June.
9. Our speaker will be Professor Anne Smith, possibly you have heard of her accomplishments in chemistry.
10. I have wondered about that for a long time, at last I know.

Singular or plural?

The singular adjectives *this* and *that* are used to point out one *kind* or *sort*. The plural adjectives *these* and *those* are used to point out two or more *kinds* or *sorts:*

This kind of hat is always flattering.
That sort of car is too expensive to run.
He had never seen *these kinds* of plants before.
Those sorts of sentences were not discussed.

Even when the noun following the singular *kind of* or *sort of* is plural, writers prefer *this* or *that* to *these* or *those:*

She likes *this kind of lamp.*   OR: She likes *these kinds of lamps.*

Although *kind of a* and *sort of a* are heard in everyday conversation, careful writers do not use the article:

That *kind of desk* is easy to make.
What *sort of apple* is that?

The adjectives *each, every, either, neither* and the indefinite pronouns *each, everyone, everybody, someone, anyone, anybody, neither, either, nobody* are singular and generally take singular verbs and singular pronouns:

Each *is expected* to do *his or her* share.
Everyone in the girls' gym classes *has her* own locker.
Neither of the cars *seems* worth the price.

Though nouns like *news, measles, mumps, smallpox,* and names of subjects ending in *ics,* like *mathematics, economics, physics, civics,* are plural in form, they are singular in meaning and take a singular verb:

Measles *is* an infectious disease.
Mathematics *was* her easiest subject.
Economics *deals* with the problems of capital and labor.

Nouns of measure — like *foot, yard, mile, pair, pound, ton, bushel, month, year* — are singular. When more than one of each is meant, the plural form is used:

Henry is six *feet* tall.
Mr. Dawes ordered fifteen *bushels* of potatoes.
Bob left three *months* ago.

When plural nouns denoting periods of time, amount, measure, or weight are thought of as a single unit, they take a singular verb:

Two days *seems* a long time to my little brother.
Ten dollars *is* the standard price.
Four yards *was* not enough for the dress.
Three tons *is* all he paid for.

Speakers and writers use the singular form *way* in such expressions as *a short way, a long way:*

The post office is a long *way* off.
They drove a short *way* with us.

When a singular subject follows *there* or *here,* use a singular verb:

There *goes* the last of my money.
Here *is* a misspelled word in your very first sentence.

When a plural subject follows, use a plural verb.

There *were* several copies of the safety pamphlet on the top shelf.
Lately there *have been* fewer complaints.
Here *are* three more questions to consider.
Here *come* the elephants.

EXERCISE 21. In each of the first four sentences, use *this, that, these,* or *those:*

1. Mother doesn't approve of _____ kind of shoe for school.
2. _____ sorts of movies did not attract many people.
3. Why did he plant so many of _____ kind of tree?
4. The complaint department often gets _____ kinds of letters.

In each of the next four sentences, use *kind of* or *sort of:*

5. We don't have the _____ pen he wants.
6. What _____ car does he drive?
7. That is just the _____ thing she would say.
8. What _____ hat are you going to buy?

In each of the next four sentences, use *his, her,* or *their:*

9 Each of the boys brought _____ own lunch.
10. Wasn't everyone told to return _____ report card before Friday?
11. Every girl on the team has _____ name on _____ uniform.
12. The treasurer wants all the members to pay _____ dues this week.

In each of the next four sentences, use *was, were, has,* or *have* in the first blank, and *his, her, its,* or *their* in the second blank:

13. Neither of the boys _____ written _____ report yet.
14. Each of the cars _____ parked in _____ assigned place.
15. All of the waiters _____ been given _____ share of the tip.
16. _____ every one of them paid _____ towel fee?

In each of the next five sentences, use *is* or *are:*

17. Five dollars _____ more than I would have paid for the picture Helen had taken at Bergen's.
18. Economics _____ just as interesting to him as chemistry to you.
19. Three weeks _____ a long time to be absent.
20. _____ mumps and measles contagious?
21. _____ fifty cents a fair price for the pen?

In each of the next five sentences, use *foot, feet, pair, pairs, ton, tons, way,* or *ways:*

22. Why don't you walk a little _____ with us?
23. I'm sure he's not more than five _____ four.
24. We burned eight _____ of coal last year.
25. He will need about twenty _____ of weather stripping for those two windows.
26. She bought several _____ of shoes at Stuart's sale.

In the next five sentences, use *is, are, was, were, has,* or *have:*

27. _____n't there any directions on the box?
28. In last month's *National Geographic* there _____ several good pictures of giant redwood trees.
29. _____n't there been enough excitement for one day?
30. By the way, here _____ a few more stamps for you to give Bill if you happen to see him.
31. _____ there enough dictionaries for everyone in class?

Wordiness

In revising sentences, watch out for unnecessary words. Make sure, for example, that the adjectives used do not express meanings expressed by other words in a sentence. For example:

Interrupting others is a *customary* habit with John.
When we moved to Elm Grove, Terry was just a *young* infant.

Since a habit is a customary act and an infant is always young, the italicized words are not needed:

Interrupting others is a habit with John.
When we moved to Elm Grove, Terry was just an infant.

Adjectives are not the only words we are likely to use unnecessarily. Think about the meaning of these sentences:

The members of our club refuse to cooperate *together*.
At times Lee's words were scarcely audible *to the ear*.
As a rule Sarah *usually* eats lunch at Turner's.

The club members could hardly cooperate except by working *together*. Lee's words could not be audible except *to the ear*. And since *As a rule* and *usually* both show that Sarah was a steady customer at Turner's, only one is needed.

The members of our club refuse to cooperate.
At times Lee's words were scarcely audible.
As a rule Sarah eats lunch at Turner's.

Predicate nominatives that add nothing to the meaning can be avoided:

My uncle is a very wealthy *man*.
Mary seemed a much happier *girl* last year.

Everyone knows that an uncle is a man and that *Mary* is the name of a girl. The predicate nominatives in these sentences are unnecessary and take emphasis away from the adjectives *wealthy* and *happier*. The sentences are more effective when only the adjectives are used:

My uncle is very *wealthy*.
Mary seemed much *happier* last year.

It is only unnecessary predicate nominatives that should be avoided. When other words follow to make the meaning more exact, predicate nominatives like *man* and *girl* are useful:

Their foreign correspondent is a *man* with a nose for news.
Clara Evans was a *girl* after his own heart.

The goal is not shorter sentences, but better sentences. Make changes only when greater clearness and effectiveness will result.

Using too many words — wordiness — is excusable in speaking, especially in conversations, where we think and talk at the same time. But there is little excuse for wordiness in writing compositions, since it can be weeded out.

One of the most common kinds of wordiness is using words that merely repeat an idea:

> Max was really worried about his dwindling bank account, *which was growing smaller all the time.*
>
> The fake paper money used on the stage *in dramatic productions* is both larger and greener than real currency *issued by the Treasury Department.*

The italicized clause in the first sentence merely repeats the idea already expressed by the word *dwindling.* And the italicized prepositional and participial phrases in the second sentence add little or nothing to the meaning of *on the stage* and *real currency.* Omitting all these unnecessary words would make a decided improvement in the sentences:

> Max was really worried about his dwindling bank account.
>
> The fake paper money used on the stage is both larger and greener than real currency.

Roundabout expressions are common in speech. But they are annoying to readers, who generally resent having to wade through many words to get at a simple idea. Sentences such as the following can make a whole composition seem tiresome and boring:

> By *the time it got to be* two o'clock in the morning, we had just about given up trying to find *the place where* the Piersons' cottage *was located.*
>
> *It has seldom been the case that* we have had such miserable weather in April.
>
> If each *and every* person does the best work *of which he or she is capable, the result will be that* the project will be successful.

The first sentence can be improved simply by dropping the italicized words:

> By two o'clock in the morning we had just about given up trying to find the Piersons' cottage.

The second and third sentences can be made more concise by omitting most of the italicized words and rephrasing:

Seldom have we had such miserable weather in April.
If each person does his or her best, the project will be successful.

Wordiness may also be caused by a desire to "dress up" writing — to achieve a formal, dignified style. Here, for example, are two sentences that would be clearer if the thought were expressed in a simpler way:

In many instances it is hard for adults to realize that high-school seniors, in spite of their *tender years,* are better informed *in the realm of politics* than many *persons who have long since attained their majority.*
Owing to the fact that my typewriter has been broken, my research paper is not yet *in a state of completion.*

Such high-sounding sentences rarely convince anyone that the writer has a way with words. Notice the improvement when the italicized expressions are replaced by single words:

Often it is hard for adults to realize that high-school seniors, in spite of their *youth,* are better informed *politically* than many *grown-ups.*
Because my typewriter has been broken, my research paper is not yet *finished.*

Some compositions are wordy because the writer explains every little detail in a separate sentence. For example:

My uniforms are made of nylon. The nylon makes them easy to launder.

The same idea can be expressed just as well in one sentence, using clauses or phrases or modifying words:

My uniforms are made of nylon, which makes them easy to launder.
My uniforms are made of nylon to make them easy to launder.
My uniforms, which are made of nylon, are easy to launder.
My uniforms, made of nylon, are easy to launder.
My nylon uniforms are easy to launder.

The most obvious kind of wordiness is caused by unintentionally repeating words. A writer is sometimes so intent on getting his ideas down on paper that he does not notice the careless repetition:

In Mexico we bought *leather* boots made of soft, pliant *leather.*
The *job* of watering the lawn was only one of many *jobs* assigned to me.

In *order* to save time in finding out who had *ordered* the case of soap, Dave went through the charge slips in alphabetical *order*.

In the summer we often go *in* swimming *in* icy streams *in* the Adirondack Mountains.

Such careless repetitions are quickly spotted and easily revised:

In Mexico we bought boots made of soft, pliant leather.

Watering the lawn was only one of many jobs assigned to me.

To save time in finding out who had ordered the case of soap, Dave went through the charge slips alphabetically.

During the summer we often swim in icy Adirondack streams.

Repetition, in itself, is not bad. Used intentionally, it may be an effective device for gaining emphasis:

Our safety campaign will be directed toward people *in* the homes, *in* the factories, and *in* the schools.

Repeating the preposition *in* shows the reader that the phrases are of equal importance and makes the sentence more forceful. But careless repetition leads to wordiness and clumsy, tiresome sentences.

EXERCISE 22. Read the sentences, and decide how to revise them to avoid wordiness. Then rewrite the sentences. Number your revised sentences. For the first one you might write: *1. The new scoutmaster is a twenty-five-year-old medical student.*

1. The new scoutmaster is a young man of about twenty-five years of age, a student who is attending medical school.
2. Because it uses so much oil and gasoline and is therefore expensive to operate, my cousin Judy is very much disappointed in her new car that she just bought.
3. Every night at twelve o'clock midnight our local radio station goes off the air and does not present any more radio programs until six o'clock in the morning.
4. Lately during the last few months my mother has increased her working hours to the point where she works so much that we seldom see her.
5. Owing to the fact that the property includes five hundred yards of lake front, it is fairly high-priced because of this added attraction.
6. It was immediately after we heard about John's accident that we arranged to take our vacations earlier than planned so that we could drive to Virginia in order that we might visit him.
7. The clerk will show you many designs from which you can choose the design that you prefer above the rest.

8. The presiding officer who conducted the meeting was obviously angry with Marcia, who kept making irrelevant comments that had no connection with the subject at hand.
9. Because of the fact that the symphony tickets are so expensive, in many cases persons who would like to attend the symphony concerts are unable to do so because they can not afford to go to the concerts.
10. The type of speaker I like is one that speaks in simple, straightforward language that is easy to understand and who sticks to a certain topic, without wandering off into various and assorted subjects.

To strengthen your mastery of standard English usage, answer the Writing Subject Test questions in Chapter 14.

Chapter 12

Seven Basic Spelling Rules

Take a look at the many pages of a newspaper. Somebody had to spell (and print) all those words — thousands of them. Rarely is there a misspelling. If the writers and printers for the newspaper can be that successful, so can any writer. Try it. Make it so.

Who can't spell? (I hate spelling!) Why, everybody can spell correctly. Look: *hippopotamus* (been to the zoo?), *Popocatepetl* (in Mexico?), *schottische* (may I have the next dance?). But, alas, I may slip when I am writing "easy" words like *too* and *its,* or *business* or *doesn't* or *writing,* or even *grammar.* And I am not alone. So many writers misspell these words so often (and some other common words) that such words are properly called "demons."

A good speller is a person with enough sense to memorize a few hundred common words (the "demons") and to learn and apply a relatively small number of fundamental spelling rules, each of which pertains to a large number of words. This Chapter covers seven basic spelling rules. The next Chapter will offer suggestions for mastering the demons.

1. Doubling a final consonant

Why is the verb *scar* spelled with one *r* — and *scarred* and *scarring* spelled with two? Doubling the *r* keeps the sound of the vowel *a* from changing. Without doubling the *r* before adding *ed* or *ing,* the *a* would have the sound of the *a* in *care,* instead of the sound of *a* in *car* and *tar.*

And notice the single *n* in *pin,* the double *n* in *pinned* and *pinning.* Forgetting to double the *n* of *pin* before adding *ed* or *ing* would change the sound of the *i.* It would no longer be pronounced like the *i* in *win,* but like the *i* in *find.*

The same thing is true of every one-syllable verb ending in a single consonant preceded by a single vowel — like *drag, step, grip, stop, rub.* To keep the sound of the *a,* the *e,* the *i,* the *o,* and the *u* in such words, double the final consonants before adding *ed* or *ing:*

drag	dragged	dragging	wrap	wrapped	wrapping
step	stepped	stepping	plan	planned	planning
grip	gripped	gripping	beg	begged	begging
stop	stopped	stopping	trim	trimmed	trimming
rub	rubbed	rubbing	stir	stirred	stirring
bat	batted	batting	rob	robbed	robbing

EXERCISE 1. Be prepared to write the following sentences from dictation:

1. Rebecca stirred her coffee vigorously, nodding her head in answer to my second question.
2. Sam Robertson was batting almost .300 until an injured wrist dragged his average down.
3. The boy gripped both ends of the cloth and polished the tips of my shoes, rubbing as hard as he could.
4. I had planned to use that wrapping paper myself.
5. Sally grabbed Tom, dragged him to the kitchen, and scrubbed his face.
6. Uncle Frank didn't feel like stopping his work to watch us trimming the tree.
7. This modern Robin Hood robbed the rich and gave to the poor — until the law stepped in and stopped him.
8. Excited at winning the race, Ken jumped up, tipping the canoe.
9. That night the man with the scarred cheek plotted his revenge.
10. Grinning with pleasure, Carol pinned the corsage to her belt.

Now, what about verbs of more than one syllable — verbs like *occur* and *instruct* and *conceal* and *benefit* and *acquit?*

If a verb ends in a single consonant, if a single vowel precedes that consonant, and if the accent falls on the last syllable, the final consonant is doubled before *ed* and *ing.*

All three of these things are true of the verb *occur.* It ends in a single consonant — *r.* That consonant is preceded by a single vowel — *u.* And the last syllable gets the main stress — oc CUR'. Therefore the *r* is doubled before *ed* and *ing: occu*rred, occurring.

Here are other examples of verbs that double the final consonant:

compel	compelled	compelling	defer	deferred	deferring
control	controlled	controlling	regret	regretted	regretting
transfer	transferred	transferring	prefer	preferred	preferring
omit	omitted	omitting	acquit	acquitted	acquitting
rebel	rebelled	rebelling	equip	equipped	equipping

The last two verbs in the list, *acquit* and *equip,* may seem to be exceptions. But they are not, since *u* has the sound of *w* after *q* and is considered a consonant in such words.

Verbs like *instruct* and *defend* do not come under this rule, because they end in two consonants. Nor do verbs like *conceal* and *redeem,* which have two vowels before the final consonant. And the rule does not apply to many common verbs that are accented before the last syllable:

develop	developed	developing	offer	offered	offering
profit	profited	profiting	listen	listened	listening
alter	altered	altering	benefit	benefited	benefiting

EXERCISE 2. Be prepared to write the following sentences from dictation:

1. Mike has never regretted transferring to West High.
2. Dad rebelled against going out to dinner two nights in a row, preferring to stay home and eat alone.
3. The idea of benefiting from the experience had not occurred to Alice.
4. The ship was fully equipped for the voyage around the Cape.
5. The storm compelled the men to stop and look for shelter.
6. Sam has been developing the films himself.
7. I listened to him for an hour, concealing my impatience as well as I could.
8. He repeated the gruesome story, omitting none of the details.
9. Since Larry always deferred to his grandmother's wishes, he offered to postpone his trip.
10. Carefully controlling her temper, Margaret altered the design a third time before handing it in.

2. Dropping final *e*

Though the *e* at the end of the verb *hope* is not pronounced, it is important because it shows that the *o* has a long-*o* sound rather than a short-*o* sound, as in *hop* or *mop.* When *ing* is added to *hope,* the silent *e* is dropped: *hope—hoping.* There is no further need for the *e;* the *o* keeps its long sound in *hoping* because of the *ing.*

A final silent *e* is usually dropped before *ing.* Study the following examples:

dine	dining	shine	shining	pursue	pursuing
use	using	write	writing	breathe	breathing
come	coming	decide	deciding	practice	practicing
hire	hiring	advise	advising	estimate	estimating

Remember these forms by thinking of them together in sentences like "Bing is *having* a hard time *deciding* where to do his *writing.*"

There are a few exceptions. The verbs *dye* and *singe* keep the *e* in *dyeing* and *singeing* to prevent confusion with *dying* ("dying like flies") and *singing* ("singing a song"). The *e* is kept in verbs ending in *oe* — *canoeing, tiptoeing, shoeing, hoeing* — to avoid an *oi* combination that might seem to have the sound of the *oi* in *coin* and *join.*

Chapter 12   Seven Basic Spelling Rules   177

EXERCISE 3. Be prepared to write the following sentences from dictation:

1. The light was shining in my eyes.
2. He is pursuing a wise course by hiring a guide for the canoeing trip.
3. Why are you dyeing the curtains blue?
4. Jane is practicing her part while we're deciding which costumes to get for Joan.
5. Estimating the cost of the tile will take only ten minutes.
6. Pat saw Dick tiptoeing past the dining room and called to him.
7. She continued advising him, hoping that he would come to his senses before it was too late.
8. Dale bandaged his blistered hand and continued hoeing until he saw Vernon coming.
9. Have you ever tried singeing the ends of your hair?
10. I almost stopped breathing when I discovered Tom using Mother's antique chair for a ladder.

A final silent *e* is usually dropped before suffixes beginning with a vowel:

value + able = valuable	typewrite + er = typewriter
desire + able = desirable	able + est = ablest
persevere + ance = perseverance	sense + ible = sensible
discipline + ary = disciplinary	refrigerate + or = refrigerator
interfere + ence = interference	grieve + ous = grievous

But notice that the *e* of words ending in *ce* or *ge* is kept before *able* and *ous* to preserve the *s* sound of the *c* and the *j* sound of the *g:*

notice + able = noticeable	service + able = serviceable
change + able = changeable	courage + ous = courageous
outrage + ous = outrageous	replace + able = replaceable

Before suffixes beginning with a consonant the *e* is usually kept:

peace + ful = peaceful	arrange + ment = arrangement
defense + less = defenseless	nine + teen = nineteen
rude + ness = rudeness	nine + ty = ninety

Most troublesome are the *e*'s before *ly.* Study the following list:

definite + ly = definitely	severe + ly = severely
immediate + ly = immediately	scarce + ly = scarcely
extreme + ly = extremely	entire + ly = entirely
sincere + ly = sincerely	separate + ly = separately
sure + ly = surely	accurate + ly = accurately

178

There are only a few common exceptions. The *e* is dropped before the consonant suffix of *ninth, truly, duly, wholly, judgment, argument.*

EXERCISE 4. Be prepared to write the following sentences from dictation:

1. He surely is changeable; yesterday he said definitely that we were to start immediately after breakfast.
2. Nineteen dollars is entirely too much for those shoes, even if they are serviceable.
3. There has been a noticeable improvement since the Student Council has taken over all disciplinary problems.
4. Attacking this peaceful and defenseless village was truly a grievous wrong.
5. I was extremely annoyed at Bill's rudeness to his mother, but decided it would scarcely be sensible to start an argument during dinner.
6. We made arrangements to pay for the refrigerator within ninety days.
7. The natives were duly warned that further interference would be severely punished.
8. On the ninth of May a typewriter and a valuable pen were stolen.
9. Millie is not wholly convinced that perseverance is always desirable or courageous.
10. We worked separately and then checked carefully to see that all figures were copied accurately in the final report.

3. Changing *y* to *i*

The plural of nouns ending in *y* preceded by a consonant is made by changing the *y* to *i* and adding *es.*

enemy	enemies	ally	allies	luxury	luxuries
city	cities	penny	pennies	colony	colonies
lady	ladies	army	armies	opportunity	opportunities

If the noun ends in *y* preceded by a vowel, the plural is formed in the regular way. No letter is changed, and only an *s* is added:

essay	essays	monkey	monkeys	decoy	decoys
doorway	doorways	chimney	chimneys	convoy	convoys

The *y* of adjectives ending in *y* preceded by a consonant is changed to *i* before the endings *er* and *est:*

happy	happier	happiest	shabby	shabbier	shabbiest
pretty	prettier	prettiest	flimsy	flimsier	flimsiest
hungry	hungrier	hungriest	busy	busier	busiest

The same change is made when *ly* is added to form adverbs:

easy easily   lucky luckily   guilty guiltily   busy busily

Or when *ness* is added to form nouns:

clumsy clumsiness   greedy greediness   busy business

Business is the most troublesome of this group, a real demon in school and out. Remember that the *i* comes after the *s,* taking the place of the *y* of *busy.* Start writing *busy* — **bus;** change the *y* to *i* — **busi;** then add *ness* — **business.**

Notice the *e* in *lonely, lovely, lively, homely, stately.* Make sure you keep these **e**'s when you add *ness:*

loneliness   loveliness   liveliness   homeliness   stateliness

EXERCISE 5. Be prepared to write the following sentences from dictation:

1. The doorways and chimneys for the street scene were made of the flimsiest wood we could find.
2. Crane's enemies speedily took advantage of these opportunities to ruin his business.
3. Bill's clumsiness is not so annoying as his greediness.
4. The hungrier and shabbier the men were, the happier the cook seemed.
5. The armies of all the allies were under one general command.
6. When he saw her, he jumped up guiltily, scattering the pennies.
7. Luckily the essays were short, and I easily finished reading them before class began.
8. The prettiest room in the world could not make up for the loneliness she felt.
9. The ladies found few luxuries in the colonies.
10. Because of the stateliness of his manner none of the people at the party noticed his homeliness.

4. *ie* and *ei*

About the only people who never have trouble with the *ie* and *ei* words are those who have photographic minds. Almost everyone else has to resort at times to a dictionary — unless he or she will take the time to learn some formula for remembering when to use *ie* and when *ei*. Since the problem is rather complicated, there is no short formula that will do. The one given here — put in the form of a jingle for easy memorizing — is in two parts.

Begin with the *ie* words. *I* generally comes before *e* when the word as a long-*e* sound, the sound of the vowels in *seen* and *greet*.

Pronounce to yourself the following words, noticing that in each *ie* spells a long-*e* sound:

believe	reprieve	grief	frieze
relieve	achieve	brief	series
grieve	belief	chief	grievance
retrieve	relief	thief	achievement

Many other words have a long-*e* sound spelled by *ie*. Remember them in groups. Think of *field, shield, wield,* and *yield* together. Link *bier* with *tier* and *pier, fierce* with *pierce,* and *frontier* with *cashier* and *chandelier.* Pronounce *siege* and *besiege;* the long-*e* sound means *i* before *e.* Pay particular attention to two demons — *piece* and *niece.* The long-*e* sound is the cue to the *ie* spelling in *priest* and *fiend* and *shriek.*

There are probably no more than a dozen exceptions — words in which a long-*e* sound is spelled by *ei.* Only six of these are common: *leisure, either, neither, inveigle, seize,* and *weird.* Since there are so few, they can easily be remembered, especially if they are put in rhyming lines:

> Seize, inveigle, either,
> Weird, leisure, neither.

These details can be summarized in the first three lines of the six-line formula:

> *I* before *e* when sound is long *e,*
>
> Except   Seize, inveigle, either,
>   Weird, leisure, neither.

Memorize these lines before doing the dictation exercise.

EXERCISE 6. Be prepared to write the following sentences from dictation:

1. With a warning shriek the cashier pointed to the swaying chandelier above our heads.
2. Bowed with grief, the chief stood beside Long Eagle's bier and vowed never to yield to the enemy.
3. Below the frieze hung a series of battered shields.
4. I don't believe anyone can inveigle my niece into giving up her leisure to work in the store.
5. Within the walls of the besieged city the priest did what he could to relieve the dying.

6. David Dawson finally achieved great success, but he never forgot his grievance.
7. Before either of the men could move, the fiend had seized the gold piece and vanished in a weird burst of flame.
8. To everyone's relief the thief was caught at the frontier.
9. It was her belief that neither of the two men involved in the plot was granted a reprieve.
10. Why should he grieve when he can so easily retrieve his loss?

Now, when can we expect *e* to come before *i?*

After c, e comes before *i:*

receive	deceive	conceive	perceive
receipt	deceit	conceit	ceiling

The only important exception to this part of the rule is *financier.*

When the sound of the vowels is something other than long *e, e* generally precedes *i.* For example, when the sound is long *a,* as in *date, ei* is the right order:

freight	reign	reindeer	veil	weigh	eight
neighbor	rein	sleigh	vein	weight	skein

The words *their* and *heir,* which have a similar sound, belong with this group. Others, less common, are *seine, deign, feign, feint,* and *heinous.*

When the sound is long *i,* as in *fight, ei* is the right order:

height	eider	sleight	Fahrenheit

When the sound is short *i* or short *e,* as in *hit* and *bet, ei* is the right order:

counterfeit	surfeit	foreign
sovereign	forfeit	heifer

Now notice the pronunciation and the spelling of the following words:

friend	view	mischief
fiery	sieve	handkerchief

All of these are exceptions to the rule that *e* comes before *i* when the sound is not long *e.*

The second part of the *ie-ei* formula can be summed up in three rhyming lines, which, when added to the three you have already learned, will give you a reliable guide for spelling the *ie* and *ei* words:

I before *e* when sound is long *e*,

Except   **Seize, inveigle, either,**
               Weird, leisure, neither.

Ei after *c* or when sound is not *e*,

Except   **Financier, fiery, and mischief,**
               Friend, sieve, view, and handkerchief.

Another jingle, not quite as complete, says it this way (followed by a sentence (!) of exceptions):

i before *e* except after *c*

"Neither leisure foreigner seized the weird height."

The best technique is to be alert to the problem and then to apply the appropriate jingle or rule — remembering exceptions!

EXERCISE 7. Be prepared to write the following sentences from dictation:

1. The counterfeit money deceived the near-sighted clerk, who handed him a receipt.
2. Her friends soon perceived that the foreign financier whom the sovereign had trusted was taking the reins of government.
3. Our neighbors paid the freight charges on the heifer.
4. The window trimmer hung a long veil from the ceiling and grouped the sleigh and reindeer behind it.
5. The duke's heir forfeited his estates by this heinous crime.
6. As soon as they received the chart, they weighed themselves and checked their weight against their height.
7. His sleight of hand was amazing, but his conceit made him unpopular with the other performers.
8. On a Fahrenheit thermometer 212 degrees marks the boiling point.
9. We could not conceive of a thing to do to calm her fiery temper or keep her out of mischief.
10. On the table in the center of the stage in full view of the audience were a handkerchief, a sieve, and a skein of yarn.

5. Possessives

The rule for writing the possessive form of a singular noun is simple: Add an apostrophe and *s* to the noun:

the doctor's office   Hugh's answer
a woman's purse   the coach's speech

If the singular noun ends in *s,* an apostrophe alone is sometimes used, especially when the word following begins with an *s:*

the governess' salary	OR:	the governess's salary
Bess' selfishness	OR:	Bess's selfishness

The rule is simple. Write the word — the complete word, without lopping off the final letter — before adding the apostrophe and *s* or the apostrophe alone. Take, for example, the proper noun *Frances Perkins* — the name of the first woman to be a member of the Cabinet.

Frances's appointment	OR:	Frances' appointment
Miss Perkins's work	OR:	Miss Perkins' work

There are two steps to follow in writing singular possessives. First, write the word — the whole word. Second, add the sign of the possessive — the apostrophe and *s* or the apostrophe alone. The first step is the one to watch. Students seldom forget the apostrophe and *s,* but many of them have no qualms about chopping off the final letter of a word. They speak of a *Miss Perkins,* but they write about the work of a "Miss Perkin." They talk of *James,* but they write about the motorcycle belonging to a boy named "Jame." Avoid such careless errors by taking time in writing. Write all of *Jones* or *actress* or *laundress* or *Harris* or *Higgins* or *Cross.* Then — and only then — add the sign of the possessive:

Miss Jones	Miss Jones's class	OR:	Miss Jones' class
the actress	the actress's wardrobe	OR:	the actress' wardrobe
Mr. Harris	Mr. Harris's garage	OR:	Mr. Harris' garage

Nouns ending in *y* — like *lady, army, family* — can be traps. Remember the first step: Write the complete word — without changing the final letter. The second step is easy: Just add the apostrophe and *s:*

lady	a lady's watch	family	my family's plans
army	the army's request	Emily	Emily's nephew

EXERCISE 8. Be prepared to write the following sentences from dictation:

1. Mr. Stevens's (*or* Stevens') car was parked in front of Dr. Harris's (*or* Harris') office.
2. Betsy's description of the lady's hat made all of us laugh.
3. His family's decision to move to Texas kept him from accepting Mr. Kelley's offer.

4. Visiting Mr. Higgins's (*or* Higgins') ranch caused another day's delay in our trip.
5. The woman's purse was lying on Mr. Rice's desk where she left it.

Most plural nouns end in *s:* three *cows,* twelve *knives,* two *ditches,* a few *keys,* many *allies,* several *heroes.* But some plurals end in other letters: six *feet,* many *women,* four *teeth,* five *mice,* several *deer.*

The possessive form of plural nouns is written in one of two ways: 1) If the plural ends in *s,* add an apostrophe. Nothing more is needed. Simply put an apostrophe after the word:

the boys	the boys' tents
the ladies	the ladies' dresses
the monkeys	the monkeys' antics
ten cents	ten cents' worth

2) If the plural does not end in *s,* add an apostrophe and *s:*

a child	the children	the children's toys
a man	the men	the men's jobs
a reindeer	the reindeer	the reindeer's names

As in writing singular possessives, the first step is important. First write the plural:

a hero	the heroes
a woman	the women

Then look at the plural word. If it ends in *s,* add an apostrophe. Do not change or omit any letter. Just put an apostrophe after the word:

heroes	heroes' trophies

If the word does not end in *s,* add an apostrophe and *s:*

women	women's purses

Writers rarely have trouble with the plurals of common nouns like *church, dish, gas, boss, fox, waltz.* Without hesitation they write *churches, dishes, gases, bosses, foxes, waltzes,* adding *es,* rather than just *s,* to form the plurals. Yet often they seem unable to write the plurals of family names ending in *ch, sh, s, x,* and *z* — which are formed in exactly the same way. The members of the Lerch family and the Standish family and the Higgins family and the Lomax family and the Metz family are the Lerches, the Standishes, the Higginses, the Lomaxes, and the Metzes. It is odd that these plural names "don't look right" and "don't sound right" to many people. But they are right, just as *bonuses* and *crosses* and *princesses* are.

Go slowly in writing the possessives of plural names. First write the plurals:

Mary Smith	the Smiths	Allen Dix	the Dixes
Pat Clemens	the Clemenses	Bill Wentz	the Wentzes

When that is done, form the possessives by adding an apostrophe:

the Smiths' invitation   the Dixes' car
the Clemenses' cottage   the Wentzes' reception

EXERCISE 9. Be prepared to write the following sentences from dictation:

1. The Stubbinses' uncle owns a men's and boys' clothing store.
2. The ladies' hats and children's bonnets are on sale today.
3. The babies' carriages were lined up in the Norrises' driveway.
4. The deer's heads were mounted on the walls of Fishermen's Lodge.
5. The monkeys' shrill cries brought their owner to the cage in a hurry.

The possessive forms of personal pronouns never have an apostrophe. The following end in *s:*

hers   its   ours   yours   theirs

The possessive of *who* is spelled *whose* — with no apostrophe:

Whose coat was stolen?   The man *whose* dog we found is here.
Whose name was drawn?   Do you know *whose* team won?

6. Contractions

In ordinary speech the adverb *not* is seldom stressed unless we want special emphasis for it, as in "Beets are all right, but I do NOT like spinach." Usually we skip lightly over the *not,* or contract it to *n't,* attaching it to the preceding word: "I *don't* like spinach or beets." "He *hasn't* enough money." "She *isn't* here yet."

No letter is ever added in writing contractions; no letter is changed. But letters are omitted, and an apostrophe shows the omission:

is + not = isn't	had + not = hadn't
are + not = aren't	have + not = haven't
was + not = wasn't	must + not = mustn't
were + not = weren't	would + not = wouldn't
does + not = doesn't	should + not = shouldn't
do + not = don't	could + not = couldn't

186

The contractions of *shall not, will not,* and *can not* are irregular. Although the *ll* of *shall,* as well as the *o* of *not,* is dropped, only one apostrophe is used: *shan't.* For *will not* use *won't,* from *woll not,* an old spelling. For *can not* use *can't.*

The first letter — or letters — of verbs are often omitted in informal speech. In writing these contractions, be sure to use apostrophes to show where the letters have been dropped:

I + am = I'm	who + is = who's	we + would = we'd
it + is = it's	what + is = what's	you + are = you're
he + will = he'll	here + is = here's	they + will = they'll
that + is = that's	we + had = we'd	they + would = they'd
you + have = you've		would + have = would've
should + have = should've		could + have = could've

EXERCISE 10. Be prepared to write the following sentences from dictation:

1. If he'd helped, we'd have finished painting before noon.
2. I didn't say you couldn't leave now; I said you shouldn't.
3. You mustn't talk when she's counting, or she'll make a mistake.
4. I'm glad you're coming to visit while they're still here.
5. It's easy to see what's happening and who's responsible.

7. Using capital letters

An important part of writing correctly is knowing which words to begin with capital letters. One general rule is all you need: **Capitalize all proper nouns and all adjectives formed from proper nouns.**

A proper noun is a special name, one that distinguishes a particular person or thing from all others of the same class or kind. Proper nouns may be the names of

Persons: Edgar Lee Masters, Emily Dickinson
Animals: Ponder, Dumbo, Mickey Mouse, Kermit
Places: Detroit, Connecticut, Asia, Luxemburg, the United States
Races, religions, languages, political parties: Mongolian, Catholic, Norwegian, the Progressive party
Days, months, holidays, holy days: Saturday, November, Fourth of July, Ascension Day, Easter
Special events, historical periods, historical documents: Operation Crossroads, the Renaissance, the Treaty of Verdun
Ships, planes, trains: The *Mayflower,* the *Independence,* the *California Zephyr*
Trade names: Mixmaster, Crisco, Post Toasties

Buildings: the Pentagon, the Merchandise Mart
Business firms: Camilla Studios, Cowles Magazines, Inc.
The Deity, the Bible, the parts of the Bible: God, the Redeemer, trust in Him, the New Testament, the Gospel of Luke

Proper adjectives — those formed from proper nouns — are capitalized, but the words modified are not, unless they are proper nouns:

Victorian manners	*Japanese* paintings
a *Portuguese* tale	a *Swedish* Christmas
an old *French* custom	a *Spanish* Benedict Arnold

Since common nouns like *street, avenue, river, lake, mountain, hotel, hospital, clinic, building, high school, college, sophomore, club, dance, prom* are ordinary names rather than special names, they are not capitalized unless they are an essential part of proper nouns. Small letters are correct for the italicized words in these sentences:

His office is in the *building* across the *street* from the *hospital.*
The *sophomores* at our *high school* want to have a *prom* this year.

But capital letters are correct here:

His office is in the *Hamilton Building* next to *Mercy Hospital* on *Twenty-first Street.*
Members of the *Camera Club* of *Wilson High School* took pictures at the *Sophomore Prom.*

Words that show family relationships and titles that show rank, office, or profession — like *uncle, aunt, cousin, general, prince, senator, doctor, professor* — are capitalized when they are used with a person's name as part of a proper noun:

Aunt Georgia and *Uncle Will* are leaving tomorrow.
General Marshall and *Admiral Somerville* were in the audience.

But:

Neil asked his *mother* for the money.
A *general,* an *admiral,* and a *senator* were members of the panel.

When a common noun is used in place of a person's name, it is capitalized, as in the second sentence of each of the following pairs:

The check was made out to *Mrs. Wiley.*
The check was made out to *Mother.*

"Mr. Ellis is here to see you, *Senator Hale,*" she said.
"Mr. Ellis is here to see you, *Senator,*" she said.

"Take off your hat, *Jerry,*" he yelled.
"Take off your hat, *Freshman,*" he yelled.

Since the common nouns *Mother, Senator,* and *Freshman* are used as substitutes for the proper nouns *Mrs. Wiley, Senator Hale,* and *Jerry,* they are capitalized.

School subjects are not capitalized unless they are names of languages:

French   economics
German   mathematics
Dick has signed up for *English, history, bookkeeping,* and *Spanish.*

Though the names of days, months, holidays, and holy days are capitalized, the names of the seasons are not:

Next *winter* the club will meet every Monday night.
The chrysanthemums won't bloom until *fall.*

Words like *north, south, east, west* are capitalized when they name or refer to the geographical sections of a country:

Sinclair Lewis was born in the *Middle West.*
His favorites are *Western* stories.

When these words show directions, they begin with small letters, as in the following examples:

Turn *east* at the next corner.
The kitchen has a *southern* exposure.

The first word, the last word, and all important words in the titles of books, newspapers, magazines, songs, plays, stories, articles, and poems begin with capital letters:

Better Ways of Growing Up   "To Tim at Twenty"
the *New York Times*   "That Heartless Young Thing"
Theatre Arts   "Out of the Scrapbook"
"Home on the Range"   "The Naming of Cats"

EXERCISE 11. Decide which words in the following sentences should be capitalized. Then write the numbers of the sentences. After them, write these words, using the necessary capitals. For the first sentence you should write: *1. Henry Ford, Dearborn, Detroit*

1. Growing tired of farm work, henry ford left his home in dearborn and walked to detroit, where he became an apprentice in a machine shop.
2. The only article aunt ruth read was "best seat in the ball park."

3. If gordon spent more time on his mathematics and latin, he wouldn't have time to direct plays for the garrick club.
4. Edward rowland sill, best known for his poems of the west, was a new englander by birth.
5. The crandall building and loan company is on twenty-third avenue, four blocks north of the townsend clinic.

Adding suffixes: a summary

It is an accomplishment to be able to spell such difficult words as *connoisseur, sacrilegious,* and *desiccate.* But it is practical — and valuable — to be able to spell such common, everyday forms as *stop—stopped, control—controlling, dine—dining, advise—advisable, worry—worrying,* and *happy—happiness.*

The first rule, studied earlier, covers words that end in a single consonant preceded by a single vowel. If the word has only one syllable, the final consonant is doubled before a suffix beginning with a vowel:

plan + ed = planned	sad + est = saddest
ship + er = shipper	snob + ish = snobbish
bat + ing = batting	tan + ery = tannery

If the word has more than one syllable, the final consonant is doubled only when the accent is on the last syllable, as it is in the following words:

prefer + ed = preferred	regret + able = regrettable
begin + er = beginner	acquit + al = acquittal
occur + ing = occurring	remit + ance = remittance

The second rule covers words that end in silent *e.* The *e* is dropped before a suffix beginning with a vowel:

desire + able = desirable	defense + ible = defensible
store + age = storage	pine + ing = pining
guide + ance = guidance	narrate + ive = narrative
hope + ed = hoped	refrigerate + or = refrigerator
advise + er = adviser	pore + ous = porous

This rule has several important exceptions. The final *e* is kept in words like *dyeing* and *singeing,* for dropping the *e* would cause confusion with *dying* and *singing.* It is kept in *oe* words like *hoeing* and *shoeing.* It is kept in such words as *noticeable* and *courageous* to preserve the *s* sound of the *c* and the *j* sound of the *g.*

The third rule covers words that end in *y* preceded by a consonant. The *y* is changed to *i* before suffixes beginning with a consonant:

busy + ly = busily   beauty + fy = beautify
lonely + ness = loneliness pity + ful = pitiful
penny + less = penniless accompany + ment = accompaniment

The same change is made before the suffixes *ed, er, es,* and *est:*

notify + ed = notified occupy + es = occupies
pretty + er = prettier   homely + est = homeliest

But the *y* is kept before *ing:*

study + ing = studying amplify + ing = amplifying
carry + ing = carrying   accompany + ing = accompanying

EXERCISE 12. Be prepared to write the following sentences from dictation:

1. We hoped that her snobbish friends would not laugh at her pitiful attempts to beautify herself.
2. Clifford repeated the narrative, amplifying the horrors of the last part.
3. Dad thought it advisable to hold up the remittance until he was sure the refrigerator was in good working order.
4. The car stopped at the corner, and we noticed that the woman accompanying the actress was much prettier.
5. His legal adviser was sure he would win a speedy acquittal.
6. Jane is busily dyeing the curtains she found in a storage box.
7. He notified us that only those with high batting averages had received desirable offers.
8. Henry was the saddest and homeliest of the beginners in the shipping department at the tannery.
9. What has occurred is regrettable, but with Ed's courageous guidance we may still regain a controlling interest in the business.
10. I had planned to use the flower pots from the window ledge in the dining room, but Sue preferred these because they are porous.

Chapter 13

Spelling Demons and Other Creatures

There are only two or three hundred real spelling demons; but since they account for almost nine-tenths of spelling errors, it is important that they be mastered.

The words printed in **boldface** type in the sentences below *seem* easy, but do not be fooled by appearances. Study each word carefully, noticing exactly what the letters are. Make sure to put each letter in its proper place.

She **asks too** many questions.	Mary **turns** the wheel.
I am **tired too.**	I **meant** to stop at **their** house.
Do you **know** that song?	He **tries** to make **sense.**
They ran **off** the **road.**	I **led** them **toward** the door.
Do you **choose those?**	She **knew its** name.

Most demons have trouble spots — one or more letters that cause the misspelling. In *separate,* for instance, the first *a* is the source of error. Want some help? Note that "pa" is in that word. Or, if a golfer or stockbroker, that "par" is there! In *February,* the danger spot is the first *r.* Study the following list, concentrating on the letters in boldface type. These are the trouble spots that cause writers to make *precisely the same mistake* in the words.

definite	doesn't	before	ninety	knowledge
until	again	recognize	doctor	interesting
answer	women	government	persuade	rough
library	pleasant	probably	grammar	believe
speak	instead	divide	separate	sentence
perhaps	trouble	piece	every	quiet
weak	often	across	stretch	enough

The best way to learn demons is to study them a few at a time, putting similar forms together so that the order of the letters becomes a familiar pattern. For example, group such forms as *speak* and *weak, rough* and *enough, know* and *knowledge.* Make up a sentence, like "The *rain* has flooded the *drain again,*" combining the demon *again* with *rain* and *drain* (which are seldom misspelled) to put firmly in mind the *ai* in *again.* Or figure out some device to secure the right letter, like "Watch for the *cog* in reCOGnize" or "Count *ten* when writing senTENce.

EXERCISE 1. Be prepared to write the following sentences from dictation:

1. Perhaps we had better wait instead, until we get a definite answer from the doctor.
2. I know Sam doesn't believe that I would recognize Mrs. Wilson if I saw her again.
3. If you could persuade Tom to be more quiet and to speak in a pleasant way, he would not get into trouble so often.
4. I meant to tell you that Laura is too tired to go to the public library with us after school.
5. Probably everyone would agree that a knowledge of grammar is important in the advertising business.
6. Someone had stretched a piece of rope across the walk, and I stumbled over it as I ran toward the house.
7. Ninety of those delegates represent foreign governments.
8. Before he copied the rough draft, he checked every sentence.
9. The women had the good sense to separate the two boys before their quarrel led to blows.
10. Though its ending was weak, the movie was interesting enough.

Mispronunciations often lead to misspellings. A good way to master the demons is to concentrate on their pronunciation. These have only one syllable:

elm   film   helm

There are only two syllables in:

ath + lete = athlete   hin + drance = hindrance
en + trance = entrance   light + ning = lightning

These have only three syllables:

ath + let + ics = athletics   pos + si + bly = possibly
dis + as + trous = disastrous   prob + a + bly = probably
li + brar + y = library   trans + la + tion = translation
um + brel + la = umbrella   mis + chie + vous = mischievous

The demon **all right** is not only two syllables; it is two separate words. Remember **all right** by grouping it with other *all* phrases: *all wrong, all over, all in, all there.*

The abbreviation **etc.** stands for two Latin words—*et,* meaning "and," and *cetera,* meaning "other things." Notice the order of the letters: **etc.** Notice the period at the end. And, of course, no one need ever write "and etc.," for the *and* is already there — *et.*

Pronounce **pattern** and **modern** and **western** and **southern.** Note the **ern** of the second syllable. Pronounce — and spell —

asparagus to rhyme with *omnibus.* Pronounce **except** in "No one *except* John cares." See the **exc** of *except?* Spell **led** in "Ted *led* Ned to the shed." Spell **led** when *Ted* and *Ned* and *shed* are not in the sentence.

EXERCISE 2. Be prepared to write the following sentences from dictation:

1. The elm near the library entrance was struck by lightning.
2. Mary's translation was a hindrance rather than a help.
3. Jimmy is quite mischievous, all right, but he won't touch your umbrella.
4. Disastrous frosts killed the asparagus in the southern part of the state.
5. Possibly Sarah isn't interested in athletics and doesn't like athletes.

The word *before* is commonly used; it is also commonly misspelled. Put the final **e** on *before.* The golfer's warning "Fore" has that same **e.** So has the verb *foretell,* meaning "tell *before.*" A person who foretells is a *prophet.* What he foretells is a *prophecy* — with the same *ph* and ending in **ecy.** Many *prophecies* are made about the *weather.*

Notice that *fascinate* has a *c* after the *s.* Also notice that *opinion* and *operate* have only one *p.* Pronounce *similar* in three syllables — "sim-i-lar" — using only two **i**'s, one before and one after the *m.* Pronounce *boundary* in three syllables — "bound-a-ry" — and don't forget the **a** before the *ry. Liable* has three syllables; the second is **a.** Put the **a** in *liable.*

See "red" when you write *hundred!* Be "strict" about having a **t** in *strictly. Humor* has an **o**; watch for that **o** in *humorous.*

Using "spelling pronunciations"

Pronounce *chocolate, interest, bachelor, vegetable, laboratory, separate.* Notice that the second *o* of *chocolate* sounds very like the first *e* of *interest,* that the *e* of *bachelor* sounds like the first *a* of *separate.* The usual pronunciation gives no clue to the spelling of the trouble spots. But mispronouncing the words may help. Think of these words as if they were pronounced with stress on the capital letters: choc-O-late, int-E-rest, bach-E-lor, veg-E-table, lab-O-ratory, sep-A-rate.

Now pronounce the syllables of the following words, emphasizing the capital letters:

rec-OG-nize	gov-ERN-ment	ARC-tic
Feb-RU-ar-y	SUR-prise	book-KEEP-er
can-DI-date	POST-pone	prob-a-BLY

Remember the letters in boldface when spelling *recognize, February, candidate, government, surprise, postpone, arctic, bookkeeper,* and *probably.*

Do not depend on the pronunciations of *Wednesday, women, restaurant,* and *prairie* to indicate their spelling. Pretend that *Wednesday* has three sounded syllables: Wed-NES-day. Remember that the plural *women* is the same as *woman,* except for the *e:* WO-men. Notice the *u* after the *a* in the second syllable of *restaurant:* res-TAU-rant. And do not forget the "air" in *prairie:* prAIRie.

In the following words the consonants printed in boldface type are not pronounced, but they are important in the spelling. Go over these words several times, looking carefully at the silent letters.

han**d**some	solem**n**	colum**n**
ras**p**berry	stret**c**h	Conne**c**ticut
cup**b**oard	ais**l**e	ans**w**er

EXERCISE 3. Be prepared to write the following sentences from dictation:

1. A handsome bachelor is the answer to many women's prayers.
2. Put the raspberry jam and the chocolate in the cupboard.
3. A column on the front page was devoted to the Arctic expedition.
4. Wesnesday he told us that he would probably postpone his trip to Connecticut until February.
5. Did you recognize the women sitting across the aisle from us?
6. Grandfather's only interest is talking and reading about vegetable and yogurt diets.
7. One of the candidates is a bookkeeper at Dad's office.
8. Donna's solemn answer was a complete surprise to the men and women at the laboratory.
9. The prairie stretches for many miles to the west of the camp, and you will probably find the drive quite dull.
10. Most of the men who work on the government project eat at the restaurant on the corner.

Words with *a*

Two of the most fiendish demons are *grammar* and *separate.* Remember that **ma** is in *grammar and* **pa** is in *separate* — and in *separated, separating,* and *separation,* as well — and these words will plague no longer.

Watch for the **ace** in *furnace,* and notice the **age** of *village.* Make sure of the **gain** in *again* and *against.* Remember that **par** is just as important in *prepare* and *preparation* as it is in golf, and you will have another group of demons under control.

The **a** in *weather* is not pronounced; neither is the first **a** in *pleasant*.

A great **many** people slight the **a**'s in pronouncing *valuable* and *liable;* but write *valuable* and *liable* without slighting the **a**'s.

Burglar and *sugar* and *calendar* and *particular* have nothing in common except the **ar** at the end. Try making up a sentence to help with this strange, demonic quartet: "This particular burglar took nothing but a calendar and a sugar bowl." Do the same with a group ending in **ary** — *secretary, salary, dictionary:* "His secretary got a raise in salary for using the dictionary." Thinking of **dance** will help with *appearance* and *allowance:* "Jim's appearance at the dance had cost him a whole month's allowance."

Affect, beginning with an **a**, is always a verb: "The new ruling did not **a**ffect the freshmen." "She was greatly **a**ffected by the poverty of their home."

EXERCISE 4. Be prepared to write the following sentences from dictation:

1. We had a pleasant time spending Peter's allowance at a small store in the village.
2. I propped the calendar against the sugar bowl.
3. Any person who drives so recklessly on icy pavements is liable to have a serious accident.
4. Aunt Helen, who was very particular about keeping up appearances, made elaborate preparations for the party.
5. Father was upset because the new furnace took most of his salary for the month.
6. Alice put the brown sugar and the white sugar on separate shelves.
7. Strangely enough, a mistake in grammar was the clue that led to the capture of the burglar.
8. A dictionary, says Miss Davis, is the most valuable reference book a good secretary has.
9. Tom is working at the separation center again.
10. Grandfather insisted that the damp weather affected his knee.

Words with *e*

The words *comedy* and *tragedy* are related in meaning — and in spelling; both end in **edy**. Remember **edy,** and never put the *g* of *tragedy* in the wrong place. Remember **edy,** and never misspell *remedy.*

Theodore Roosevelt's favorite expression for showing approval was "DE-lighted." Think of this exaggerated pronunciation of *delighted* when writing other **de** words. **De**scribe, **de**scription, **de**spair, **de**spise, **de**stroy, and **de**struction are especially **de**monic.

The Latin word *bene* — with two e's — means "well." **Bene**factor means "a well-doer." Notice that same **bene** in **bene**dic*tion,* **bene**vo*lence,* **bene**ficial, **bene**fit, **bene**fiting. Most students can spell *petition,* derived from the Latin *peto,* meaning "ask." See *petition* in *re***petition** and *com***petition?**

The trouble spot in *competent, superintendent, dependent, independent* is the e in the last syllable. Watch for the **tent** in the first of these words; watch for the **dent** in the others. Watch for the **ten** in *exis***tent**ce and *sen***tent**ce, for the **den** in *ten***den**cy.

Notice *cemetery* — almost every other letter is an e. *Stationery* should be easy; like *letter paper, stationery* has an er. The only vowels in *whether* are e's; the only vowels in the noun *effect* are e's. *Quiet* should rhyme with *diet.*

Three verbs, and only three, belong to the "double-trouble" group, ending in **ceed.** Look *twice* every time you write *succeed* or *proceed* or *exceed,* to make sure of doubling the e of *succeed* and *proceed* and *exceed.*

EXERCISE 5. Be prepared to write the following sentences from dictation:

1. The only remedy was to get a more competent superintendent.
2. There are no words to describe how much I despise that fellow.
3. He has a bad tendency to despair if he does not immediately succeed.
4. Mr. Grimes wondered whether the increased competition would have any effect on their sales.
5. He brushed me aside and proceeded with his report of the tragedy.
6. She is dependent on them for everything from food to stationery.
7. The natives owed their very existence to his benevolence.
8. Michelle's description of the comedy was funnier than the play itself.
9. Exceeding the speed limit is a short cut to the cemetery.
10. Even the noisiest tourists became quiet on seeing this destruction.

Words with *ly*

A number of adjectives are made by adding *ly* to nouns: *friend* — a *friendly* manner, *month—monthly* meetings, *brother* — *brotherly* advice. But the *ly* ending is more commonly added to adjectives to form adverbs: *frank* — speaking *frankly, cool* — stood *cooly* by, *evident* — *evidently* angry, *particular* — *particularly* good, *discreet* — *discreetly* silent, *peculiar* — dressed *peculiarly.* The final *y* of adjectives like *sloppy, easy, busy, lazy* is changed to *i* before the *ly* is added: *sloppily, easily, busily, lazily.*

Though a final *y* may be changed to *i,* no final consonant is ever dropped before the addition of the *ly.* Add *ly* to the adjective *equal:* the adverb *equally* will have two *l*'s. Add *ly* to *personal: Personally* will have two *l*'s, as will adverb forms of all *al* adjectives:

final + ly = finally   especial + ly = especially
usual + ly = usually   accidental + ly = accidentally
real + ly = really   continual + ly = continually
natural + ly = naturally   original + ly = originally

First write the adjective — the whole adjective. Then add the *ly.*

The adverb form of *public* is *publicly.* But most *ic* adjectives add *al* before the ending *ly:*

dramatic + al + ly = dramatically
optimistic + al + ly = optimistically
sarcastic + al + ly = sarcastically
systematic + al + ly = systematically

EXERCISE 6. Be prepared to write the following sentences from dictation:

1. Evidently the last problem was particularly hard.
2. Naturally we disliked his speaking so sarcastically about our work.
3. Everything in the office was usually systematically planned.
4. Finally she appeared, dressed sloppily as always, and coolly asked what we wanted.
5. He paused dramatically, then continued with his brotherly advice.
6. Sam was equally certain that Jim had been hurt accidentally.
7. Though the food was really not bad, Clara complained continually, especially when Mr. Evans was there.
8. Originally we had planned to hold monthly meetings.
9. I personally think she spoke too optimistically about our chances.
10. He seemed particularly interested, though his manner was unfriendly.

Words with *ia* and *ai;* One *s* and two *s*'s

Pronounce the following words: *brilliant, William, valiant.* The *y* sound is in each of the words — "brill-yant," "Will-yam," "val-yant." The *y* sound is there because the *i* comes before the *a* in the second syllable.

Now pronounce *villain, chaplain, porcelain, bargain,* none of which has a *y* sound.

Notice the *i* before the *a* in *Christian,* pronounced "Chris-chan." But there is no *chan* sound in *captain, certain, curtain, mountain, fountain* — in which the *a* comes before the *i.*

Let pronunciation guide spelling, whenever possible. For example, say to yourself *mission, session, profession.* Notice that each ends with the sound "shun." When the *shun* sound follows a vowel,

as it does in these words, it is always spelled by two *s*'s before *ion.*
Here are other examples: *omission, admission, permission, discussion, succession, concession.*

Now look at *decision* and *division,* which end with the sound
"zhun." A *zhun* sound following a vowel is always spelled by one s
before *ion.*

EXERCISE 7. Be prepared to write the following sentences from
dictation:
1. The chaplain was certain that ten of the men in his division would
   volunteer for this dangerous mission.
2. The discussion at the afternoon session was about preventing erosion.
3. After a bit of persuasion, Mother gave me permission to buy new curtains for my room.
4. William Foster, our football captain, hopes to become a professional
   golf player.
5. On one occasion the careless omission of a single word in an ad cost
   the company hundreds of dollars.
6. Later we discovered that three of the porcelain dishes, which Aunt
   Helen thought were such a bargain, were cracked.
7. The general admission was a dollar, but we spent much more than that
   at the concessions on the grounds.
8. Occasionally the valiant Rhett Butler seemed more like a villain than a
   hero.
9. The collision was followed by a succession of lawsuits.
10. Katherine does brilliant work, but she cannot make prompt decisions.

Words with *ful* and *mit*
   The adjective *sorrowful,* made by adding the suffix *ful* to the
noun *sorrow,* means "full of sorrow." The adjective *dreadful,* with
the same suffix, means "full of dread." Though in these words the
suffix means "full of," it is spelled with only one *l:* **ful.**

With one exception, words ending in *e* keep the *e* before **ful:**
useful, careful, wasteful, hateful, hopeful, spiteful, peaceful. The
exception is a very common word — *awful.*

Words ending in *y* change the *y* to *i* before **ful:** *pity* + *ful* =
pitiful, beauty + *ful* = *beautiful, bounty* + *ful* = *bountiful, plenty* + *ful* = *plentiful.*

The plural of nouns of measure ending in *ful* — like *cupful,
handful, teaspoonful* — is made by adding *s* to *ful: cupfuls, handfuls, teaspoonfuls, carfuls, bushelfuls, armfuls.*

The base word of several common verbs is *mit,* derived from the Latin *mittere,* meaning "to send": *omit, permit, transmit, admit, submit, commit.* Since each of these verbs is accented on the last syllable and ends in a single consonant preceded by a single vowel, the final consonant is doubled before *ed* and *ing.* Remember the double *t*'s in *omitted, omitting; permitted, permitting; transmitted, transmitting; admitted, admitting; submitted, submitting; comitted, committing.* Do not forget the double *m,* the double *t,* and the double *e* in *committee.*

EXERCISE 8. Be prepared to write the following sentences from dictation:

1. Life in the small village was peaceful and beautiful; few crimes were committed there.
2. Though he never admitted it, Mike is the one who submitted Jane's story to the contest committee.
3. Grandmother is very careful about money, never permitting anyone in the household to be wasteful.
4. Did you ever find out whose coat had been left in place of yours?
5. Apples were plentiful, and we gave bushelfuls of ours away.
6. Within a short time the awful message was being transmitted to a shocked and sorrowful nation.
7. Both suggestions are good, but hers is more useful than theirs.
8. Because George felt spiteful, he gave Helen only part of the message, omitting what she most wanted to hear.
9. The foghorn repeated its dreadful warning throughout the night.
10. She measured out two cupfuls of flour and three teaspoonfuls of baking soda, before admitting she couldn't remember the recipe.

Words with *o* and *ous*

The preposition *among* looks like an easy word; yet, because the **o** has a sound like that of *u* in *blunt, among* is often misspelled. *Forty* is a strange word — strange and demonic. Logically its first syllable ought to have two vowels; it has only one, an **o.** Remember *forty* by pairing it with *fort.* Put another **o** demon, *porch,* with these. "The boys built a **fort** forty yards north of the porch." The nouns *mayor, visitor, author, governor, doctor, proprietor, conductor* all end in **or.** A number of common nouns end in **on:** *carton, lesson, pardon, apron.* Keep the **on** when **er** is added to *prison* and **ous** to *poison:* "The pris**on**er had no fear of the pois**on**ous snake."

Adjectives ending in **ous** are common: *enormous, jealous, generous.* The sound of the last syllable can trick a writer into forgetting the **o.** Watch for the **ous** in *mischievous, momentous,* *famous, perilous.* Watch for the **ous** after the **i** of *various, furious, victorious,* and *curious.*

The **c** in *curious* has a *k* sound because of the following *u.* Notice that same sound, spelled the same way, in *conspicuous, inconspicuous,* and *innocuous.*

Notice the *sh* sound in *delicious, ferocious, precious, vicious.* The **c** in these words sounds like *sh* because of the **i.** If the **i** were omitted, the *c* would have the sound of *k,* as in *cousin.* Make sure of the *sh* sound by putting **ci** before the *ous* of *gracious, spacious, suspicious, vivacious.* Three adjectives — *conscious, unconscious,* and *luscious* — deserve special attention. Each has an **s** before the **ci.**

The **g** in *religious* has a *j* sound because of the following **i.** Without the *i,* the *g* would have a "hard" sound, as in *Gus.* Do not forget the **i** after the **g** in *religious, contagious, prodigious.*

EXERCISE 9. Be prepared to write the following sentences from dictation:

1. Forty people, the mayor and the governor among them, were on hand to welcome the visitor, a famous and gracious author.
2. The doctor assured us the snake was innocuous, not poisonous.
3. In the middle of the spacious hall stood an enormous carton covered with various hotel and steamship labels.
4. Most conspicuous of all was a vivacious, gray-haired woman, dressed in blue and wearing a necklace of precious stones.
5. The banquet for the victorious team was a momentous occasion.
6. I was furious at Jimmy's mischievous behavior and decided to teach him a lesson.
7. Freda was not conscious that anything was wrong until Sam's questions made her suspicious.
8. The proprietor laughed at our terror, insisting that the dog on the porch was neither vicious nor ferocious.
9. Realizing that we were curious about the luscious fruit, the conductor explained that it was not so delicious as it looked.
10. Great faith is often contagious, as many religious people know.

Words with *u* and *ou*

The trouble spot in *guard* is the **u,** because that **u** is not pronounced. An unpronounced *u* after a *g* is commonplace. English spelling has it in *guardian* and *guilty* and *guest* and *guarantee* and *guess* and *guide.* Look carefully at these words; get used to the **gu** pattern.

The *u* is troublesome in other common words. Study the following four, paying special attention to the **u**'s in boldface type: am**a**teur, chauff**eu**r, mourn**f**ul, conq**u**er.

We spell *custom* with a **u** in the first syllable and an **o** in the second. Spell *accustomed,* getting the *u* and the *o* in the right places. Spell *bury* with a **u**, and *minute* with a **u**, though neither of the words as a *u* sound in the pronunciation. And notice the *u* in the first syllable of *surround* and *pursuit* and *pursuing;* it is this first *u* that causes the trouble. Since the **u** in *pronunciation* has a *u* sound, it should not cause trouble; yet it does.

The **ou** combination spells several different sounds. It spells the long-*o* sound in *four* and *fourteen* and *course,* in *though* and *thorough,* in *boulder* and *shoulder.* It spells the short-*u* sound in *double* and *trouble.* The diphthong sound "ou," which rhymes with *cow* and *how,* is always spelled **ou** before *nd* — *bound, found, pound, ground, sound, wound* — and before *d* — *cloud, loud, proud.* The only exception is *crowd,* which has an *ow* before the *d.* Put the *w* in *crowd.*

EXERCISE 10. Be prepared to write the following sentences from dictation:

1. Can you guess which of the fourteen guests was found guilty?
2. A minute later Hilda had buried her nose in a book, her troubles completely forgotten.
3. England was conquered by the Normans in 1066.
4. While the guard was pursuing Sam, the other four boys scrambled over the fence and disappeared in the crowd.
5. Though I soon grew accustomed to his strange pronunciation, I never could stand his mournful air.
6. Our clocks are guaranteed, but they must be wound carefully.
7. After a thorough search of the grounds, they gave up the pursuit.
8. The guide pointed to the dark clouds overhead and advised us to pitch camp in the shelter of a large boulder.
9. A group of fans surrounded the proud winner of the amateur title.
10. The chauffeur skillfully guided the car onto the shoulder of the road.

Words with *al*

Be sure of the spelling of the following adjectives ending in **al**: *actual, real, physical, practical, capital, neutral, technical, usual, legal, principal.* The most troublesome are the demons *capital* and *principal.* Think of the *a* of *al* as an **a** for *adjective:*

a capit**al** letter   their princip**al** objection
a capit**al** ship   my princip**al** reason

Trouble with the nouns *capital* and *principal* is avoided with the reminder that a *capital* is the "capital city of a state or country," that *capitals* are "capital letters," that a *principal* is the "principal person in a school," and that the *principal* is the "principal sum of money."

Words with *el;* Double letters

The following nouns all end in **el**:

ang**el**	tunn**el**	barr**el**	pan**el**
nick**el**	shov**el**	flann**el**	mant**el**
lab**el**	parc**el**	chann**el**	couns**el**

These words are common and simple, yet they are often misspelled, probably because the sound of the last syllable is the same as the sound of words ending in *le.* Pronounce each word by syllables, emphasizing the syllable containing the trouble spot — in these the **el**. Try to visualize the word. A clear mental picture of *angel* and *nickel* and *label* will secure these words.

Use this scheme of visualizing words for learning the spelling of the following demons with double letters:

app**ro**ach	**ne**cessary	exa**gg**erate	a**cc**ount
para**ll**el	o**pp**ortunity	a**pp**arent	a**rr**ival
a**pp**reciate	perso**nn**el	a**pp**earance	de**ss**ert

Concentrate especially on the two sets of double letters in:

add**r**ess	su**cc**ess	asse**ss**ment	emba**rr**a**ss**ment
su**cc**eed	su**cc**essful	posse**ss**ion	a**gg**re**ss**ive

A few words have three sets of double letters. Can you spell *committee* and *Tennessee* and *Mississippi?*

EXERCISE 11. Be prepared to write the following sentences from dictation:

1. He had the right address, all right; but somewhere between Tennessee and Mississippi the label had been torn off the parcel.
2. The arrival of these guests meant that I went without dessert.
3. Because he was aggressive and took advantage of any opportunity that came his way, he was quite successful financially.
4. However, it was apparent to those who knew him that the newspaper account greatly exaggerated his success.
5. The committee decided that an extra assessment was necessary.
6. The parallel lines in the drawing show where the tunnel will be.
7. The only one of his many possessions that Alice envied was the angel figurine on the mantel in the living room.
8. I nervously approached the office of the personnel manager.

9. To my embarrassment the flannel cost a nickel more than I had.
10. Though I disliked his appearance, I appreciated his wise counsel.

Words with *dis, mis, un, ness*

Words like *disagree, disappear,* and *dissatisfied* consist of two parts: a prefix *dis* and a "base" word — *agree, appear, satisfied* — to which the prefix is joined to change the meaning.

There is no need to make a point of remembering how many *s*'s to use. Simply write the prefix *dis;* then add the base word, whatever it is; and the *s*'s will take care of themselves. If the base word begins with *s*, there will be two *s*'s:

dis + satisfied = dissatisfied   dis + similar = dissimilar
dis + satisfaction = dissatisfaction   dis + service = disservice

Otherwise there will be only one *s:*

dis + agree = disagree   dis + appear (two *p*'s) = disappear
dis + continue = discontinue   dis + appoint (two *p*'s) = disappoint
dis + honor = dishonor   dis + approve (two *p*'s) = disapprove

Other related forms are *disagreement, dishonorable, disappearance, disappointment, disapproval.*

Deal with *mis* words the same way. Write the prefix *mis* and add the base word, whatever it is:

mis + spell = misspell   mis + place = misplace
mis + state = misstate   mis + print = misprint
mis + statement = misstatement   mis + use = misuse

Un words follow the same pattern:

un + natural = unnatural   un + fortunate = unfortunate
un + necessary = unnecessary   un + usual = unusual

The pattern is similar at the ends of words. What happens when the suffix *ness* is added? If the base word ends in *n*, there will be two *n*'s:

stern + ness = sternness   plain + ness = plainness
mean + ness = meanness   stubborn + ness = stubbornness

Otherwise there will be only one *n:*

great + ness = greatness   expensive + ness = expensiveness
pleasant + ness = pleasantness   coarse + ness = coarseness

Of course if *ness* is added to a word ending in *y*, the *y* is changed to *i:*

busy + ness = business   greedy + ness = greediness
tardy + ness = tardiness   ready + ness = readiness

EXERCISE 12. Be prepared to write the following sentences from dictation:

1. The disapproval of dissatisfied customers can ruin our business.
2. It is unusual for him to misuse his authority.
3. Three misprints and two misspellings on one page are unnecessary.
4. Sally's pleasantness made up for Aunt Helen's stubbornness.
5. That unfortunate misstatement cost him his job.
6. Though we disagreed about most things, we all disapproved of Tim's greediness and meanness.
7. Two sisters could not be more dissimilar than Martha and Kay.
8. To add to our disappointment, Sam had misplaced the car keys.
9. Mr. Hill's dishonorable campaign was a disservice to the whole party.
10. After Flora's mysterious disappearance the weekly golf games were discontinued for the rest of the summer.

Words with *per, com,* and *ac*

Notice the order of the letters in the first syllable of *perform* and *performance* and *perspiration* — **per**. These words are not only spelling demons; they are sometimes pronunciation demons. And the trouble spot is the first syllable — **per**. To pronounce that syllable correctly, put the *e* before the *r*. Another *per* demon is *perhaps*. Two other *per* words are hard: *permanent* and *persuade*. Watch for the "man" in *permanent;* be sure you have a *u* before the *ade* of *persuade*.

A number of common words have the Latin prefix **com**: *compare, combine, complain*. Prefixing *com* to a base word beginning, with *m* results in a double *m*, as in:

commit	commercial	commend
commerce	commuter	recommend

Before a base word beginning with *l, com* becomes *col*. That is why there are two *l*'s in:

collide	collect	colleague
collapse	collection	collaborate

Before a base word beginning with *r, com* becomes *cor*. Do not forget the two *r*'s in:

correct	corrupt	correspondence

Another common Latin prefix is **ad**, as in *admire* and *advise*. Before a base word beginning with *c, ad* becomes *ac*. Concentrate on the two *c*'s in:

accuse	accumulate	accident
accept	accomplish	accurate

206

Remember that there are two *c*'s and two *m*'s in *accommodate.*

EXERCISE 13. Be prepared to write the following sentences from dictation:

1. Bruce sent us copies of the article commending his performance.
2. An hour after that accident two trucks collided at the very same spot.
3. Perhaps you can persuade Honora to collaborate with you on a skit for assembly.
4. Uncle Al, who is usually most accommodating, refused to perform in the community benefit.
5. Professor Danvers would have accomplished little without the help of her colleagues.
6. Within a month Dave had accumulated quite a collection of coins.
7. The commuters sent a petition to the Illinois Commerce Commission.
8. The next candidate denounced the council as corrupt and accused the members of accepting bribes.
9. For those interested mainly in business correspondence, Mr. Wilson recommends the two-semester commercial course.
10. When news of Mary's promotion reached us, our plans for making San Francisco our permanent home collapsed.

Words with *le;* Single letters; Other demons

Concentrate on the last two letters of *vehicle, obstacle, article, axle, angle,* and *principle;* for the **le** causes trouble in spelling these words. Watch *angle* and *principle* especially; misspelling these words often makes whole sentences ridiculous. "He drew a right ang**le** on the board." "Can you explain the princip**le** by which this engine works?"

Do not forget the **t** — even though it is silent — in spelling *wrestle, whistle, trestle, hustle, gristle,* and *bristle.* There is more to these words than meets the ear.

Imitate has only one **m** — with an **i** before and after the **m;** so have *imitation* and *imitator.* There is only one **r** in *around* and *arouse. Britain* and *British* have only one **t** — as in "Tommy," a nickname for a British soldier. Let "Sahara" recollect the single **s** in *desert,* a place where anyone would hate to be *deserted.* The **p** in *politeness* will help recall the single **p** in *apology, apologies, apologize.*

Watch for demons like the ones in **boldface** type in the following sentences:

He **knew** his **speech** was **too** long.
His father **told** him to stay **here until** next **week.**
Do you **know which road** he **meant?**
Every person **there** was **quite** sure he had been **there once before.**
She was **thrown** from her horse on the home **stretch.**

EXERCISE 14. Be prepared to write the following sentences from dictation:

1. Dan knew that if he whistled once more he would be thrown out of the study hall and told to report to the office.
2. I'm quite sure that Terry meant to apologize for imitating Hugh's British accent.
3. They will have to hustle to get here before the noon whistle blows.
4. Philip makes it a principle to save part of his allowance every week.
5. The article told of their being deserted in the mountains and of the many obstacles they had to overcome before reaching safety.
6. Are the angles of an equilateral triangle equal?
7. The steak I had there last week was nothing but fat and gristle, and the potatoes were too soggy to eat.
8. The crowds gathered around the strange vehicle stalled in the road aroused my curiosity.
9. Great stretches of desert lay between them and their destination.
10. The speech which she had so carefully prepared had to be postponed until the next meeting.

Words with *i, ism,* and *ize*

The second syllable of *delicate, privilege, medicine, similar, positive,* and *diligent* consists of a single letter — **i.** Concentrate on that **i;** it is the trouble spot that makes demons of these words.

Notice the first **i** in *divide* and *divine,* another pair of "i" demons. The second **i** of *original* and *originally* is the source of many errors. Remember that these words are derived from *origin,* ending in *gin.* That same *gin* is in *original* and *originally.*

It is easy to spell *finite;* its pronunciation tells its spelling. Thinking of *finite* when you write *definite, indefinite, infinite,* and *definition* will help you put the demonic *i*'s in the right places.

The following common words have an *i* before the *ble:*

visible	sensible	possible	indelible
invisible	horrible	impossible	eligible

A number of common nouns are made by adding the suffix **ism** to nouns or adjectives:

hero + ism = heroism   feudal + ism = feudalism
social + ism = socialism   American + ism = Americanism

Though **ism** is always pronounced in two syllables, as if it rhymed with "Quiz 'em," it has only one vowel — an **i.** Remember **ism** in *critic + ism = criticism, journal + ism = journalism, symbol + ism = symbolism.*

208

Adding the suffix **ize** to nouns and adjectives changes them to verbs:

critic + ize = criticize   civil + ize = civilize
ideal + ize = idealize   capital + ize = capitalize

If **ize** is added to a word ending in *y*, the *y* is dropped:

apology + ize = apologize   sympathy + ize = sympathize
economy + ize = economize   colony + ize = colonize

EXERCISE 15. Be prepared to write the following sentences from dictation:

1. Fred has been more diligent lately; he wants to be eligible for the team.
2. I am quite positive that Sally chose Americanism, not socialism, for her topic.
3. Mother sympathized with Jerry, but insisted that he apologize as soon as possible for criticizing Dad's definition of symbolism.
4. Because Mildred was delicate and had to take medicine, she was given more privileges than the rest of us.
5. Miss Ellis divided the work, assigning the divine right of kings to me and feudalism to George.
6. In the original, written in indelible ink, all nouns are capitalized.
7. Wouldn't it be more sensible to economize by buying a similar hat made of less expensive material?
8. It was impossible to believe that the horrible scar, so clearly visible that morning, was now invisible.
9. If criticism is indefinite, it is useless.
10. Her report on journalism definitely idealized the cub reporter.

Solid words

Taken singly, the words *never* and *the* and *less* are easy, harmless words that cause no one any trouble. But when they are put together — in *nevertheless* — they become a demon, causing confusion. "Is *nevertheless* three words or one?" "Does it have one hyphen or two?" *Nevertheless* is one word, one solid word with no hyphens between the parts — **nevertheless.**

Inside and *outside* are solid words; so are *upstairs* and *downstairs.* Another pair is *without* and *within.* Still another is *somewhere* and *nowhere.* Notice the four italicized in *"Whatever* happens, *wherever* you are, *however* you feel, write *nowadays* as a solid word."

Three common solid words begin with *a* — *apiece, across,* and *awhile.* Learn to write them as one word in sentences like these:

Those melons cost fifty cents **apiece.**
They live **across** the street from our house.
Can't you stay **awhile?**

Watch the **al** group: *almost, already, although, always, altogether.* Each is a solid word; each has only one **l**. Remember "Albert." "*Although* Albert is *already altogether* altered, he is *almost always* alert."

Consider *throughout* or *moreover* or *semicolon* or *tomorrow.* All are written as solid words. So is *instead.* And *pastime* is troublesome. Remember that it is a solid word with only one *s.*

EXERCISE 16. Be prepared to write the following sentences from dictation:

1. Oranges like these are almost always ten cents apiece in the store across the street.
2. Nevertheless, Mother went upstairs and rested awhile.
3. Although Sam has promised to help us tomorrow, we're not altogether sure he will.
4. Annie, however, would go nowhere without Sandy.
5. He'd better be back within an hour, wherever he is.
6. Moreover, I would have used a period instead of a semicolon in the second sentence.
7. By five o'clock it was already too dark to take pictures outside.
8. Hal's only pastime throughout the summer was playing chess with the man downstairs.
9. Kenneth and I were sure he had hidden the bag of money somewhere inside the house.
10. Nowadays whatever Grace wants, her parents buy for her.

Chapter 14

Taking Objective Tests

Almost everyone has encountered or will encounter the necessity of taking some kind of standardized objective test. Most of these tests deal, at least in part, with the ability to read, write, and edit standard written English.

Students who plan to go to college will generally be asked to take a series of College Board examinations, consisting of a Scholastic Assessment Test (SAT) and one or more Subject Tests.

Academic record is the most important evidence of preparation for college. However, since secondary schools differ greatly in their courses, academic standards, and grading practices, the SAT and the Subject Tests are offered as a standard measure of abilities generally considered important in college work.

The SAT is offered as a standard measure of general scholastic ability. It is not an intelligence test, nor is it an Achievement Test. Included in the SAT test of verbal ability (there is also a section that measures quantitative ability) are vocabulary questions, verbal reasoning questions, and reading comprehension questions.

The Writing Subject Test

The College Board offers a number of challenging tests in specific subject areas. Each test lasts one hour and is designed to assess what has been learned in a subject and thus provide one indication of preparation for college study. College admissions officers consider Achievement Test scores along with other information such as school record, recommendations, and other evidence of accomplishment and promise. Some colleges use the scores for placement, especially in placing freshmen in English, mathematics, and foreign language courses.

The Writing Subject Test is designed to help colleges evaluate ability to use standard written English. Standard written English is the kind of English found in most books, magazines, and newspapers, and it is the kind of language in which students will write the papers for most college courses.

Each form of the Writing Subject Test consists of several kinds of multiple choice questions selected from the kinds of examples given in this Chapter. These questions examine your ability to express ideas correctly and to use language with sensitivity to tone and meaning. The two types of questions listed in this chapter are:

Type One: Identifying Sentence Errors
Type Two: Improving Sentences

Basic Verbal Skills and objective tests

The sample questions that follow have all appeared in pamphlets published by the College Board that describe the SAT, the Writing Subject Test, and other objective examinations. Almost every one of these questions can be answered by applying a skill or set of skills studied in this book.

The directions and the questions appear on each righthand page. Discussions of each question and each proper answer appear on each lefthand (facing) page. Therefore, while answering the questions, *keep the lefthand pages covered.*

The first and most important step in taking any examination is to be sure to *read the directions thoroughly.* The directions that appear on the next pages appear in actual Writing Subject and SAT Tests. Therefore, it is to your advantage to become thoroughly familiar with them before taking the tests. Carelessly hurrying through directions may lead to incorrect answers for whole sections of the test.

Guess intelligently. Students often ask whether they should guess if they are uncertain about the answer to a question. The general directions to a test will usually tell whether or not it is worthwhile to guess. In most objective tests, including the College Boards, scores will be based on the number of questions answered correctly minus a fraction of the number answered incorrectly, with the answers left blank not counting either way.

Therefore, it is unlikely that random or haphazard guessing will change a score significantly. However, if some knowledge of a question helps eliminate one or more answer choices, it is generally an advantage to answer such a question. Such an attempt is not a wild guess; it is an intelligent guess.

After answering the questions, study the discussions that appear on the facing pages. If you have answered a question incorrectly, turn to the pages in *Basic Verbal Skills* that are mentioned in the discussion and review the principles and exercises. Then examine the question again.

Type One: Identifying Sentence Errors
EXAMPLE: See *Chapter 11,* page 155, Pronouns as appositives.

The correct answer is (C). We use the form *we* as a subject and *us* as an object even when an appositive noun follows the pronoun. Since *spectators* is an object of the preposition *to,* the sentence should read: "He spoke bluntly and angrily to us spectators."

1. See *Chapter 10,* page 131, *Have* and *of.*

The correct answer is (C). The verb form *have* and its contraction *'ve* sound like *of* in rapid speech. But we do not write *of* for *have* or *'ve.* The sentence should read: "Had we known of your desire to go with us, we most certainly would have invited you to join our party."

2. The answer is (C). The prepositional phrase should read: "in response to his innocent query."

3. See *Chapter 11,* page 156, Reference of pronouns.

The correct answer is (C). The error is one of vague pronoun reference. In the test sentence there is no clear antecedent of the pronoun *they.* The sentence should read: "Just listening to a little of Wagner's music will make clear to almost anyone that it represents an entirely new technique, something quite distinct from the conventional conception of opera." Now it is clear that the antecedent of *it* is *music.*

4. See *Chapter 11,* page 139, Agreement of subject and verb.

The correct answer is (A). The error is one of agreement of subject and verb. A singular subject takes a singular verb even when a phrase beginning with *as well as* comes between the subject and the verb. The sentence should read: "The Secretary of State, as well as the other members of the cabinet, was summoned suddenly to the bedside of the ailing President."

One kind of multiple-choice question consists of a sentence with four of its parts underlined and lettered. You are required to decide either that one of the four underlined parts of the sentence is unacceptable or that the sentence has no error. Each of the underlined parts of the sentence presents a problem of usage, some of which are more complex than others. Therefore, consider carefully *all* the underlined parts of the sentence before you choose your answer.

Directions: **The following sentences may contain problems in grammar, usage, diction (choice of words), and idiom.**

Some sentences are correct.

No sentence contains more than one error.

You will find that the error, if there is one, is underlined and lettered. Assume that all other elements of the sentence are correct and cannot be changed. In choosing answers, follow the requirements of standard written English.

If there is an error, select the *one underlined part* that must be changed in order to make the sentence correct, and blacken the corresponding space on your answer sheet.

If there is no error, mark answer space E.

EXAMPLE: He spoke <u>bluntly</u> and <u>angrily</u> to <u>we</u> <u>spectators</u>. <u>No error</u>
                A   B   C D   E

           A B C D E
ANSWER: ☐ ☐ ■ ☐ ☐

---

1. <u>Had we known</u> of your desire to go with us, we <u>most</u> certainly <u>would of</u> invited
     A   B   C

  you <u>to join</u> our party. <u>No error</u>
        D   E

2. Schmidt was <u>ill-prepared</u> <u>to cope with</u> the many letters that came in response
             A   B

  <u>about his</u> innocent <u>query</u> concerning Keats. <u>No error</u>
      C   D   E

3. Just <u>listening</u> to a little of Wagner's music <u>will make clear</u> to almost anyone
     A   B

  that <u>they represent</u> an entirely new technique, something quite <u>distinct from</u>
        C   D

  the conventional conception of opera. <u>No error</u>
                            E

4. The Secretary of State, as well as the other members of the cabinet, <u>were</u>

  <u>summoned</u> suddenly <u>to</u> the bedside of the <u>ailing</u> President. <u>No error</u>
      A   B   C   D   E

5. See *Chapter 11,* page 156, Reference of pronouns.

The correct answer is (C). The error is one of vague pronoun reference. In the test sentence there is no clear antecedent to the pronoun *they*. The sentence should read: "Prefabricated housing is economical because it reduces labor costs considerably." Now it is clear that the antecedent to *it* is *housing.*

6. See *Chapter 5,* page 39, Gerunds; and page 43, Infinitives.

The correct answer is (B). The sentence awkwardly combines a gerund *Giving* with an infinitive *To give.* The result is an idiom — a combination of words — that does not exist in standard written English. The sentence should read: "Shirley Chisholm is clearly determined to give blacks more voice in the selection of national candidates."

7. See *Chapter 11,* page 166, Singular or plural?

The correct answer is (B). The noun *life* must be in the plural to parallel the possessive modifier *their* and its antecedent *people.* The sentence should read: "It is startling to realize that in this rich country thousands of people live out their lives without ever having enough to eat."

8. See *Chapter 11,* page 156, Pronouns in adverb clauses of comparison.

The correct answer is (D). Because *than him* is an elliptical clause in which the verb *was* is understood, the pronoun subject should be *he.* The sentence should read: "The senator had voted against the Wilson bill; yet no one was more interested in reforestation than he."

9. See *Chapter 11,* page 142, Avoiding shifts in time.

The correct answer is (B). The structure of the sentence is faulty because the tenses of the verbs shift awkwardly from present *turns* to past *rolled.* The sentence should read: "Every time he turned the book in his enormous hands, the muscles of his big arm rolled slightly under the smooth skin."

10. See *Chapter 11,* page 156, Reference of pronouns.

The correct answer is (D). The error is one of vague pronoun reference. In the sentence there is no clear antecedent of the pronoun *it.* The sentence should read: "Jane Austen, unlike many of her contemporaries, cannot be called a sentimentalist; in fact, she mocked sentimentalism in her novels."

11. See *Chapter 3,* page 21, Conjunctions.

The correct answer is (D). The sentence should read: "The king, whom the people loved, had given the Prime Minister neither overt nor tacit encouragement."

5. Prefabricated housing <u>is</u> economical <u>because</u> <u>they reduce</u> labor costs <u>consider-</u>
                             A   **B**   **C**   **D**

<u>ably</u>. No error
  E

6. Shirley Chisholm is clearly determined <u>to giving</u> blacks <u>more</u> <u>voice in</u> the selec-
                 A   **B**   **C**   **D**

tion of national candidates. <u>No error</u>
                       E

7. It is startling to <u>realize</u> that in this rich country, thousands of people live out
             A

their <u>life</u> without ever <u>having</u> <u>enough to eat</u>. <u>No error</u>
  B   **C**   **D**   **E**

8. The senator had <u>voted</u> <u>against</u> the Wilson bill; yet no one <u>was more</u> interested
              A   **B**   **C**

in reforestation <u>than him</u>. <u>No error</u>
           D   **E**

9. Every <u>time</u> he <u>turns</u> the book <u>in his</u> enormous hands, the muscles of his big
      A   **B**   **C**

arms rolled <u>slightly</u> under the smooth skin. <u>No error</u>
          D   **E**

10. Jane Austen, <u>unlike many</u> of her contemporaries, <u>cannot be</u> called a sentimen-
             A   **B**

talist; in fact, she <u>mocked it</u> in her novels. <u>No error</u>
           C **D**   **E**

11. The king, <u>whom</u> the people <u>loved</u>, <u>had given</u> the Prime Minister neither overt
         A   **B**   **C**

<u>or</u> tacit encouragement. <u>No error</u>
D   **E**

12. See *Chapter 11*, page 150, Use parallel forms.

The correct answer is (B). The sentence shifts awkwardly from the third person (*Most people*) to the second person (*you*). To correct such nonparallelism, the sentence should read: "Most people will find it easier to adjust to the metric system if they become familiar with it before the changeover occurs."

13. Although the ideas expressed in the sentence might be conveyed with different words and expressions, the sentence contains no grammatical, idiomatic, logical, or structural errors. The answer is (E).

14. See *Chapter 11*, page 139, Agreement of subject and verb.

The correct answer is (A). In this sentence the plural subject, *Holes,* does not agree in number with the singular verb, *suggests.* The sentence should read: "Holes in the skulls of people from certain ancient civilizations suggest that modern physicians are not the only doctors who have attempted to operate on the brain."

15. See *Chapter 11*, page 143, Double negatives.

The correct answer is (B). In standard written English we do not use two negative words to express one negative meaning. Since the adverb *hardly* is negative in meaning, it should not be combined with *without.* The sentence should read: "If Shakespeare were alive today, he would, without a doubt, not want his name associated with last night's presentation of 'Hamlet'."

16. See *Chapter 11*, page 148; Parallel forms; page 154, Pronouns with gerunds.

The correct answer is (A). Parallel ideas should be expressed in parallel forms. To parallel *the Beatles' breaking up,* the subject of the sentence, here awkwardly cast in a verb form, should also be cast as a gerund. The sentence should read: "Dylan's turning thirty, as well as the Beatles' breaking up, signified the end of a distinctive period in rock music."

17. Although the ideas expressed in the sentence might be conveyed with different words and expressions, the sentence contains no grammatical, idiomatic, logical, or structural errors. The answer is (E).

18. See *Chapter 11*, page 166, Singular or plural?

The correct answer is (A). The adjective *every* is singular and should take the singular verb *has urged.* The sentence should read: "Every one of the city's newspapers has urged its readers to vote in the special election to be held on Tuesday."

12. Most people will <u>find it easier</u> to adjust to the metric system <u>if you become</u>
       A   B
familiar <u>with</u> it before the changeover <u>occurs.</u> <u>No error</u>
          C   D   E

13. One of the <u>activities of</u> women's organizations <u>is to encourage</u> projects that
                    A   B
will <u>make</u> life <u>easier for</u> working mothers. <u>No error</u>
      C   D   E

14. Holes in the skulls of people from certain ancient civilizations <u>suggests</u> that
                                                                                           A
modern physicians are <u>not the only</u> doctors who <u>have attempted</u> <u>to operate</u> on
                             B   C   D
the brain. <u>No error</u>
                  E

15. If Shakespeare were alive today, he <u>would,</u> <u>without hardly</u> a doubt, not want
                                              A   B
his name <u>associated with</u> last night's <u>presentation of</u> "Hamlet." <u>No error</u>
                  C   D   E

16. <u>Dylan's turned thirty,</u> <u>as well as</u> the Beatles' breaking up, <u>signified the end</u> of a
       A   B   C
distinctive period <u>in</u> rock music. <u>No error</u>
                         D   E

17. There are several places in Yellowstone National Park <u>where</u> fish <u>can be caught</u>
                                                                      A   B
in a freshwater pool <u>and then</u> cooked in a hot spring <u>close by.</u> <u>No error</u>
                           C   D   E

18. Every one of the city's newspapers <u>have urged</u> <u>its</u> readers to vote <u>in</u> the special
                                              A   B C
election <u>to be held</u> on Tuesday. <u>No error</u>
              D   E

Chapter 14   Identifying Sentence Errors   219

19. See *Chapter 11,* page 142, Avoiding shifts in time.

The correct answer is (B). Because the main clause precedes the introductory phrase in time, the verb tense should be past perfect. The sentence should read: "To have performed the trick so smoothly, the dealer would have had to know the order of the cards in advance."

20. See *Chapter 11,* page 153, Pronouns as objects.

The correct answer is (A). The pronoun *she* cannot be used as an object of a preposition, in this sentence *between.* The sentence should read: "The discussion between Professor Barron and her centered on what they thought Hitler would have done had he known how weak England was in 1940."

21. See *Chapter 11,* page 148, Parallel forms.

The correct answer is (C). In this sentence, the compound verb lacks parallelism, shifting from the past tense *(helped)* to a participial form *(serving).* With the two verbs properly parallel, the sentence should read: "Once regarded as 'Africa's Guiding Light,' Kwame Nkrumah helped the West African colonies win independence and served as the first prime minister of Ghana."

22. The sentence is correct.

23. See *Chapter 11,* page 139, Agreement of subject and verb.

The correct answer is (A). The correlative conjunctions *neither* and *nor* are singular and take singular verbs, in this case *was.* The sentence should read: "Neither the contractor nor the architect was willing to estimate when the work would be completed because each suspected that a strike might occur."

24. See *Chapter 11,* page 162, Sentence errors.

The correct answer is (A). In this sentence, two independent clauses are improperly joined by a comma instead of a semicolon. The sentence should read: "The city needs more public housing; taxes must be increased in order to finance the construction."

25. See *Chapter 11,* page 139, Agreement of subject and verb.

The correct answer is (C). Even though the subject follows the verb in the main clause the two must still agree. The subject *question* must take a singular verb *is.* The sentence should read: "Not to be ignored as part of the problem of describing American dialects is the question of social and economic influences on linguistic patterns."

19. To have performed the trick <u>so smoothly</u>, the dealer <u>would have to know</u> the
                                  A   B

    <u>order</u> of the cards <u>in advance</u>. <u>No error.</u>
     C   D   E

20. The discussion between Professor Barron <u>and she</u> centered on <u>what they</u>
                                           A   B

    <u>thought</u> Hitler would have done <u>had he known</u> <u>how weak</u> England was in
                                       C   D

    1940. <u>No error</u>
          E

21. Once <u>regarded as</u> "Africa's Guiding Light," Kwame Nkrumah helped the
          A

    West African <u>colonies win</u> independence and <u>serving</u> as <u>the first</u> prime minister
                       B   C   D

    of Ghana. <u>No error</u>
             E

22. A good many modern musicians have <u>begun</u> <u>composing</u> pieces that <u>call for</u>
                                     A   B   C

    using electronic devices <u>as</u> musical instruments. <u>No error</u>
                    D   E

23. Neither the contractor nor the architect <u>were</u> willing to estimate <u>when</u> the
                                          A   B

    work <u>would be</u> completed <u>because</u> each suspected that a strike might occur.
              C   D

    <u>No error</u>
      E

24. The city needs more public <u>housing</u>, taxes <u>must be increased</u> in order <u>to</u>
                                A   B

    <u>finance</u> the construction. <u>No error</u>
     C   D   E

25. <u>Not to be</u> ignored <u>as</u> part of the problem of describing American dialects <u>are</u>
     A   B   C

    the question of social and economic influences <u>on</u> linguistic patterns. <u>No error</u>
                                              D   E

26. See *Chapter 11*, page 144, excessive predication, page 148; Parallel forms.

The correct answer is (D). The sentence awkwardly shifts from a participial form *choosing* to a verb *would employ*. In correct parallel form the sentence should read: "O'Neill experimented with each of his plays, skillfully choosing difficult subjects and employing unusual dramatic techniques."

27. The correct answer is (D). The prepositional phrase should read: "of all of its students."

28. See *Chapter 11*, page 156, Pronouns in adverb clauses of comparison.

The correct answer is (B). Because *than him* is an elliptical clause in which the verb *is* is understood, the pronoun subject should be *he*. The sentence should read: "Although Elen is a better tennis player than he, Henry insists on competing with her and usually loses."

29. See *Chapter 11*, page 156, Reference of pronouns.

The correct answer is (D). In this sentence it is clear that the collective noun *country* is referring to a single unit of people. Therefore, all pronouns that refer to *country* should be singular. The sentence should read: "Pride alone is usually enough to induce a country to support its athletes in international competition."

30. The sentence is correct.

31. See *Chapter 10*, page 131, *incredible* and *incredulous*.

The correct answer is (C). *Incredulous* means "unbelieving," while *incredible* means "unbelievable." The sentence should read: "The accidental meeting of the distant cousins came about through an incredible series of coincidences."

32. See *Chapter 10*, page 132, *less* and *fewer*.

The correct answer is (B). *Less* means "not so much," while *fewer* means "not so many." The sentence should read: "In those cities where public transportation is adequate, fewer traffic problems occur and pedestrians are rarely involved in traffic accidents."

26. O'Neill experimented with each of his plays, skillfully choosing difficult sub-
       A   B   C
    jects and he would employ unusual dramatic techniques. No error
                        D   E

27. Unless bilingual and bicultural programs are developed and funded, the school
    A   B
    district will not be able to meet the needs for all of its students. No error
                        C   D   E

28. Although Ellen is a better tennis player than him, Henry insists on competing
        A   B   C
    with her and usually loses. No error
    D   E

29. Pride alone is usually enough to induce a country to support their athletes in
          A   B   C   D
    international competition. No error
                              E

30. Some genetic research has become highly controversial because the results of
    A   B   C
    the studies suggest that people may eventually be able to manipulate the
                                      D
    development of the human race. No error
                                   E

31. The accidental meeting of the distant cousins came about through an
                  A   B
    incredulous series of coincidences. No error.
    C   D   E

32. In those cities where public transportation is adequate, less traffic prob-
        A   B
    lems occur and pedestrians are rarely involved in accidents. No error.
        C   D   E

33. See *Chapter 11,* page 139, Agreement of subject and verb.

The correct answer is (B). Because the subject of the sentence is "two electron microscopes, three scales, and a notebook," the verb should be cast in the plural form, *were.* The sentence should read: "Missing from the laboratory after the robbery were two electron microscopes, three scales, and a notebook containing detailed entries about the experiment."

34. See *Chapter 11,* page 148, Parallel forms.

The correct answer is (B). The sentence awkwardly shifts from an infinitive, *to ride,* to a gerund, *explaining.* In correct parallel form the sentence should read: "It is far easier to ride a bicycle than to explain in words exactly how a bicycle is ridden."

35. The sentence is correct.

36. See *Chapter 11,* page 142, Comparison of adjectives and adverbs.

The correct answer is (D). The sentence is afflicted by an illogical comparison. One cannot compare artists with prior times. The sentence should read: "Because they painted scenes of life as ordinary people lived it, rather than scenes from myths, many nineteenth-century American artists differed from artists of prior times."

37. See *Chapter 11,* page 162, Sentence errors.

The correct answer is (A). Because *having been improved* is a participle and not a verb, the example is a sentence fragment. The sentence should read: "The living conditions of some migrant workers has been improved primarily through the efforts of people like Cesar Chavez."

38. See *Chapter 11,* page 139, Adjectives and adverbs.

The correct answer is (B). *Constant,* which modifies the participle *changing,* is incorrectly cast in adjective form. The sentence should read: "The research study reveals startling proof of a constantly changing seafloor that comprises the major part of the underwater landscape."

39. See *Chapter 11,* page 153, Pronoun cases.

The correct answer is (B). *He,* the object of the preposition *by,* should be cast as *him.* In addition, the pronoun referring to the speaker, Alexander, should come after *the committee.* The repaired sentence should read: "The report Alexander is discussing, a report prepared jointly by the committee and him, does not take into account the socioeconomic status of those interviewed."

33. Missing from the laboratory after the robbery was two electron micro-
          —————————   ———
          A   **B**

scopes, three scales, and a notebook containing detailed entries about the ex-
                                        —————————   —————
                                            C   **D**

periment. No error.
           ————
             E

34. It is far easier to ride a bicycle than explaining in words exactly how a
           ————————   ——————————   —————————
              A   **B**   **C**

bicycle is ridden. No error.
        ————————— ————
            D   **E**

35. Each of Beethoven's many acts of ungraciousness seems to have been
                          ——————————   ———— ——————————
                              A   **B**   **C**

balanced by an act of kindness. No error.
——————————   ————
    D   **E**

36. Because they painted scenes of life as ordinary people lived it, rather than
        —————————   ———————— —————————
            A   **B**   **C**

scenes from myths, many nineteenth-century American artists differed from
                                                                        ————
                                                                         D

prior times. No error.
—————————— ————
    D   **E**

37. The living conditions of some migrant workers having been improved
                                                      ——————————————————
                                                              A

primarily through the efforts of people like Caesar Chavez. No error.
————————— —————————————— ——————————   ————
    B   **C**   **D**   **E**

38. The research study reveals startling proof of a constant changing seafloor
                          ———————   ————————
                             A   **B**

that comprises the major part of the underwater landscape. No error.
     —————————   ————   ————
         C   **D**   **E**

39. The report Alexander is discussing, a report prepared jointly by he and the
                             ———————————   ——————————
                                  A   **B**

committee, does not take into account the socioeconomic status of those inter-
                      ——————————————   ———————————
                            C   **D**

viewed. No error.
—————— ————
         E

40. See *Chapter 11,* page 145, Modifying errors.

The correct answer is (D). "When traveling in some foreign countries" is a dangling modifier that modifies nothing in the rest of the sentence. The sentence should read: "Although malaria has been eradicated from the United States, this disease is still a threat when one travels in some foreign countries."

40. Although malaria has been eradicated from the United States, this disease
$\quad$ **A** $\qquad\qquad$ **B** $\qquad\qquad\qquad\qquad\qquad\qquad\qquad\qquad$ **C**
is still a threat when traveling in some foreign countries. No error.
$\qquad\qquad\qquad$ **D** $\qquad\qquad\qquad\qquad\qquad\qquad\qquad$ **E**

Type Two: Improving Sentences

41. See *Chapter 11,* page 142, Avoiding shifts in time; *Chapter 5,* page 50, Use a participle; and *Chapter 6,* page 65, Use an adverb clause.

The best answer is (E). The first problem with sentence (A) is that the tense of the first clause is incorrect. A completed action should not be expressed in the present tense. Second, the relationship between (1) the man's living in New York for eight years and (2) his inability to find Yankee Stadium is one of concession. That is, even though the first fact is true, the second is also true. Sentence (A) states the relationship in a loosely compound way. (B) implies a cause and effect relationship, certainly illogical; and (C) with its time relationship is also imprecise. Of the two possibilities remaining (E) is preferable to (D) because of the rather stiff expression — *eight years' existence* — in (D).

42. See *Chapter 11,* page 142, Comparison of adjectives and adverbs; page 145, Modifying errors; and *Chapter 1,* page 5, Active and passive verbs.

The best answer is (C). There are two errors in the original version of the sentence. First, there is an illogical comparison. One cannot compare a gardener *he* with a garden. Second, the adjective clause at the end of the sentence seems to modify *garden,* when it should be modifying *neighbor.* Answers (A), (B), and (D) each retain one or both of these errors. (E) contains an awkward and unnecessary shift from the active to the passive voice.

43. See *Chapter 11,* page 145, Modifying errors; page 144, Excessive predication; and page 169, Wordiness.

The best answer to this difficult question is (B). (A), the original sentence, contains an adjective clause (the *which* clause) that is at an unnecessary and confusing distance from its antecedent *Walden Pond.* (C) and (D) solve the problem, but they contain excessive predication and wordiness because of their two main clauses. In (E) the two participial phrases are stilted and weak. And the total of four *-ing* words — *being, becoming, setting* and *living* — bangs upon the ear.

228

A second kind of question requires you not so much to identify unacceptable usage as to choose the best way of phrasing a sentence.

Directions: **In each of the following sentences some part of the sentence or the entire sentence is underlined. The underlined part presents a problem in the appropriate use of language. Beneath each sentence you will find five ways of writing the underlined part. The first of these repeats the original, but the other four are all different. If you think the original sentence is better than any of the suggested changes, you should choose answer A; otherwise you should mark one of the other choices.**

This is a test of correctness and effectiveness of expression. In choosing answers, follow the requirements of standard written English; that is, pay attention to acceptable usage in grammar, diction (choice of words), sentence construction, and punctuation. Choose the answer that produces the most effective sentence — clear and exact, without awkwardness or ambiguity. Do not make a choice that changes the meaning of the original sentence.

41. <u>For eight years he lives in New York and</u> he still does not know how to find Yankee Stadium.

   (A) For eight years he lives in New York and
   (B) Having lived for his last eight years in New York,
   (C) After his having lived eight years in New York,
   (D) Despite eight years' existence in New York,
   (E) Although he has lived in New York for eight years,

42. The young amateur gardener was delighted when he produced more vegetables than his neighbor's garden, who had been growing vegetables for years.

   (A) his neighbor's garden, who   (B) the garden of his neighbor, who
   (C) his neighbor, who   (D) his neighbor's garden produced, who
   (E) was done by his neighbor, who

43. <u>Henry David Thoreau first saw Walden Pond at the age of five years, which was later to become famous as the setting of his experiment in simple living.</u>

   (A) Henry David Thoreau first saw Walden Pond at the age of five years, which was later to become famous as the setting of his experiment in simple living.
   (B) When he was five years old, Henry David Thoreau first saw Walden Pond, which was later to become famous as the setting of his experiment in simple living.
   (C) When he was five years old, Henry David Thoreau first saw Walden Pond, and later this became famous as the setting of his experiment in simple living.
   (D) At the age of five years, Henry David Thoreau first saw Walden Pond, and this place was later to become famous as the setting of his experiment in simple living.
   (E) Henry David Thoreau, being five years old, first saw Walden Pond, later becoming famous as the setting of his experiment in simple living.

44. See *Chapter 11,* page 143, Double negatives.

The correct answer is (E). In standard written English we do not use two negative words to express one negative meaning. Since the adverbs *hardly* and *scarcely* are negative in meaning, we do not combine them with *no, (can)not,* and other such negatives. Hence, sentences (A) and (D) are incorrect because they contain double negatives. The gerund form *being* in (E) is preferable to the awkward and unidiomatic infinitive forms in (B) and (D).

45. See *Chapter 11,* page 142, Comparison of adjectives and adverbs.

The correct answer is (A). It is illogical to compare two things that are not alike in any way. (C), (D), and (E) are not acceptable because they compare a person with an emotion, while (A) does compare one person with another. The comparison in (B) is logical, but the sentence contains language not ordinarily used in standard written English *(had anger* for *was angry).*

46. See *Chapter 4,* page 34, Appositives; *Chapter 11,* page 156, Reference of pronouns; and page 156, Sentence errors.

The best version of this sentence is (C). (A) is a sentence fragment because the noun *actress* has no verb. *Born* in sentence (A) is a participle. Sentences (B) and (D) contain awkward transpositions of the subject and predicate nominative or verb, transpositions that serve no useful purpose. In addition, the *being* phrase at the end of (D) is quite weak and gives the sense that Bernhardt was a famous actress at the time of her birth. Sentence (E) begins with a vague pronoun, *she,* that has no antecedent. As a result we cannot tell whether the sentence is talking about one or two women.

47. See *Chapter 11,* page 139, Agreement of subject and verb.

The best answer is (E). The singular subject *outlook* must take a singular verb, thus eliminating answers (A) and (B) from contention. (C) and (D) contain constructions that are not characteristic of native English speakers. Only (E) is grammatically and idiomatically correct.

48. See *Chapter 11,* page 145, Modifying errors.

The best answer is (D). (A), the original sentence is afflicted by a dangling modifier. (B) contains both an unnecessary passive construction and an incorrect verb form, *forbade.* (C) still lacks a subject in the main clause to which the opening phrase can relate. The opening phrase in (E) is unidiomatic and unnecessarily complex.

230

44. The reader of "Manchild in the Promised Land" <u>cannot scarcely help but be</u> moved by the experiences Claude Brown describes.

    (A) cannot scarcely help but be

    (B) can scarcely help to be

    (C) can but scarcely help be

    (D) cannot scarcely help but to be

    (E) can scarcely help being

45. <u>Eddie was as angry as Linda was</u> when he discovered that thieves had stripped her car.

    (A) Eddie was as angry as Linda was

    (B) Eddie had anger like Linda's

    (C) Eddie's anger was like Linda was

    (D) Eddie's anger was as great as Linda

    (E) Eddie had an anger as great as Linda

46. <u>The world-famous actress, Sarah Bernhardt, born in 1844.</u>

    (A) The world-famous actress, Sarah Bernhardt, born in 1844.

    (B) A world-famous actress was Sarah Bernhardt, born in 1844.

    (C) Sarah Bernhardt, the world-famous actress, was born in 1844.

    (D) Born in 1844 was Sarah Bernhardt, being a world-famous actress.

    (E) She was a world-famous actress and Sarah Bernhardt was born in 1844.

47. Despite his youth and the limited number of his publications, his outlook on our world and its problems <u>are enough to have shown us</u> his greatness as a humanist.

    (A) are enough to have shown us

    (B) are enough to be showing us

    (C) is enough that it shows us

    (D) is enough for showing us

    (E) is enough to show us

48. <u>Forbidden by his father to study music, his first violin lessons were taken secretly.</u>

    (A) Forbidden by his father to study music, his first violin lessons were taken secretly.

    (B) Although forbade to study music by his father, he took his first secret violin lessons.

    (C) His father having forbidden him to study music, so his first violin lessons were taken secretly.

    (D) Because his father forbade him to study music, he took his first violin lessons secretly.

    (E) Because of his father forbidding him as to studying music, he took his first violin lessons secretly.

49. See *Chapter 11,* page 156; Reference of pronouns.

The best answer is (C). In (A), the original sentence, the pronoun *it* is an example of vague reference. (B), (C), and (D) each correct the reference error, but (C) is the clearest and most concise version of the three.

50. (A), the original sentence, is by far the best of the five versions presented. The other four choices are examples of (B) a run-on sentence, (C) wordiness, (D) a sentence fragment, and (E) a dangling modifier.

51. See *Chapter 7,* page 79, Use a complex sentence.

In the underlined sentence, the writer has used *and* to join two statements about Althea Gibson. The sentence is not effective because *and* does not adequately convey the relationship between the two statements. A more interesting sentence would indicate which one of the ideas was more important to the writer. The only sentence to do so is (D). While choices (B), (C), and (E) are either fragments or run-ons, (D) is a well-constructed sentence, one with appropriate subordination and emphasis.

52. See *Chapter 11,* page 145, Modifying errors.

The best answer is (D). In the original sentence, the introductory phrase *Placed in the time capsule* seems to modify *the scientists.* Choice (B) contains a similar error and adds to it by using the pronoun *it* without a clear antecedent. (C) contains a dangling modifier and is further weakened by the distance between *them* and the word to which it refers. Choice (E) manages to avoid any modifying error, but it uses the passive voice awkwardly and is unnecessarily wordy. The intended idea of the original sentence is expressed clearly and logically only in (D).

49. In Malthus' celebrated essay, <u>it</u> discusses the evils of overpopulation.

   (A) In Malthus' celebrated essay, it

   (B) In Malthus' celebrated essay, he

   (C) In his celebrated essay, Malthus

   (D) In the celebrated essay by Malthus, he

   (E) In a celebrated essay by Malthus, it

50. <u>During her appearance on the talk show, Germaine Greer discussed her book, "The Female Eunuch."</u>

   (A) During her appearance on the talk show, Germaine Greer discussed her book, "The Female Eunuch."

   (B) Germaine Greer appeared on the talk show, she was discussing her book, "The Female Eunuch."

   (C) Her book "The Female Eunuch" was what Germaine Greer discussed and it was on the talk show.

   (D) Germaine Greer, who appeared on the talk show, and discussed her book, "The Female Eunuch."

   (E) In appearing on the talk show, Germaine Greer's book "The Female Eunuch" was discussed.

51. <u>Althea Gibson was the first black American to win major tennis championships and played in the 1950s.</u>

   (A) Althea Gibson was the first black American to win major tennis championships and played in the 1950s.

   (B) Althea Gibson, being the first black American to win major tennis championships, and playing in the 1950s.

   (C) Althea Gibson, playing in the 1950s, being the first black American to win major tennis championships.

   (D) Althea Gibson, who played in the 1950s, was the first black American to win major tennis championships.

   (E) Althea Gibson played in the 1950s, she was the first black American to win major tennis championships.

52. <u>Placed in the time capsule, the scientists did so in the hope that the documents</u> would be found by future generations.

   (A) Placed in the time capsule, the scientists did so in the hope that the documents

   (B) When they were placed in the time capsule, the scientists did it in the hope that the documents

   (C) By placing them in the time capsule, the hope of the scientists was that the documents

   (D) The scientists placed the documents in the time capsule in the hope that these documents

   (E) The placing of the documents in the time capsule by the scientists was in the hope that these documents

53. See *Chapter 11,* page 148, Parallel forms.

The best answer is (C). The original sentence is afflicted with faulty parallelism because of a gerund *understanding* and infinitive *to control* are paired. Choices (B) and (D) perpetuate the same error, and choice (E) is quite awkward and wordy.

54. See *Chapter 11,* page 145, Modifying errors.

The best answer is (B). Again we are confronted with a modifying error in that the introductory phrase appears to modify the word *attempt* in the main clause. Only choice (B) makes clear the idea that it was Perez who was prepared for the violent opposition he encountered.

55. See *Chapter 1,* page 7, Use an active verb; *Chapter 11,* page 150; Use parallel forms.

Because it lurches from the active voice *relunctantly acknowledge* to the passive voice *stopped by them,* the original sentence is faulty in its parallelism, as is choice (B). Of the remaining choices only (E) is concise and correct in its tense.

56. See *Chapter 11,* page 162, Sentence errors.

The original choice, (A), is a run-on — two sentences written as one, with only a comma between them. Choices (D) and (E) contain expressions that do not appear in standard written English; choice (B) transforms the second clause into a sentence fragment. By subordinating the second idea in an adjective clause, choice (C) is by far the most effective sentence.

57. See *Chapter 11,* page 145, Modifying errors.

The best answer is (E). In the original sentence, the introductory phrase *When arriving at the station* seems to modify *the parking lot.* Choices (B) and (C) repeat the error of the dangling modifier, while (D) is overly complex and wordy.

53. Modern governments try <u>not only understanding but also to control</u> economic forces.

   (A) not only understanding but also to control
   (B) to not only understand but at controlling
   (C) not only to understand but also to control
   (D) not only to understand but also controlling of
   (E) for not an understanding, only, but the control, as well, of

54. Prepared for the violent opposition he met with, <u>Perez's attempt to organize the boycott succeeded.</u>

   (A) Perez's attempt to organize the boycott succeeded
   (B) Perez succeeded in his attempt to organize the boycott
   (C) the attempt by Perez at organizing the boycott succeeded
   (D) there was success for Perez's attempted organization of the boycott
   (E) success was the result of the attempt by Perez to organize the boycott

55. Most cigarette smokers reluctantly acknowledge that they would feel better if <u>smoking were to be stopped by them.</u>

   (A) smoking were to be stopped by them
   (B) smoking was stopped by them
   (C) they would have stopped smoking
   (D) they were to have stopped smoking
   (E) they stopped smoking

56. Though a chronicle of actual events, the story of the survivors is an extraordinarily well-written <u>book, it reads</u> like an exciting tale told by a master storyteller.

   (A) book, it reads
   (B) book, and reading it
   (C) book that reads
   (D) book being that it reads
   (E) book reading it being

57. <u>When arriving</u> at the station, the parking lot was full; however, we soon found a spot in a nearby garage.

   (A) When arriving
   (B) Arriving
   (C) Upon arriving
   (D) As of our arrival time
   (E) When we arrived

58. See *Chapter 11,* page 162, Sentence errors.

The best answer is (B). The underlined portion of the original sentence forms a sentence fragment because *writing* is a participle rather than a main verb. Choice (C) creates a loose sentence consisting of three main clauses and two coordinating conjunctions. (D) perpetuates the sin of the sentence fragment, while (E) contains an awkwardly repetitive *Although . . . but* combination. Only choice (B) expresses the intent of the original sentence with clarity and grammatical accuracy.

59. The verb forms and, therefore, the original sentence itself are correct.

60. See *Chapter 11,* page 145, Modifying errors; page 156, Reference of pronouns.

The best answer is (E). The sentence is marred by both dangling modification (the introductory infinitive doesn't modify anything) and a pronoun *it* that has no antecedent. Choices (B) and (C) perpetuate one or both of the errors. Choice (E) is clearer and more concise than (D), especially with the confusing *the* in the latter.

61. Choice (A) is the clearest and most idiomatic of the five that are offered.

62. See *Chapter 11,* page 150, Use parallel forms; page 166, Singular or plural?

The best answer is (D). The sentence shifts awkwardly from the third person *a person* to the second person *you.* Choices (B) and (C) remedy the problem with another error — a clumsy shift from singular *a person* to plural *their.* (D) concisely and clearly maintains the parallelism of the infinitive phrases, unlike choice (E).

236

58. Early in her career, Gwendolyn Brooks writing poetry about a variety of subjects, but in recent years her writing has focused on the human concerns of black Americans.

    (A) Early in her career, Gwendolyn Brooks writing poetry
    (B) Early in her career, Gwendolyn Brooks wrote poetry
    (C) Gwendolyn Brooks wrote poetry early in her career and it was
    (D) Gwendolyn Brooks having written poetry early in her career
    (E) Although the early poetry of Gwendolyn Brooks's career was

59. Napoleon has been and probably always will be fascinating to students of history.

    (A) has been and probably always will be
    (B) always has and probably will always be
    (C) was and always probably will be
    (D) has always and probably always will be
    (E) has been and probably will have been always

60. To deal with the problems raised by the women's liberation movement, it demands basic changes in our assumptions about the organization of society.

    (A) it demands basic changes
    (B) basic changes are what it demands
    (C) there are basic changes demanded
    (D) people must make the basic changes
    (E) we must make basic changes

61. According to linguists, the Hopi language is unlike any other in that it does not have verb forms.

    (A) unlike any other
    (B) unlike any others
    (C) opposite to the others
    (D) opposite of the others
    (E) opposite of any other

62. It is still quite common in rural areas for a person to be born and then you spend your whole life in the same community.

    (A) then you spend your whole life
    (B) then they spend their whole lives
    (C) to spend their whole lifetimes
    (D) to spend his whole life
    (E) then he would spend his lifetime

63. See *Chapter 1,* page 5, Active and passive verbs; *Chapter 11,* page 148, Parallel forms.

A clumsy shift from the active voice *helps* to the passive voice *are better understood* creates a faulty parallelism in choices (A) and (B). Of the remaining choices only (C) contains parallel structures — here the infinitives *(to) learn* and *(to) understand.*

64. See *Chapter 11,* page 156, Reference of pronouns.

The correct answer is (B). The pronoun *their,* having no clear antecedent, is vague in its reference. Choice (D) perpetuates the reference error, while (C) and (E) contain overly complex expressions not common in standard written English. (B) retains the intention of the original statement, and the pronoun *they* in this version clearly refers to *oil refineries.*

65. See *Chapter 6,* page 57, Use an adjective clause.

The correct answer is (D). The original sentence presents two main facts — that Booker T. Washington founded Tuskegee University and that he wrote *Up From Slavery.* The relationship is best stated by using an adjective clause as in choice (D).

66. The original sentence, choice (A), is by far the best of the five offered.

67. The correct answer is (E). The original sentence is afflicted by an unidiomatic expression *as identical as* and an illogical comparison, in which *characteristics* are compared to *people.* Choice (C) remains unidiomatic, while (B) and (D), both offering *is,* lack proper verb agreement. Only (E) is correct in its verb number and idiomatic in its expression.

63. A thorough study of a foreign language helps people learn about other cultures and <u>attitudes different from theirs are better understood</u>.

   (A) attitudes different from theirs are better understood
   (B) different attitudes from their own are better understood
   (C) understand attitudes that are different from their own
   (D) their understanding of different attitudes is better because of it
   (E) a better understanding of different attitudes is possible

64. Old oil refineries are generally heavy polluters <u>because of their building them</u> when technology was still relatively crude.

   (A) because of their building them
   (B) because they were built
   (C) insofar as they had been built
   (D) inasmuch as they built them
   (E) for such have been built

65. Booker T. Washington founded Tuskegee Institute, also writing "Up From Slavery."

   (A) Booker T. Washington founded Tuskegee Institute, also writing "Up From Slavery."
   (B) Writing "Up From Slavery," Booker T. Washington founded Tuskegee Institute.
   (C) The author of "Up From Slavery," Tuskegee Institute was also founded by Booker T. Washington.
   (D) Booker T. Washington, who wrote "Up From Slavery," founded Tuskegee Institute.
   (E) Booker T. Washington wrote "Up From Slavery," founding Tuskegee Institute in addition.

66. Frank decided to visit the <u>area because he wanted to see</u> the Navajo craftsmen at their work.

   (A) area because he wanted to see
   (B) area, it was for seeing
   (C) area, he wanted to see
   (D) area because of seeing
   (E) area for seeing

67. The characteristics of the people in Langston Hughes's writing <u>are as identical as</u> the people he lived with in Harlem.

   (A) are as identical as
   (B) is identical to
   (C) are identical as those of
   (D) is the same as
   (E) are the same as those of

68. (A), the original sentence, is the best of the five choices offered.

69. The correct answer is (D). Once again we see an illogical comparison in the original sentence, with *nuclear power* being compared to *the use of other fuels.* Choice (D) most clearly and idiomatically corrects the illogicality.

70. See *Chapter 11,* page 162, Sentence errors.

The correct answer is (B). (A), the original statement, is a sentence fragment, as is choice (D). (C) and (E) are faulty in the relationships they establish between the first and second ideas.

68. The new state law banning all billboards except those on business premises has generated a legal battle that could affect the future of outdoor advertising throughout the nation.

    (A) banning all billboards except those on business premises
    (B) that bans any billboard unless they are on business premises
    (C) in which all billboards, but not those on business premises, are banned
    (D) placing a ban against billboards, except where they are on business premises,
    (E) bans billboards, but it excepts any one on business premises, and

69. The report suggests that nuclear power raises more practical and ethical problems than the use of other fuels.

    (A) than the use of other fuels
    (B) than using other fuels does
    (C) compared to alternative sources of power
    (D) than do alternative sources of power
    (E) as against other forms of energy

70. During the summer, the children in the neighborhood playing in the spray from open hydrants.

    (A) playing in the spray from open hydrants
    (B) play in the spray from open hydrants
    (C) play in the spray while having opened the hydrants
    (D) playing in the spray when having opened the hydrants
    (E) play in the spray, and the hydrants have been opened